I Followed My Heart to Jerusalem

I Followed My Heart to Jerusalem

– Yale Roe –

BARRICADE BOOKS

Fort Lee, New Jersey

Published by Barricade Books Inc.
185 Bridge Plaza North
Suite 308-A
Fort Lee, NJ 07024

www.barricadebooks.com

Library of Congress Cataloging-in-Publication Data

Roe, Yale.
    I followed my heart to Jerusalem / Yale Roe.
        p. cm.
    ISBN 1-56980-288-2
    1. Roe, Yale. 2. Jews--United States--Biography. 3. Jews, American--Israel--Biography.
4. Television journalists--Israel--Biography. I. Title.

E184.37.R64A3 2005
956.94'004924073'092--dc22
[B]
                                                                          2005050813

Manufactured in the United States of America
First Printing

Contents

For my children, who shared the journey,
Laura, Devorah, David and Becca

Introduction

Ernest Hemingway turned thirty the year I was born. We never met even though we were both from Oak Park. The one in Illinois, not Michigan.

People are middle class in Oak Park. Hemingway's father was a doctor. My dad was a dentist.

Our homes were only about a mile apart, but he'd already left by the time I was growing up. He went and drove an ambulance in World War I. Later he ran with the bulls in Pamplona. It seems people are always looking for something.

I had the same problem. Oak Park was nice, but I was looking for something, too. That's how I ended up in Jerusalem.

Chapter 1

The Adventure Begins

Like a dancer sensing the movements of her partner, the Greek ocean liner, *Queen Anna Maria,* moves in rhythm with the ocean. For two weeks, I have watched the dark waves dive right and left to escape its force, the waters around us constantly moving, churning, lurching upward and falling back. Fingers of foam reach out to touch our ship and then withdraw into the deep. It is almost the end of our journey. And the beginning.

Ahead of us—we know it's there though we cannot see it through the darkness—lies the land that will be our new home. No one knows us there.

It is our last night at sea, actually almost morning by now. In the distance, the night recedes imperceptibly, softening the darkness ahead. The motion of the ship retreats into a slower rhythm as if it, too, is uncertain of what awaits it.

The dampness darkens the wooden planks of the deck. A fine mist sprays our faces as I stand there with Rosalind and our four children, huddled together against the chill of both the weather and the unknown. Porters push carts with huge rubber wheels, carts heavy with passengers' suitcases. We see ours among them. Each has a bright green tag.

Laura, at twelve and a half, is our oldest. She peers into the darkness searching for the sight of land. I see her chin jutting out and her upturned nose. She is on the brink of womanhood, and except for her thick curly hair, she looks like her mother. So much hair, her first growing-up act of defiance. Born in San Francisco, she is living the seventies as a spiritual child of the sixties, the decade of Aquarius and the musical, *Hair*, and the love-and-let-love and let's-demonstrate spirit of California. Since the day she was born, she's been charged with energy like a squirrel sniffing and darting in every direction, always ready to dash somewhere. But this night, she is restrained, sidling up to me, seeking reassurance.

"Who's meeting us?" she asks.

"No one," I tell her. Her question was answered. But not her feelings.

David is sleepy at four-thirty in the morning. At age six, he comes up to my waist, almost. Standing there, he pushes his hands deep into his pants pockets, completing the stretch that began with a huge yawn into the darkness. Becca, our four-year-old whose head is a chrysanthemum of brown curls, and Devorah, blonde and shy at ten, press themselves against their mother's skirt. Their arms wrap around her legs. The darkness that envelops them is different from the darkness of their bedrooms. That's familiar darkness. Here there is not even the comfort of the small night-light. As they press against her, they feel a protective warmth against the chill of the ocean. She is an element of nature. They do not see her as an attractive young woman, only thirty-four, caught up in her own excitement and apprehension at our new adventure that lies ahead. She is an essence, the reassurance that nothing has changed despite their quiet forebodings.

The first light of dawn obscures the distance rather

than reveals it. A veil of misty haze hides what lies behind, but the mist is a tease that will soon disappear. And then slowly, ever so slowly, like God creating life from a void, from nothingness, forms begin to emerge. The ship is moving slowly now, and we are more conscious of it rising and dipping through the waters. There is the hint of hills in the distance and then more shapes, rectangular ones that outline a landscape, until from the darkness, a city emerges, the port of Haifa. And we are not tourists.

Chapter 2

Growing Up American

"**O**f the nine hundred families in our congregation..."

That's how Rabbi Dresner began his sermon that Friday night in March 1972. I was in the third row with Rosalind and the four children.

Everyone was staring at us. Devorah squirmed in her chair, sensing what was coming.

"Of the nine hundred families, the last one I would have expected to move to Israel would have been the Roes."

Devorah squirmed some more, hoping to disappear.

"He's right," I thought. I wanted to disappear, too.

Not many people were rushing to Israel in 1972. I was forty-three with a nice suburban family in a nice suburban home in the nice Midwest. What could be better?

Nine hundred families in the congregation and not only was I jumping to the head of the line—the fact is, there was no line. No interest at all in leaving comfortable America.

Rabbi Dresner went on, but his words disappeared into the background of my thoughts. I was still caught up in those first words. "Of nine hundred families..." I don't remember much after that except a dull feeling that Rabbi Dresner was right.

I had grown up Christian. Not literally, of course, but in the 1930s, in the Chicago suburb of Oak Park, Christian was the way of life. Stores were closed on Sundays because that was the Christian Sabbath. Schools were closed on December 25 because that was the birthday of our Lord.

There was always a chubby Santa Claus in the toy department at Marshall Field's that time of year. Little kids would climb up on his lap and tell him what they wanted for Christmas. Kids weren't so cynical back then. Even kids a little bit older who already knew that the funny fat man in the red suit and wool cap with a white cotton ball on top couldn't possibly be Santa Claus climbed onto his lap. After all, you never can tell.

Wherever you turned, everything had turned to Christmas. When my boyfriends and I plodded through the snow to neighbors' front doors to raise money to fight tuberculosis, the decorative stamps we were selling weren't called Tuberculosis Seals, they were called Christmas Seals. Every year, the stamps had a different decoration. Sometimes a big smiling Santa Claus, just his face because that way the smile was bigger. Some years, a green Christmas tree. I never did understand what tuberculosis had to do with Christmas, but that's the way it was, which was all right with me because it was fun going door to door through the snow and little Jewish me was one of the guys, the Christian guys that is.

The Christmas Seals with the trees on them were my favorites because they were like the trees sprouting up in living rooms all over our neighborhood. On every street brown plastic reindeer were leaping across snow-covered lawns. Strands of small light bulbs—red and green and yellow—stretched across their sleek bodies.

There were lights sparkling, too, from the living rooms of all the houses. It got dark early those winter days. So on my way home I'd make a point of walking slowly past a lot of those houses to peek in and see the chunky Christmas trees laced with different colored bulbs that flashed on and off in a way that made their lights seem to be chasing one another. There were other decorations, too, stars and moons and bells. And angels.

It seemed that every house except ours had a Christmas tree. Far away even a very important house called the White House had one. I knew all about the White House because I saw it in the newsreels they showed at the movies. That's where I went every Saturday afternoon to watch a triple feature of cowboy films. There were cartoons, too, and Flash Gordon in the twentieth century, and then even more cartoons.

My mother would give me fifteen cents. The movies cost ten cents. The other five cents was for penny candy. That bought me a whole bag stuffed with chewy Mary Janes and hard, red jawbreakers and pumpkin seeds and a chocolate treat called moth balls with still one penny left over for chewing gum. I figured out how to eat the candy at just the right speed so it would last to the very end of that long afternoon.

Between the cartoons and Flash Gordon, about the time I was eating the jawbreakers, I would suddenly hear the sonorous voice of a man called Westbrook Van Voorhis. I'd hear a great musical fanfare and then that voice from atop Mount Sinai, announcing "The March of Time!" That's where I saw it, that place called the White House, with all sorts of famous people there, even the president of the United States or somebody like that turning on the lights of a Christmas tree. It was the biggest Christmas tree I had ever seen.

The trees in Oak Park were smaller than the one at the White House but it didn't matter. In the weeks before

Christmas they transformed our lives. Forests suddenly emerged from what used to be empty lots. My older sister, Charlotte, and I watched with envy as children my age, together with their mothers and fathers, actually touched those trees, walked all around them and talked about them in hushed, intimate tones, deciding which one was the right size for their living room.

Charlotte and I would wait while the tree man tied up the tree the family picked out. He tied it with strong twine so they could drag it home. That's when a few branches would fall off. We would stand there watching until the family was out of sight, and then when no one was looking we would bend over, pick up the abandoned branches, press them against the sides of our coats and rush away, walking faster than usual but not so fast as to attract attention. At home we would examine them closely, thrilled at the excitement of their prickly touch. We would press them against our faces and breathe in deeply that tingling aroma and close our eyes and feel we were somewhere high up in the mountains. The sensation was like a vibrating current we could feel right down to our toes. Then we would hang the branches on the walls of the bedroom we shared, climb into our beds and softly sing Christmas carols until we fell asleep.

We knew every song by heart. The radio stations played them over and over again as Christmas got closer. A lot of the songs were about snow. And about mangers, too. I had no idea what a manger was but I figured that whatever it was, it must have had snow piled up all over it. A lot of the words were about a virgin. That was like manger, another of those words I didn't understand.

I never thought of the songs as religious. They were just something that happened at Christmas time that made you feel happy. And they were something you could share with your friends. I felt a special sense of belonging at school when we sang Christmas carols, all of us kids together, even if I didn't understand everything. Words like "*Holy virgin, mother and child.*" Who were all those people? Three of them, including the virgin. And what was a virgin anyway? It was confusing if you thought about it, but I didn't think about it too much.

And virgins weren't the only thing. There were places too. Like *Little Town of Bethlehem*. I knew about Oak Park, of course, and some towns around Chicago. But Bethlehem? Where in the world was that? I had no idea. Neither did any of the other kids. It's funny how things work out because I was the one who ended up going there. But that's another story. Back then none of us paid much attention to what words meant, words like *harktheheraldan-gels* and a lot of other strange sounds. It just didn't matter. We liked the singing.

With one exception. There was always one word that like a jack-in-the-box jumped out from all the others. "Jesus," the one everyone kept singing about. I didn't know anything about him, but I did know—I don't know how I knew it, I just did—that Jesus was the one word a nice Jewish boy shouldn't be saying. Standing in the back row of the singers where the teacher placed the tallest kids, when-ever I came to the Jesus word I would look down and pre-tend I was singing, but I would never say it. Singing about Christmas was all right, but there are some things you just didn't do. At least not if you're Jewish.

It's not that my family was so religious or even tradi-tional. Matter of fact, we were about as 100-percent American as you can get and still stay Jewish. Our Jewish memories had been dimmed by neglect, cultural assimila-tion and, perhaps on some subconscious level, may have even been dimmed deliberately. No matter. Even as I stood with my nose pressed against the window of Christmas celebrations I knew I could only look.

"It's not that we're different," my mother once told me. "But we're not quite the same."

We weren't. About the same time everyone else was celebrating Christmas we had our own holiday, Chanukah. My parents did their best to make it as much fun as Christmas but it never was.

I didn't know a lot about Chanukah. It seemed that some people called Greeks or Syrians or something like that were making trouble for the Jews and wouldn't let them pray in their temple. Somehow the Jews fought those people and won and went back to their temple and lit some oil that was supposed to burn for just one day and instead it burned for eight days and that was the whole story. So we were supposed to light candles for eight days.

At Sunday school, each kid was given a tin candle holder called a menorah. The tin was so thin it could easily be bent but I knew I wasn't supposed to bend it. It was colored gold but I knew it wasn't really gold. It was long enough to hold eight candles.

When I got my menorah I also got a small box of candles. They were all sorts of different colors—blue, white, green, yellow and red. I was supposed to light one candle the first night, two candles the second night and so on. So the first night I lit my first candle. It wasn't much bigger than a birthday candle. Charlotte and my parents watched me proudly. I watched the candle as it flickered, tossed off small shadows and then disappeared in a small pool of wax. My Chanukah candle didn't last nearly as long as the neighbors' Christmas candles. Those were electric and never went out.

After I lit the candle I quietly sang the few words of the traditional Chanukah song that I had been taught.

Actually, there were two Chanukah songs but I only knew the words to one of them. There were a lot of Christmas songs. When I grew up I learned that one of the most popular was "White Christmas." It was written by a Jew named Irving Berlin. He also wrote a song about another Christian holiday, "Easter Parade." But even Irving Berlin couldn't find a tune that worked for Chanukah.

On the second night of Chanukah, I lit two candles. That was the extent of my attention span. No more candle lighting after that. The remaining six days of the holiday went on without me. That was Chanukah. Something like Christmas, but not as exciting.

My dad tried to split the difference and brought me a small plastic Christmas stocking from Walgreens. It was filled with hard candies and tiny metal toys made in Japan. I hung the pretend Christmas stocking over our pretend brick fireplace. I wasn't expecting any Santa Claus to arrive and even if he did, he couldn't put anything inside the stocking without breaking the plastic. I didn't care. I already knew that Walgreens was more reliable than Santa Claus. I already knew that's as good as it gets.

Oak Park in those days was as American as Plymouth Rock. It wasn't a small town. Sixty-five thousand people lived there, but they insisted on calling Oak Park a village. That way they could say it was the largest village in the world. There were no liquor stores. A person would have to cross the street into Austin for that kind of vice.

My childhood was like the Norman Rockwell covers of the *Saturday Evening Post* that I sold door to door. In fall, I was the kid who would rake the crisp autumn leaves into big piles and then after all sorts of warnings and admonitions be allowed to use matches, just the way grown-ups did, and start a miniature bonfire with all those leaves, mesmerized by the sight of them curling into ashes. That was the best part. I would stand there hypnotized at the sight of the leaves crackling and burning and by the earthy aroma of the smoke, all the time feeling very grown up and responsible.

In winter, I was the kid shoveling snow from the neighbors' sidewalk for thirty cents an hour, intoxicated by the cold air that tasted like freshly pumped well water. I had a part-time job at the local drugstore where I'd make sodas and banana splits and ice cream sundaes untroubled by my job description, soda jerk. I was the awkward kid with the sweaty palms who would try to be nonchalant sitting next to his thirteen-year-old girlfriend whom I wouldn't dare touch but whose angora sweater stretching ever so slightly over tentative breasts set off feelings I didn't understand.

Just about all the kids had magazine routes, going door-to-door trying to sell copies of the *Saturday Evening Post*. I would climb up and down the stairs, pressing doorbells and asking the lady who opened the door if she wanted my magazine. It never occurred to me to develop a sales pitch. It was just "Hi, do you want the *Saturday Evening Post*?" The answer was usually a polite no but I quickly learned that if you kept ringing, somebody was bound to say yes. And with every sale, you earned a couple of pennies. And those pennies quickly added up to nickels.

Best thing of all, if you switched your loyalty from the *Saturday Evening Post* to its rival, *Colliers*, you would get a pocketknife for free, yesterday's equivalent of a "signing bonus." Having a pocketknife was great. You could open it and send it twirling into the ground, doing it just right so the blade would slice through the earth and leave the knife quivering victoriously.

Another challenge was to send it spinning toward a tree so it embedded itself into the trunk. But it rarely did. The trunk was hard and my knife-twirling skills were limited.

Successful or not, there was nothing like that big-shot feeling of having my very own knife inside the special pocketknife holder on the side of my high-top boots. Not a bad reward for climbing up and down stairs.

Oak Park emanated reassurance. From Harlem Avenue to Austin Boulevard, from North Avenue to Roosevelt Road, you knew that everything was all right. Walking to high school I passed homes designed by Frank Lloyd Wright. The school paper had once been edited by a guy—back when he was a kid—named Ernest Hemingway. Year after year the Oak Park football team, the Huskies, won the league championship. Every day, as three thousand of us entered the high school, we passed under an arch where elaborately carved Greek letters spelled out the school motto. We were told it meant "The best is none too good for us." Oak Park could mark you for a lifetime. Maybe two.

It was a time when everyone may have been created equal but that equality stopped at birth. None of the familiarity between young people and adults that exists today. Teachers were there to teach you, not to understand you. The principal was addressed as Mister and the teachers as Miss, never by their first names, although once I tried. Hormones had begun to race around inside me, tipping me off to what a knockout my tall, blonde, Spanish teacher was. She had a boyfriend who was in the navy during those World War II days but I was fearless enough to seek out a special relationship of my own. I asked her one day if I could call her by her first name. She smiled at me, radiating warmth and dazzling beauty. But not a hint of encouragement. I understood in a second. She was his alone. The answer was no.

My parents belonged to a Reform temple, a place of worship for Jews who don't know much about Judaism. They rarely went to religious services, didn't know the prayers, and like most American Jews, couldn't read Hebrew. But they did know that Jewish boys were supposed to have a bar mitzvah, the ceremony marking the passage into so-called manhood at age thirteen. So three afternoons a week I was sent to a Hebrew school taught by a refugee from Hitler's Germany, a man who knew nothing about teaching but did know Hebrew. We kids were so unruly that the poor man spent most of his time trying to control chaos while we spent most of our time trying to avoid studying.

My haftarah, the week's reading from the Prophets, was from the writings of the prophet Zechariah. I had no idea who Zechariah was. I wasn't even curious. My own disinterest was matched by my teacher's. It was many years later that I learned that Zechariah was pretty important and that all those sounds I was chanting meant things like "Not by might, nor by power, but by my spirit, says the Lord." At the time, though, Zechariah was just another one of those unpronounceable words like *littletownofbethelehem*. But at least, it was a Jewish word.

By the time my bar mitzvah was approaching I had learned the sounds the Hebrew letters make. I learned the rest by imitation. The tutor dutifully sang to me the sounds of the haftarah—you were supposed to chant it, not read it— and I dutifully memorized those sounds. I was a windup doll who sings on cue. And that's what happened on a beautiful day in June as I chanted all those Hebrew words I didn't understand, standing in front of the open Torah in the tiny building that used to be a dance studio. There weren't enough Jews in Oak Park for a real synagogue.

The moment everyone was waiting for was the speech that every bar-mitzvah boy delivers in English. This was the highlight of the ceremony because after the thirteen-year-old thanked the rabbi and his teachers he would get to the part where he thanks his mother and father for being wonderful parents. Everyone listened closely, especially the parents. This might be the only time they would hear such words.

In those days divorce was rare so everyone knew who the parents were. It was easier than today when a bar mitzvah boy may be surrounded by a father with his new wife, a mother with her new husband, and assorted children from all four, today's extended family. In the less-complicated time when I delivered my bar mitzvah speech, all eyes were focused on only two people, my biological parents. I stepped forward to the front of the stage. There was a hush in the room. A few sniffles, too, and I hadn't even said anything.

And then I began. I talked about how for years my father would come into my room every night as I lay sleeping and pull the blankets up snug around me. I told about the time I brought home a stray puppy, wanting desperately to keep it, knowing the answer would be no and then seeing my mother smile and nod that it was okay, that I really could have it. The congregants started to cry. A lot of them. Crying was good. It meant the speech was a success.

But a bar mitzvah happens only once. Holidays happen all year long. In Oak Park, most of them were Christian. The big one after Christmas was Easter. It was easy to tell when Easter was coming because the dime-store windows would fill up with pink bunnies and straw baskets stuffed with narrow strips of green and yellow paper and chocolate eggs. My friends were busy coloring hard-boiled eggs. Later on their parents would hide them and on Easter day the kids would look for them. They did that at the White House too, on the lawn out front. I learned that in still another newsreel, between Flash Gordon and the cartoons.

In our house we didn't do anything about Easter and yet every year I got in the mail a big chocolate bunny from my

Cousin Ann. It was hollow inside but that was okay because the chocolate was really good. I rarely saw my Cousin Ann because she lived in New York and was an old maid. My mother told me that. It wasn't until years later when I was going through a bunch of yellowing family photos that I noticed that Cousin Ann was a darn good-looking woman. That's when I was finally let in on the family secret that she had several lovers. That's when I realized she wasn't such a poor thing after all. Meanwhile, her chocolate bunny was my connection to Easter. I was a Jew for all seasons.

I didn't mind not having Easter because in our own dysfunctional way we were busy celebrating the Passover Seder, the traditional dinner when the whole family gets together for the annual ritual of reading the haggadah, the story of the exodus from Egypt. My mother put out the good china and silverware on a richly embroidered white tablecloth and everyone would come, her sister, Aunt Sarah, who weighed about 300 pounds and Uncle Dave, who weighed about half that, and their children too, Ruthie, Dava Lee, and Lou Ann.

And there was Uncle Ned who had ended fifty years of bachelorhood when he married Aunt Irene whose dark eyebrows were constantly twitching and whose intensely black hair spread confusion over one of the family myster-ies, whether she was really older than Uncle Ned which is what everyone suspected. I thought she was a nice lady but my mother had reservations about her. After all, fifty-year-old Uncle Ned, a shoe salesman, was her baby brother, and she found it hard to believe that anyone was good enough for him.

When the family finally got organized my sister, Charlotte, would pass around the haggadah booklets so that everyone could take turns reading the traditional story of the Exodus. That's what Jews all over the world do that night. I'd often think about that but I'd quickly give up because it was too complicated figuring out all the different time zones and realizing that in some countries Jews had already finished, and in other places they were just getting up for breakfast and also wondering if anyone in China was celebrating Passover since people in China didn't look Jewish.

In many countries haggadahs have been produced as stunning works of art with exquisite illustrations and rich designs. Our haggadahs were a collection of disparate editions including paperback copies that extolled the virtues of Empire Kosher Poultry.

The head of the household—in this case my dad—conducted the Seder. He was a good-looking man standing there in his narrow tie and starched white shirt which curved just slightly over a modest middle-age spread that connoted affluence even if there was none. He parted his hair on the right but the part went virtually unnoticed within his full dark hair that was combed straight back. People said he looked like the romantic film star of the day, John Barrymore. A carefully trimmed mustache beneath his aquiline nose framed an easy smile that revealed his genuine liking of people. His gray eyes, peering through narrow glasses, threw a friendly glance to the world. Tolerant of the quirks of others, he was perfect as the impresario of the haggadah reading while managing the more demanding task of keeping everyone focused on the evening's rituals.

One of the first ceremonies, the highlight of the evening, was to hear the youngest child at the table recite the traditional four questions. In every Jewish home the youngest boy or girl, often just five or six years old, is brought to the head of the table while everyone leans forward and beams—*cvells nachas* as they say in Yiddish—as the child timorously recites, "Why is this night different from all other nights?" Embarrassed, the child begins to squirm and then no louder than he has to finally recites those traditional questions. He has no idea what they mean but he knows they are important. Finished at last, he lowers his head and dashes back to his seat, dodging the pinches and kisses that follow him. For years, I was the youngest child.

After the four questions, each person takes turns reading the actual story. We did that, too. We also read prayers and psalms that are in the haggadah and even tried our discordant best at singing some traditional songs. And we read about four rabbis deep in philosophical discourse in a town in Israel called B'nai B'rak. That was like Bethlehem to me, another place that could have been on another planet. Many years later I was actually there, just an hour from Bethlehem. It's a small world, especially in Israel.

As we continued to read the Passover story we would recite blessings over wine and parsley and matzoh, the unleavened bread, until inevitably we would hear a fifth question that after so many years had become almost as traditional as the holiday's official four questions. The fifth question—there was always someone who would ask it—was, "So when do we eat already?"

My father would give way to the popular mood. "Turn to page twenty-four," he would say, suddenly skipping over six pages of text and moving closer to the moment when dinner would be served. Someone would read another paragraph and then before you knew it, Dad would announce, "Page thirty-two."

The Seder wasn't just reading. There were all sorts of symbols along the way, a kind of Jewish show and tell. There were the bitter herbs to remind us of the embitterment of being slaves in Egypt. There was the flat matzah to remind us of Jews fleeing Egypt so fast that there wasn't enough time for the dough to become bread. There was the lamb shank to remind us of the sacrifices in the Temple. And there was the hard-boiled egg. The haggadah doesn't even mention a hard-boiled egg, but it was always there. Tradition. With different interpretations. One was that the egg, dipped in salt water, was to remind us of the hardships and the tears of the Jews. Such a Jewish thing, I thought. Sad eggs. Why couldn't they just be something you colored and had fun with?

Besides the holiday rituals there were the family rituals such as the annual sibling rivalry contest between my mother and Aunt Sarah regarding who made the better gefilte fish, the traditional Ashkenazi delicacy of chopped carp. With the possible exception of Coca-Cola, no secret formula is as jealously guarded as the private recipes of serious gefilte fish makers.

My mother, a petite, smartly dressed woman, was the official hostess. Her younger sister, Sarah, was the antithesis of my mother. Aunt Sarah had lived much of her adult life in gingham in small towns in Oklahoma and Colorado as the wife of an army doctor. Aunt Sarah's face was round and jovial, her arms an array of folds, her dress that covered her spread legs a modest frock. My aunt didn't look Jewish and my mother didn't act Jewish. Both were very American, each in her own way, but Passover was a return to roots.

Sarah: "So how do you like the gefilte fish?"

Mother, being polite: "Very good." Then she would take another small bite and chew it thoughtfully. "Maybe a little too much pepper."

Sarah says nothing. She knows it is not her destiny to hear a compliment.

"I like it spicy," my father says. My father, with a natural bonhomie, likes to keep peace in the family.

"Herman likes it spicy," my mother says. Then she passes around some of her gefilte fish. "Try this," she says.

Sibling rivalry never ends, though with the passing years we learn to hide it better. But not much better.

Uncle Ned was the exception. Everyone liked Uncle Ned. He was a sweet, gentle, bald man who sold shoes to everyone and was a threat to no one. The 1930s were different from today. There were no self-service stores. In the midst of what came to be known as the Great Depression wages were low and stores provided personal service. So every day my Uncle Ned would slip his shiny metal shoehorn along the backs of dozens of different women's shoes, run downstairs and then back upstairs to bring each customer the exact size and color she asked for even though she usually wasn't sure what she wanted or, for that matter, whether she wanted anything at all beyond the adventure of looking. Every day was like that, Uncle Ned opening, closing, and returning to their places boxes upon boxes of shoes. Sometimes he would even sell a pair. At the Passover table, with whatever strength he had left after all that running up and down with a heart condition, Uncle Ned would laboriously read his paragraph. Everyone held their breath as he inevitably mispronounced several words. Then at last he would finish, and we would all breathe again.

Uncle Dave, small and compact, was always dapper in a gray tweed suit. When it was his turn to read the words seemed to part from him reluctantly, exhausted perhaps as they struggled through his bushy mustache. During the 1930s, Uncle Dave couldn't make a living as a private doctor, so he joined the CCC, the Civilian Conservation Corps, part of the army and one of the many New Deal projects designed to create employment. In those days, he and my Aunt Sarah lived in a tiny house in Gunnison, Colorado. I spent a summer there the year I was nine. It was long before the uranium boom that put Gunnison on the map. Back then, nothing was booming in Gunnison.

Nothing was booming throughout America. One out of every four American men was out of work. Many of them—they were called hobos—rode the rails swinging themselves unseen into one of the empty train carriages, going from one town to another looking for work or just trying to find a life. Every couple of days a hobo would knock on the paint-chipped screen door of the small wooden house my aunt and uncle rented and politely ask for something to eat. Aunt Sarah would amble over to the rickety table next to the iron stove where she did her cooking—my favorite spot in the kitchen because that's where every now and then she would open the heavy metal door and toss chunks of wood into the fire—and reach for two slices of bread, spread some margarine or mayonnaise across them, and if the man was lucky even put some cheese inside. With a big smile on her full cheeks she would hand the man his sandwich and then the smile would dissolve into a stern expression as she warned him not to talk to the children. The man would thank her and disappear into the distance with his sandwich and his fears.

In time Uncle Dave and his family moved to Maywood, Illinois, not far from Oak Park. That's how they became part of our Passover gathering. Uncle Dave always seemed to be lost in some other world until every now and then, one of his enormous sneezes would shake his small frame and return him to this world. His appearance as an absent-minded professor belied an intelligence and wit that I came to appreciate only years later.

All that is now a distant past and hardly anyone of that long-ago family with its craziness and feuds and good times and shared sadness is here anymore. Every problem seemed so important back then and every slight so hurtful, and now all is swept away in a fog of time as if none of those things ever happened. I find myself wishing that all those crazy people were alive and that once again we could celebrate Passover together. We would be contemporaries and I would be more understanding and less judgmental. It takes a lifetime to learn how to live.

Thanksgiving was my favorite holiday. It was neither Jewish nor Christian. On Thanksgiving we were all Americans. At the community religious services we were all together, Christians and Jews. Jesus was conveniently absent. And there were no rabbis from B'nai B'rak to worry about. I was grateful at Thanksgiving time, not only for my blessings but because I wasn't conflicted. On Thanksgiving my friends and I had the same forefathers and came from the same place, Plymouth Rock. Not Russia, not Poland. Plymouth Rock.

We didn't have much money in those years of the Depression but we were comfortable. My dad was a dentist, making fillings for five dollars and then waiting months to get paid. Dentures were as much as five hundred dollars but only one or two patients could afford them and they made him wait for his money longer than the poor people did.

One time my dad even had the embarrassment of having to borrow money. I knew that by accident because one day when he was in charge of taking care of me he brought me along when he met with a man I didn't know and asked him for a loan, a couple of hundred dollars. My dad told me not to tell my mother where we had been. That night, at the dinner table, my mother asked me how our day was. I started talking about different things, and then suddenly I let it slip. I mentioned the man we had met. I didn't mean to. As soon as I said it I could feel the silence. Without looking up, I knew my parents had exchanged glances. Nobody said anything more about it, at least not in front of me. We all kept eating. But I knew I had done something terrible.

We couldn't afford a car, but my dad bought me a shiny red-and-cream-colored Schwinn bicycle which was the best gift I ever got in my whole life. I was on it every day, quickly learning how to ride with "no hands." It had a big basket that I would fill with groceries when my mother sent me on errands. Other times, I would race the cars down Ridgeland Avenue, catching up with them when they had to stop for a red light and then pedaling past them while dodging the cars turning in front of me. Every now and then I would lose control and fall down with the bicycle in the middle of traffic. But God tends to take care of little children and I would just get up again and continue pedaling, ignoring the cuts and bruises and, of course, never letting anyone at home see them.

Like all families, we had our share of personal problems. I still remember standing at the side of my grandmother's open coffin when I was six years old. Her hair was pulled back tight. The wart on her chin that always looked to me like a little red cherry was still there. She looked as clean and neat as she had been in real life, but there was no life. I tried to understand that. A year later, more death. My grandfather was dying and my mother moved him into our small apartment and set up a bed for him in the living room. I remember the day I left for school and his nurse asked me if I wanted to say goodbye to him. I always said goodbye. I could feel deep inside me she was telling me something more. I fumbled a goodbye as best I could and went off to school, trying to think about something else. When I came home for lunch he wasn't there and the bed wasn't there. No one said anything to me about it but of course I understood. Later at the funeral parlor, I stepped over to his coffin and touched his chest and forehead. His chest felt like it was stuffed with sawdust. I didn't know anything about sawdust, but I was sure that's what it felt like.

Other family problems—cousin Yonny's father, Isadore, visiting us and sitting with his belt undone and the top of his pants open so the cancer inside his stomach would have more room. And the death of Yonny's son, Ralph, a couple of years later. Ralph was older than I was, maybe three years older.

When summer came we rarely went anywhere. At best, we would spend a week at a farm in nearby Indiana, getting there on a smoke-clogged train that rumbled out of the grime of Chicago's South Side, past isolated wooden buildings near small railroad crossings and then through passive fields. For the rest of the summer months I was on my own. No one worried about me being bored, being dyslexic or being socialized. I was just supposed to grow up.

On summer days I would run out of the kitchen, let the screen door bang shut behind me and race down the stairs. I would find a friend or two and we would play ball or ride our bikes all day. Then between five and six in the afternoon we would be back home, lying on our backs on the living-room floor with the radio turned on, listening to the fifteen-minute programs, Two of my favorite characters were the Lone Ranger and his faithful guide, Tonto. Those were the days before people were politically correct. I never knew Tonto was a Native American. Tonto was an Indian. I had no problem with that, and I doubt if Tonto did either.

Another favorite was Jack Armstrong, the All-American boy. He was sponsored by Wheaties, "The Breakfast of Champions." If Wheaties was good enough for Jack, it was good enough for me. I began every morning with a big bowlful and sent in the box tops for every promotion that was offered. I can still remember the Hikeameter that measured how far I walked. I clipped it proudly onto my belt and even though I knew how far everything was in my little neighborhood I would dutifully check my Hikeameter at every corner just to be sure it was clocking the distance. That's what Jack would have wanted me to do. More than anything else, that's all I wanted—to be like Jack Armstrong. The All-American boy.

Chapter 3

Rita and Mike

*T*he snowy Sunday afternoon when Rita and Mike came to visit changed all that.

It was 1971. I was forty-two that year. Rosalind and I had been married thirteen years. We had four children. We were living in Winnetka, a Chicago suburb that was a lot like Oak Park.

That's when it all began, though it's hard to be sure when anything begins. Sometimes feelings are so deep inside you that they're already there waiting to happen.

Rosalind and I had met Rita and Mike a few months earlier at a small dinner party. We liked them immediately, Mike outrageous with his dramatic storytelling, Rita intrinsically refined. We felt we had always known them. We didn't know that knowing them would change our lives forever.

Years later I would sometimes lie in bed wondering what our lives would have been like if we hadn't met them that night. What if a child had been sick and we had missed the party? What if something else had kept us away? What if.... But when you're young and master of your destiny you don't think about things like that. What if is for later years.

We felt like old friends by the time they visited that day. I guess you would call it chemistry. Or maybe fate. Somehow we just connected. While we waited for them we drifted into our weekend ritual of exploring world events and mindless gossip in the Sunday papers, Rosalind comfortable in her favorite chair while I spread out across the sofa, relishing the warmth of the fireplace and the sputtering of flames dancing across the pile of logs. Outside the January storm tossed clouds aside and sent snow plummeting across the entire Midwest. We couldn't even see the hedges beyond the bay window. They had disappeared within the deep drifts of snow.

Turning a page, I looked up and before they even rang the bell spotted Mike and Rita coming toward the house. They had just stepped out of their car and were leaning into the wind as they came toward us, their boots crunching across the snow. It was a short walk, but already their faces were flushed by the wet cold. We jumped up and pulled the front door open. The sharp wind tried to elbow us aside as it swept into the house. Mike and Rita all but fell into our arms as the four of us bunched together in a mixture of windmill gestures of hands brushing off snow, arms pulling off coats, fingers tugging at scarves until, with the wet garments finally cast aside, we dragged our friends into the warmth of the pillowed sofa.

The glow of the see-through fireplace sent friendly shadows dancing across the mantle's rough stones. Rosalind brought out a carafe of mulled wine whose pungent spices drifted into the aroma of the burning logs. We filled waiting glasses and sipped slowly, all of us. The warmth of the wine meandered through our bodies, a blissful numbing that lulled our senses into a warm drowziness as we watched the hypnotic movements of snowflakes twirling through an improvised ballet.

I had already kicked off my shoes and stretched out my legs so that my thick white socks rested on the edge of the low-lying coffee table, a wicked indulgence that was part of being grown up and free from parental admonitions about hurting the furniture.

Devorah was nine that year. Laura had just turned eleven. David and Becca were four and two. Nice ages when they would be in their rooms, Laura playing the adult and busily bossing Devorah around, David and Becca acting out stories with their stuffed animals. It was a comfortable time of life when everyone still loved Mommy and Daddy, long before the days of inevitable teenage rebellion and nights worrying about the kids driving safely.

Rita nestled into the pillows, her feet pulled up under her legs. Her features were petite in a childlike way with pudgy cheeks and an easy smile.

Rita was the financial and emotional support of her parents and even her adult brother. She worked as an interior designer and came home after a long day to be the mother to her two sons and apparently to Mike as well. Mike was older and wiser and dependent. Rita was one of those people who spends her life fulfilling other people's expectations. She died of cancer at fifty, perhaps from the stress of always smiling. That afternoon, however, death was far away, something that happened to others. We were still young and immortal.

Mike was older than the rest of us, the top of his head already bald while the sides of his face were ringed by dark curls that made his formidable mustache seem even more foreboding. Like a monk who has left the monastery he projected the tension between the devil and the saint.

Given to mood swings, he was as unpredictable as he was mannered. That Sunday, his mood was benign. Almost contemplative.

Rosalind was the youngest, beautiful with her fair skin, blue eyes, and light hair. She had just turned thirty-six and looked even younger. As a matter of fact, a couple of years earlier while I was working at ABC-TV in New York, the president of the network, Ollie Treyz, came by to drop off a script at our home in Scarsdale. He rang the doorbell and Rosalind came running down the steps wearing a white sweater, plaid slacks and white socks. Ollie had never met her before and greeted her warmly.

"When he gets home," Ollie said as he handed her the manila envelope, "please give this to your daddy."

Even during our days in Winnetka, she didn't look much different than she did when I first met her. She was a rebellious Berkeley coed back in 1958, racing around town in a red MG convertible so covered with dirt and grime as to no longer be shiny red and yet red enough to attract attention. Especially with Rosalind driving.

I was a bachelor at the time, sent to San Francisco by ABC to work at its TV station, KGO. I wasn't there long when from my circle of single men I heard about an attractive girl at Berkeley. Not only that, but one of my friends even had a blind date with her. A few years earlier, with the mystique if not the salary of a young TV executive, I would have been embarrassed to date a girl of college age. But as I approached thirty I was no longer intimidated by such prurient predilections, especially since my friend who had the blind date, Norman Ascherman, was even older at thirty-three.

I had known Norman since he was eighteen. He was a twin—his brother had become a doctor and Norman a dentist—and he was living in San Francisco when I was transferred there. Norman was short, had bushy hair, and spoke in a voice that sounded like a truck driving on gravel.

"Bring your date over to see me," I told Norman one day.

"Why should I do that?" Norman graveled.

"So you can return the book you borrowed," I said.

"But I never borrowed a book," Norman said.

As I said, Norman was a dentist. A good dentist, but not a creative thinker.

"You'll pretend you borrowed a book," I said. "Bring over any book."

"With my date?" he said.

"Of course with your date. I want to meet her." I was getting impatient. There is only so much you can expect from a dentist.

Norman looked puzzled. But he was nothing if not loyal. On the night of his date he returned a book I had never seen before. That's when I saw Rosalind. She was a knockout, warm, animated and even Jewish. Norman gave me the book and I invited them to sit down for a few minutes. We talked. We talked about F. Scott Fitzgerald, a concession to the college girl. We talked about the stock market, a concession to the junior executive. Norman joined in. He talked about leaving, and then they did.

As they left I decided that having borrowed Norman's fictitious book, I would borrow his girlfriend as well. Or at least I'd try. Norman was as good a friend as he was a dentist. He never complained. And besides, she wasn't really his girlfriend. Just a blind date.

Years later, Rosalind admitted that she wrote my name in her datebook that night so she would remember it when I called. She knew I would call. Women always know.

That was the beginning of the end of my bachelor days. The next weekend we drove up to Marin County in her dirty MG. A week after that we met for dinner and a few days after that for lunch at Fisherman's Wharf and then there was that day when we were meandering down a street of San Francisco decorators.

Stopping in front of one of the display windows, Rosalind took my arm and pulled me over toward one of the open rolls of wallpaper.

"Do you see that one over there?" she said. "That blue?"

I looked over to where she was pointing. "The blue," I said.

"That blue," she said.

I looked at the blue.

"It would look nice in our home," she said.

I'm not sure we ever did use that color blue but suddenly everything was different. That December we were married at the Fairmont Hotel.

In Winnetka thirteen years later we were the perfect couple with four children, two television sets and a brick home on a corner lot. As with any married couple there were moments of tension as we went beyond romantic bliss to the realization that neither of us was perfect. But we were not married long enough for annoyances to grow into resentments. Life was good in Winnetka, a sheltered world of suburban self-satisfaction where, as Rosalind mused years later, "no one ever got sick or died." Or so it seemed. As with Rita, Rosalind's words were always framed within a smile. Like Rita, she died of cancer two decades later. Right then, however, it was the best of times.

Beyond Winnetka it was not the best of times. A half-million Americans were at war in a country hardly anyone had ever heard of, Vietnam. In the beginning, there were only seven hundred Americans there. They were called "advisors" and they were supposed to help the South Vietnamese government hold off the North Vietnamese Communist regime that wanted the whole country.

President Kennedy decided that seven hundred advisors were not enough so he increased the number to 16,000.

Then in 1964 President Johnson told the country that Vietnamese gunboats had attacked American destroyers in another place no one ever heard of, the Gulf of Tonkin. That never really happened but the president said it happened and the newspapers wrote that it happened and so everyone believed that it happened. The pundits of print journalism, precursors of today's screaming heads, put it all in context by echoing the government's line about the domino theory, the idea that if Vietnam fell so would every other small country along the Pacific Rim. Ninety-eight senators quickly expressed their patriotism by voting for the Gulf of Tonkin resolution that gave Johnson a free hand to pursue the war. Before long, Johnson decided that what America really needed was to have more than a half-million American soldiers in Vietnam.

One of the two senators who voted against the war was Wayne Morse of Washington. Morse, an intelligent, handsome man of great presence who had served in the Senate with distinction for almost a quarter of a century, continued to argue against American involvement. For his disloyalty, he was defeated for reelection four years later.

For several years dissonance was muffled. Most people were just not emotionally involved. Vietnam was a long way away. It was a war against people with dark skin fought by America's volunteer army that had a lot of other people with dark skin. There was a disconnect in the country that brought to mind the Korean War movie, *The Bridges at Toko-Ri*. The night before his dangerous bombing run to take out the bridges, Bill Holden can't sleep. He's scared. His life is on the line. On the radio he hears eighty thousand people screaming their excitement at a Rams–49ers football game. Eighty thousand people screaming for a touchdown, eighty thousand people oblivious to Bill Holden risking his life.

The Vietnam War was something like that. For a long time most people didn't give it much thought. There were a few antiwar demonstrations in places like San Francisco but everyone knew that San Francisco was radical and not to be taken seriously. Insofar as Winnetka was concerned, Winnetka could never be confused with San Francisco. Winnetka was not even like nearby Chicago where during the 1968 Democratic convention, hippies, protesters, and other troublemakers battled police in Grant Park. People don't do things like that in Winnetka. We are very polite. We discuss world affairs over drinks and dinner, not in the streets. Dissension is rare. If expressed at all, it is always with restraint. Winnetka is Republican, and Republicans don't raise their voices.

I had moved to Winnetka after fifteen years as a migrant worker for ABC Television, years that took me from Chicago to New York to San Francisco and back to New York. I hadn't really planned to work in television. I was thinking about going from Northwestern University to the State Department. The pay there was fifty dollars a week, not much, but nobody was paying much in those days.

That was 1950 and something unusual was happening, something magical. It was called television. So six months before graduation I started looking for a job in TV. Five months later I got my chance. There was a job open for a writer at WBKB in Chicago. They also paid fifty dollars a week. So I figured that for the same money I would go for the magic.

The first magic was the disappearance of my promised salary. On my first day at work, my boss, Red Quinlan, told me that his boss, John Mitchell, told him that fifty dollars a week was too much to pay a young kid. On payday I found out that instead of getting ahead in the world I was going backward. My pay was cut to forty-five dollars a week. But I couldn't bring myself to leave. As the old joke goes: "What? And quit show business?"

The years may not have been lucrative but they were exciting. When I started in 1950 television programs from New York could be seen only as far west as Chicago. Just a couple of years later we all watched Edward R. Murrow from CBS in New York show us a television shot of the Atlantic Ocean and then turn in his chair, as if to look out a window, and show us a live scene of the Pacific. Talk about magic!

ABC, like most big corporations in those days, constantly moved its executives and even junior executives around the country. It wasn't unusual after chatting with a fellow commuter at the train station in Scarsdale to run into him again a year later at the train station in Winnetka. During those years, I lived in bedroom communities from Belvedere, California, to Scarsdale, New York, but my life was not like the best-seller of those days, *Peyton Place*. Nobody ever invited me into her bedroom. We were all young marrieds, happy with one another, with the fun of rearing small children and with our rapid progress through the corporations. After fifteen years, though, I was in the mood for a new adventure and left the network to join a small broadcasting company in Chicago and work for a man who remained a close friend until his death more than thirty years later, Irving Harris.

That's when I moved to Winnetka, replicating my pattern of suburban living. I bought a modern beige brick home on a corner with the reassuring names of Berkeley and Ash near the local elementary school called Crow Island, a name deferential to the area's Indian roots. We were a community of achiever husbands, beautiful wives, and mannered children. Five nights a week Rosalind joined the suburban end-of-the-day ritual of rushing the kids into the shiny family station wagon and driving into a bumper-to-bumper line of loyal wives and bouncing children, all waiting for their hard-working husbands and fathers to alight from the train.

Five nights a week at 5:40 P.M., like scores of other commuting husbands in their serious suits and conservative ties, I would jump down from the train and slide comfortably into the front seat of our station wagon and be driven home amid the screaming of children's greetings and the internecine torment going on in the backseat. I was happy to be back after a hard day's work and not terribly sensitive to how much harder and longer Rosalind had worked that same day with dinner, bathing the children, and getting everyone ready for bed still looming ahead of her. It was the generation before husbands shared children chores with their wives, not much different from about a thousand generations before then. I still feel the guilt.

Winnetka was as predictable politically as it was sociologically, overwhelmingly behind the Vietnam War. I was troubled by the war. I was troubled a lot. But I was too hopelessly middle class to be a radical and too Midwestern to seethe with indignation. People don't seethe in the Midwest. And yet deep down, the war gnawed at me. I remembered listening to the newscasts of Edward R. Murrow back in 1954 and hearing his reports of the Vietnamese driving out their former colonial rulers, the French. A decade later we had replaced the French. I remembered my student days at Northwestern University where my political science professor taught us that foreign policy should grow out of national self-interest. I saw no American self-interest in Vietnam. It was not Czechoslovakia in 1939, the precursor to Hitler's madness. It was not Europe, vital to America's economy and security. I just couldn't see how Vietnam was critical to American well-being. It was a point of view not widely shared, especially in Winnetka.

In 1966, a year after we arrived, the big political news was that one of our neighbors, a man from our suburban North Shore, was going to run for the United States Senate. His name was Chuck Percy.

His opponent was the formidable Democratic incumbent, a craggy-faced giant and intellectual giant as well, Senator Paul Douglas who had been a full professor at the University of Chicago. His devoted followers embraced him for his strong liberal views and admired him for joining the United States Marines at age fifty and fighting the Japanese in Peleliu and Okinawa in the Pacific during World War II. Douglas was wounded, underwent five operations and spent the rest of his life with a left arm that he described as being little more than "a paperweight." Douglas's supporters were primarily New Deal liberals who conveniently overlooked his hawkish position on Vietnam that few of them shared. Politics is like love. The mind easily adapts to the heart.

Chuck Percy, the Republican candidate, was the antithesis of Douglas. Percy lacked Douglas's overpowering persona, the enormous intellect that matched his large, lumbering body. Percy was short, lithe, athletic and beautiful. If Hollywood had made the story of his life Robert Redford would have starred.

Percy had lived the Horatio Alger story, especially as Republicans would have written it. Though born poor, he did not come out of the Chicago slums the way poor Democrats did. Instead, Percy had been poor in respectable North Chicago. He worked hard, got ahead, was always neat and mannered, married a handsome young woman and grew up to become the successful CEO of a fast-growing camera company, Bell & Howell. Percy was one of those people who, quite simply, did everything right. He gave you the feeling that at age six he decided he would never again perspire.

As a political junkie, I watched the race closely. Douglas was the towering presence. Percy was charismatic, a fast take and could learn anything. But in a stunning bit of role reversal the darling of the Democratic liberals was outspoken in his support of America's growing involvement in Vietnam while Percy failed to share the Republican commitment to the war.

Late one night, seeing Percy as a possible outlet for my own antiwar sentiments, I sat down at a typewriter and undeterred by my complete lack of political experience laid out an entire campaign strategy for him. I was certain that the last thing he needed was unsolicited advice but I decided I would write to him anyway. If money were as available to a candidate as unsolicited advice no one would ever need a fund-raiser.

I worked hard on my letter. I developed my ideas carefully. I integrated them into an overall campaign. I tried to keep the presentation as concise as possible. I finished the letter and mailed it the next day.

A week went by and I still hadn't heard from him. No doubt he received a lot of mail, I thought. It was unreasonable to expect an answer so soon. Two more weeks went by and still no response. Well, the letter was unsolicited and there was no reason why he should answer, I thought.

Three weeks went by. "It would have been nice," I told Rosalind, "if he had at least acknowledged the letter. Even a brief thank-you." Four weeks went by. There was something worse than my ideas being rejected, I realized. Worse was being ignored. "You would have thought," I said as we were doing the dishes together, "that he would at least have wanted my vote." My pique overroad my antiwar sentiments, I was ready to throw my support, my entire one vote, to Paul Douglas.

And then one night the phone rang. It was eleven o'clock. People didn't usually call after ten. Rosalind answered and heard a deep, resonant voice ask for me. An improbable time and an improbable voice. Her eyes darted upward in a look of exasperation. "It must be an insurance salesman," she said as she shoved the phone into my hand.

I grabbed the phone from her, annoyed by then at both her and the late-night caller. And then I heard the voice, as mellifluous as a CBS announcer introducing the president of the United States. "Yale," the voice said. "This is Chuck Percy."

That's how I got involved in Republican politics and opposition to the Vietnam War. Percy talked about my letter and my ideas in detail. Clearly, he was aware of every suggestion. He asked me to meet his campaign manager. The next day, I arrived at an office suite in the middle of Chicago's Loop, rooms that had already succumbed to the campaign disarray of papers, pamphlets and posters. Presiding over it all was a thickly built son of a German tavern owner, who himself looked like a balding German butcher. I introduced myself to Tom Houser. Like two cocks preparing for their life-and-death encounter, we looked each other over with mutual suspicion. Tom got right to the point. "Percy told me about your talk and I don't know a damn thing about you. You might even be a son of a bitch," he said, "but at the end of the day, remember that I'm the top son of a bitch."

His street-smart aura and tough talk did little to hide his sense of decency. But he was protecting his turf. He was running the campaign and knew exactly what to do. I was running nothing and lost no time in letting him know how I could do things better. A couple of arrogant, bright guys in their thirties. Despite the bravado and the bluff, we immediately liked each other, went on to work well together, and have remained close friends ever since.

Within a week, I was out campaigning with Chuck, flying from town to town in a small Cessna. Chuck was in the back seat shouting strategy over the sound of the motor to his aide, Scott Cohen, formerly of the CIA. I sat in the front seat with the pilot wondering what the hell I was doing risking my life in that two-bit plane. But when we landed, magic happened. Chuck started working the crowd. Not very big, he soon disappeared within a maze of women wearing white bouffant hair and men in red-and-black checkered shirts, all shaking hands and making small talk. Chuck was good at that. "Glad to see *you*," he would say with the "*you*" left vibrating in the air on the resonance of that improbable voice, leaving the voter at the other end of the handshake with the firm conviction that there was nothing Chuck would rather be doing that morning (afternoon/night) than hear what the guy had to say. How much he actually heard was open to question because, unknown to most people, Chuck had a serious hearing problem. I never asked if he considered that a problem or a blessing.

Chuck moved through the crowd in a grab-your-partner kind of dance step, his right hand shaking the voter's hand and his left hand gripping the voter's right shoulder in a dozey-doe movement that created intimacy (clutching the arm as well as the hand) while the hand-on-the-shoulder gesture moved the voter on past him so he could reach out to the next voter. It was sort of a country-and-western dance step guaranteed to smoothly sashay the candidate through the throng of voters.

Though Chuck had invited me to barnstorm with him he never told me what he wanted me to do. So I made it up as I went along, meandering through the crowd, jotting down one-liners that he might use in his impromptu speeches and then timorously shoving my notes into his hand while he was talking to somebody else. And then a funny thing happened. I was walking along the fringes of the crowd, Chuck had started to speak, and I wasn't paying particular attention to what he was saying when suddenly I heard some words that sounded familiar. Chuck was delivering my lines. When was he able to glance at them? I thought. And how could he remember them so precisely? I knew he was fast but I didn't know he had total recall. No question about it, ours was a libretto made in heaven. Or were we in Kankakee?

It was late when I got home that night after touching down in a few more towns, but my spirits were soaring. I was a player. Maybe only a bit player, but no matter. It was exciting.

There were moments of guilt, as well. Returning home one night a week later I was greeted at the door by Devorah, who was four years old and hadn't gone to bed yet. My enthusiasm at seeing her was immediately dampened by her greeting. "Why," she looked up and asked me, "do you spend so much time with your friend, Percy?" I picked her up in my arms and told her about all the things we were doing, trying to share my excitement with her. As the memory of that greeting lingered over a lifetime I finally understood that what she was really saying was that she missed her daddy. But back then I was too consumed with my own feelings to be more sensitive to hers.

The campaign continued and in time that giant oak of a man, Paul Douglas, was toppled as Chuck Percy emerged as one of the most exciting Republicans on the national scene. There was talk of him becoming president. He was on his way to fame. I returned to anonymity.

My son, David, was born that campaign year. Our

third daughter, Becca, was born two years later, and our lives settled into suburban respectability, mowing the lawn on Saturdays, chatting with neighbors walking by, riding the kids one at a time on my bicycle as I pedaled along the path that wound through large trees in a nearby park. As we rode, I explained to them in a deep and serious voice that this was a forest and that all sorts of mysteries lay within it.

I remained a political junkie and persisted in one of my parental shortcomings, scanning the newspaper at the breakfast table. One morning in 1969 there was big news, big for our community. The local congressman from our thirteenth district was resigning to join the Nixon administration. His name was Don Rumsfeld.

Bells went off in my head. An off-year election. Several candidates would run from that group that had worked for Percy, knew Rumsfeld, and were a part of the local Republican establishment. With that many contenders, the winner would need only a plurality. A perfect setup for an unknown. I thought about it. I certainly qualified on that score. I was very unknown. But I did have that fascination with politics. Maybe . . . maybe . . .

I like to think that I gave the matter serious thought, but the fact is that my gut had the answer before my mind did. Of course, I would run. I knew that as soon as I finished the front-page story.

I've often thought about the value of ignorance. With too much knowledge, you know what can't be done. With ignorance, you try for it anyway. And who knows? I certainly wouldn't get elected if I didn't run, so running was the only choice there was—if one ignores saner alternatives such as having a normal life.

The trick was to win the Republican primary. There was always a candidate from the Democrats in the general election but he never had a chance. The North Shore elects only Republicans. Having worked for Percy I had my Republican credentials although they were somewhat suspect, as were Percy's, because they were liberal Republican credentials. In the suburbs of the Midwest, it is all right for Democrats to be liberals because everyone knows they are fools. But Republicans who are liberal are worse than fools. They are disloyal. And yet, all I needed was that plurality.

All anyone needed to win was a plurality. I wasn't the only one to notice something so obvious. With that tantalizing prospect, twelve of us Republican bit players decided to try for stardom even as we all knew that old cliché that for every light on Broadway, there are a million broken hearts. The same goes for Washington.

The campaign, lasting only three summer months, remains with me as a mélange of memories such as standing at the Old Orchard shopping center with ten-year-old Laura and Devorah, who was eight, trying to get signatures from passers-by so that I could get on the ballot. They didn't have to be supporters, just anybody who would add his name to the number of signatures required to get a person on the ballot. Winnetka is a civic-minded community. While most people just walked past many did, indeed, sign up in the interest of free elections. Of course, there are always spoilsports. Laura approached one man who briskly turned her down, telling her that her daddy was a bad man. That one hurt. She had never heard anyone call her daddy a bad man before. She was too young to know it was a synonym for liberal Republican.

There were many acts of kindness. My boss, Irving Harris, called and *asked* if he could contribute a thousand dollars to the campaign. Irving is a smart man and he knew my chances were slim. My name was hardly a household word, and I had lived in Winnetka for only a few years. But some people are just nice.

My mother, who had spent a lifetime making a dime look like a dollar, shopping carefully and then buying only on sale, came over one Sunday and just between the two of us gave me a check for $1,500. She had probably spent a lot of years saving that up.

David Hardin, one of the members of the inner circle of the North Shore Republican establishment, stepped forward to help me. Dave was a marketing man who had been a longtime friend of Rumsfeld and just about everyone else in that Republican power group that had decided to support one of the other candidates. Dave, whom I had known only a few years, told them he couldn't do that. Referring to the candidate they were backing, Dave said to them, "He's like one of my family but Yale, he's like my brother." That made me feel really good.

Dave became my political advisor. He had a lot of experience in politics and ran one of the largest market research companies in America. I felt I was in good hands. The first thing Dave told me was that I had to separate myself from the other candidates to create a niche that would attract the plurality we were looking for. That was easy because of the twelve candidates running, I was one of only two who opposed the Vietnam War. So I was already "niched" in a congressional district where, when campaigning in Arlington Heights one day, a woman came up to me and with her face close to mine announced, "If I have to stand behind my son with a pitchfork, he's going to Vietnam." In Arlington Heights, as in much of my district, being against the Vietnam War was like being a traitor to America.

The challenge was how to turn my negative into a positive. How could my antiwar position become a rallying point for the disaffected? Dave came up with the idea. It was a perfect bit of niche marketing. The only thing wrong was that it consigned me to a niche of opprobrium. Dave Hardin decided I had to speak out sharply against one of the most popular United States senators in American history, the brilliant legislator, magnificent orator and accomplished drinker, Republican Everett McKinley Dirksen. Attacking Dirksen in Winnetka was like attacking the pope in Rome. If my campaign had ever been important enough to be studied in Harvard's classes in American politics or in Wharton's classes in business, it would undoubtedly stand out as one of the worst political-marketing decisions of all time.

We fired our salvo on the official opening night of the campaign when several hundred conscientious citizens of the North Shore, most of them passionate Republicans, gathered at a town meeting in Winnetka to look over the newly assembled cadre of candidates. One by one, each of the candidates took his turn speaking. Each of us was well groomed, well mannered, and congenial. One by one, the candidates laid out their positions of probity that were manifestly similar promises for America—better education, more efficient use of federal funds and the support of our men overseas.

Then it was my turn. My arguments were tightly reasoned, my rhetoric carefully honed and the speech well rehearsed. All the polite people in the audience with their white hair and blue eyes sat there in respectful attention until the moment when it seemed you could actually hear everyone in the room, in unison, sucking in his breath. I had just jabbed my forefinger out at the crowd exactly the way I had seen President Kennedy do it so many times. I pointed that finger at the crowd and loyally delivered David's own copy line specifically designed to separate myself from my fellow campaigners. "If you're a Dirksen

Republican," I said, finger jabbing away, "if you're a Dirksen Republican, then I'm not your man."

I could feel the audience tighten into tension. I could feel the hostility that swept through the room. People don't usually speak out against the pope. I had created a niche, no doubt about that. But it was beginning to look like one of those niches that goes six feet down.

Life seemed hopeless and the campaign irredeemable and yet much to my surprise wonderful things happened. Strangers walked into our home and offered to work on the campaign. People we knew, and people we didn't know, had coffees for me so I could meet their friends and try to get their votes and sometimes donations. Even on the North Shore, there were people who opposed the war. Maybe not enough, but the only way to find out was to try. One night I spoke before perhaps a hundred people in a private home. The mood was electric, and I felt loved and reassured. Another day I drove for more than an hour to a daytime coffee and only three women showed up. It was nice of them to do that. They certainly didn't owe me anything. But I was heartbroken and even angry. What was I doing knocking myself out for maybe three votes? And maybe not even that?

In the middle of all that, my campaign manager quit. I felt like I was dangling in the wind. Rosalind quickly rushed in, cut down the rope and said she would take over. Within days she had organized friends to sit around tables in our home, fold mailers and stuff them into envelopes. I came home one night to find David sitting alone at the table with a sheaf of papers and crayons, but he wasn't drawing. He was folding sheets of paper into thirds, just the way the volunteers had been doing. At age three he thought that's what you did with paper.

Life became an emotional roller coaster. One moment,

I would feel the exhilaration of being on the political stump fighting for my beliefs. But then in the car on the way to the next appearance, I'd slump back into the seat completely exhausted, wondering how I could possibly get up the energy for another speech. Even on Broadway, only twice a week does an actor have to perform twice a day. If the actor is called a candidate, and all candidates are indeed actors, he performs many more times than that day in and day out.

One night, I complained to Percy that I was already tired even though the length of my campaign was shorter than his and I didn't have to campaign through the entire state the way he did. Our congressional district did have as many voters as the entire state of Wyoming but all the same it was a much smaller area. "Yale," he said with compassion, not for me but for himself, "at least you get to sleep in your own bed at night." He was right, of course. Instead of staying with strangers and having to be charming every moment or instead of staying in another depressing hotel room, I was at least home every night. But even at home I would wake up at three in the morning with the terrible feeling that I just couldn't go on. Campaigning is hard on the body and even harder on the emotions.

The meetings and public appearances continued. The twelve candidates were beginning to feel like a touring road company. There we were night after night, each of us repeating essentially the same lines. Worst than that, night after night, we had to listen to the same lines of our opponents, lines we knew as well as our own. Real actors do that all the time, of course, but they seem to like what they do. We candidates were doing it only for the promise of fame. But who knows? Maybe that's what keeps real actors going, too.

To overcome my own boredom as much as to do something the voters would remember I tried to think up new ways to deliver my small bits of theater, resorting one night to picking out items one by one from deep inside a shopping bag so I could point out how much more expensive each item had become and thereby turn an economic argument into show-and-tell. Other nights, Phil Crane, the most right-wing candidate among us and ironically the one I enjoyed listening to the most, would conspire with me to gratuitously bait one another just for the challenge of having to think of something new to say. I don't know if our little repartee did anything to enlighten the audience or gain any votes for either of us, but it did help us get through the boredom.

It was Phil whom I was sure would win. I told that to a few close friends just two weeks after the campaign started. Crane was a first-rate speaker, handsome, charismatic and something of a 1930 Midwest Republican in our 1969 race, a perfect fit for the North Shore of Chicago. There was no doubt about it in my mind, no candidate more precisely matched the constituents than Phil Crane with his unquestioning commitment to the war and all things Republican. Crane did, indeed, win and won happily ever after for more than three decades.

My campaign theme was that the Vietnam War would end some day, as all wars do, but that 50,000 Americans would die. For nothing. When the war finally did end, I was proven wrong. The number of American dead was 58,000.

The number of Vietnamese dead was three million.

That was six years after my campaign. That's when in 1975 President Gerald Ford presided over America's abandonment of South Vietnam. Not long after that, the North Vietnamese, who had battled the French and then the Americans since the 1950s, finally took over the whole country. Despite hysterical warnings to the contrary, Southeast Asia did not fall to the communists. And only a decade later, America was filled with travel brochures and advertisements extolling the exotic beauty of Vietnam. American tourists flocked to the country as if nothing had ever happened and the word "domino" was returned to its original usage, a game.

With my political career over, my inner Walter Mitty succumbed to the comforts of suburbia with just a few emotional bumps along the way. A few weeks after the campaign, I was walking out of a Kentucky Fried Chicken store with the kids, absent-mindedly going out through the door marked Entrance. A man about my age brushed against me, muttering, "You still can't get it right."

A few months after that, another stranger stopped me in the middle of town. He seemed shy and his voice was almost a whisper. I bent down to hear him better. "I just wanted to tell you," he said, "I was against you in the campaign. I didn't vote for you. But I've been thinking it over. I think maybe you were right." He paused a moment to gauge my reaction. "I know it sounds silly," he said, "but I hope that makes you feel a little better." I told him no, it didn't make me feel better. Not even a little bit better. That memory stays with me, not because of his kindness but because of my sharp response. Politics is not necessarily ennobling.

By the time Rita and Mike came to visit us that snowy Sunday, I was back to shoveling snow rather than tilting at windmills. Suburban once again. The events and emotions of the campaign were tucked away in the memory book of my mind.

Chapter 4

Move to Israel?

In Winnetka the world of young couples was one of shared small talk, gossip, and dreams. Whatever problems we had were hidden from others behind our practiced charm. They were often hidden from ourselves.

There were exceptions, of course, a few people with whom we felt close enough to share real feelings. It's funny, but even though they were new friends we felt that way about Rita and Mike.

We carried our wine over to the dining-room table and settled ourselves around an array of cheeses and salads Rosalind had laid out. I leaned over a big loaf of olive bread and started slicing away while Rita and Mike filled their plates. The small talk didn't miss a beat as we resettled ourselves around the table.

Mike was now animated, propounding his views on the day's political problems. He was something of an anomaly, Mike. You felt his presence more than you saw him. Centuries of Jewish suffering lay deep within his eyes. He spoke with intellectual intensity, but even his vitality couldn't hide the heaviness of all that history. I had a professor once who thought that over time cultural experiences were transmitted genetically. I don't know if he was right but when I looked at Mike I thought he might be.

When Mike stopped talking, it didn't feel like the end. He was looking down at his plate and pushing some food around, and there was silence. He seemed to have disappeared into some mist of contemplation as if struggling with himself, reluctant to let his thoughts become words. There was more silence than there should have been. I took a sip of wine to have something to do.

"I was reading an article the other day," Mike finally said, "in *Advertising Age*. It was about a guy who worked at Procter and Gamble." Mike was speaking slowly now. "He'd been there twelve years and had become one of their top brand managers. He said he'd increased the market share of Crest toothpaste every year he was there."

We waited to see where he was going with all this. "And do you know what he told the reporter?" Mike's eyes looked past us as if he was seeing the magazine in front of him, actually reading from the article. "He said that one day he realized he didn't really care whether Crest increases its market share. Here's a guy who has a top job at a major company and he is a big-deal success and then one day he starts thinking about things and decides there's more to life than selling toothpaste."

"I guess after that interview they got rid of him pretty fast," I said.

"He may have been unhappy," Mike said, "but he wasn't stupid. He didn't talk to the reporter until he had left the company. With his stock options." Mike smiled.

It wasn't the first time I'd heard a story like that. The economy was booming in the 1960s, and people weren't worried about quitting their jobs. There were plenty of other jobs out there.

And a lot of people had already made a lot of money, especially in the corporate world where many middle-level as well as top-level executives had stock options. The stock market was wild, like the market of the 1990s, except that instead of stocks soaring because they were all about dot-coms, the stocks in the 1960s were all about technology.

At the same time, a do-your-own-thing mood was sweeping the country. In California, young people were turning marijuana and LSD into a lifestyle. In New York, people were taking their clothes off onstage before thousands of strangers in the musical, *Oh Calcutta!* Even people who thought it all extreme got a kick out of reading about it.

The mood was infectious. Even the hard-working middle class was often envious as the hippies kept repeating, "Do your own thing." The people best able to do it were corporate executives, young men in their thirties or forties who could become the best of all possible hippies, hippies with money.

Their parents before them had worked hard until they died. Suddenly, there was a generation of people with a stock-market windfall who could take the money and run. The *Wall Street Journal* featured a story about an executive who quit his job and opened an antique store in New England. The next week, there was another story, this time about a young technology whiz who cashed in and bought a farm in New Mexico. There were a lot of ways to do your own thing.

That's what Mike was leading up to. He finally said it.

"I want out," Mike said. "I'm tired of the traveling and calling on clients and waiting in waiting rooms and being friendly and . . ." His feelings spilled out, almost tumbling over one another until suddenly his words stopped, and we all sat there stunned.

It was all right for others to talk about doing their own

thing, but not Mike. He wasn't in that league. He didn't have that kind of money. They don't give you options in the diamond business. And when you quit your job there aren't a lot of other jobs waiting for you. It was different from the corporate world. In the corporate world people were interchangeable parts.

I looked over at Rita. She must have known all about this. She must have known exactly how he was feeling. Her smile showed sympathy. No matter. I didn't feel good about her smiling.

"I like the diamond business," Mike said. "I mean, I like it, I'm even good at it." He was talking to himself as much as to us. "But there are times when it's not really me." His shoulders slouched, and his head bent down as if looking deeper into himself or perhaps to avoid looking at us. I could see fear in his dark eyes, fear about thoughts whose dim drumming for attention were muffled by the rhythm of routine, fear about thoughts usually kept distant. Or hidden altogether.

Then he thrust his chin up as if to stop at the precipice of thought, as if to save himself. His eyes scanned the ceiling. "Maybe I'll go to Minneapolis," he said. "I know people who live in Minneapolis. Or maybe Texas. Rita and I used to live in Texas."

And then, from out of nowhere, "Why don't we all move to Israel?" He looked straight at us. "Hey, there's an idea," he said. "Why don't we all move to Israel?"

"Why don't we all go to the moon?" I said. I pushed back my chair. At least I had broken the tension.

I looked at Rosalind. She smiled slightly. I looked back at Mike, but Mike wasn't laughing. I looked at him closely. This time I didn't have to look for Jewish history to see the suffering in his eyes. I could see his own suffering. He was afraid. Life wasn't working out the way it was supposed to.

He was afraid of where he was going. Or where he wasn't going.

I didn't know anything about depression in those days but looking back, I now think that Mike's problems were not just about a job, nor about his past. He was looking at his future and he was scared and flailing around to reach out to—maybe reach back to—something reassuring

Mike grew up in an Orthodox Jewish home in Brooklyn and studied in a yeshiva. Maybe he wanted what we all want at some time or other but don't admit wanting because we're supposed to be grown up. Maybe he wanted to return to a time when life was simpler and there were big people to take care of us. Maybe he thought that Israel would be like his Jewish past. There's an old Yiddish expression, "Change your place, change your luck." Maybe on some level, Mike felt that Israel was that kind of place where everything would be good again.

I certainly didn't feel that way. No one would ever confuse Israel with Oak Park. I clung to my first impression. Might as well talk about going to the moon.

I glanced over to Rita and then to Rosalind, looking for their reactions. Certainly there would be some response, some light banter about the absurdity of the idea. At least a little laughter. Move to a different country where we don't even know the language? That's kind of funny, isn't it? Isn't that what humor is all about, a story with an unexpected ending? Isn't that when you're supposed to laugh?

No one laughed.

Mike's question hung suspended in air. Why the silence? I thought. Rita was looking down. Of course, I thought, Mike's problems might be new to me, but they certainly weren't to her. I looked at Rosalind who turned and looked away. No one said anything, each of us drifting into different streams of thought. Israel?

The whole idea was ridiculous. I was surprised to find myself smiling as I became lost in my own thoughts. "Running for Congress when I didn't have a lot of money and when I had no following—that was pretty ridiculous, too." But I pulled myself up short. Even that wasn't like suddenly moving a whole family to a strange country.

Rosalind said nothing. Israel? For Rosalind, Israel wouldn't be like going to the moon, it would be like going to another universe, a million light-years away from the San Francisco where she grew up, a city where virtually all Jewish families were culturally assimilated. A few were even accepted, even prominent, even part of the establishment. Something like Berlin in the 1930s. Jewish, yes, but not too much so. Jewish culturally more than religiously. San Francisco itself was a religion, one that worshiped itself. Just to live there was a reason for living. It was beautiful. It was comfortable. Ennui by the Sea.

In the home where Rosalind grew up religion was little more than a memory dusted off once a year for the family gathering at Passover which was little different from Thanksgiving except that on Passover a child asked four questions. Rosalind's parents were members of a Reform congregation. They quit the congregation after we were married. No need for that anymore. Their daughter had found the traditional nice Jewish boy.

She was in her last year at the University of California at Berkeley when I met her, a time when students in general and especially at Berkeley basked in their self-styled roles as intellectual challengers to the hypocrisy of middle-class values including, of course, religion. At Berkeley, protest was as important as grades. Maybe more important. By the time we were married, Rosalind had not only rejected the idea of God but seemed to resent that the concept might even be considered.

Our first shared synagogue experience did nothing to discourage her skepticism. The Reform rabbi who would marry us suggested we meet a week before the ceremony. I felt guilty taking up his time. After all, he was the chief rabbi of one of the city's largest congregations, a leader in the community and a spiritual father figure. I was touched that he would meet with us. I imagined he would talk about the seriousness of our decision. Or maybe about how our marriage would bring us into the 4,000-year-old tradition of Jewish values. I was already close to thirty when we married and less cynical than when I was younger.

There was a downpour in San Francisco that November night when we went to meet him. We sloshed up the steep San Francisco streets while the rain washed down toward us. At last we got to the top of the hill, entered the synagogue and found the rabbi's private office. He was standing in front of a mirror that hung on the open door of his clothes closet. Instead of wearing the usual Jewish head covering, a yarmulke, he wore an embroidered silk crown of sorts, the kind that might be worn by an Episcopalian minister in England.

He turned to greet us, turned back to the mirror to adjust the angle of the crown, and then sat down behind his desk. He smiled warmly. I was happy. I was flattered by the attention. I looked forward to his words. Probably something about the sanctity of our marriage, its obligations, its spiritual significance. He might even ask some questions to learn more about us.

He did begin with a question. Still smiling. "Tell me," he said, "what day are you planning to be married?" He was thumbing through his datebook.

"December 21," I said. Rosalind didn't say anything.

And then another question.

"And what time of the day?" He leaned back in his chair and adjusted the black silk crown, slightly.

We answered and he sat there looking at us, still smiling. I sat there looking at him. Then somehow I realized the meeting was over. We got up to leave.

"Have you any questions?" he asked as I was reaching for my raincoat.

"I don't think so," I said. I couldn't think of any. Rosalind mumbled a thank-you. I offered him an awkward handshake and we stepped back out into the rain.

The experience reinforced Rosalind's hostility to religion. Even without Berkeley she would have been a freethinker who could have lived a bohemian life and enjoyed it. She would have been happy married to a professor in a rented frame house that needed painting and had broken front stairs. But freethinking has its limits, especially when a young woman is a product and even a prisoner of the same middle-class background she despised. A decade before Betty Frieden argued that women should be what they want to be, Rosalind was one of the last of a generation who grew up thinking that careers were for men and marriage was for women.

"You were supposed to be married by the time you graduated," she told me one day. "But I never thought about what happens the day after." And so her marriage became an extension of her past, repeating with me the docility she had always shown her father. In a sense, she went from being a daughter to being a daughter. Yet on another level, she sensed that was not the way it was supposed to be. The first book she bought after our marriage was called *The Woman You Want to Be*.

The anomaly is that deep down she was steel. Her favorite person was her Grandma Esther, a tough little lady who was born in the Old Country, spoke English elegantly, had manners to match and who reared eleven children, six of her own and five whom she inherited from a sister who died young. Grandma Esther lit *Shabbat* candles every Friday night in the tradition of every observant Jewish woman preparing to welcome in the Sabbath. When we were married, Rosalind did the same thing. It was a mark of respect for Grandma Esther. She could separate that from her contempt for religion.

Within an aura of pleasing others Rosalind struggled with her conflict between her internalized middle-class values and a spirit of rebellion that rejected them. She lived a lifetime with those two tensions, looking for the woman she wanted to be. The answer lay elsewhere than in a book.

The spirit of Grandma Esther must have settled into Rosalind's soul because after we were married we not only joined a synagogue in San Francisco, but at Rosalind's insistence we joined a Conservative synagogue. In the Conservative movement, most of the prayers are in Hebrew. We couldn't read Hebrew, barely recognized the letters and could only follow the service in those merciful moments when the congregation prayed in English.

Joining a Reform temple like the one her parents had belonged to would have made more sense. In Reform services, except for one or two prayers, the rabbis and the congregation speak English. Fortuitously, God understands English. But the spirit of Grandma Esther would not be denied.

By the time we met Mike and Rita we belonged to a Conservative synagogue in nearby Highland Park, a large brick building sprawled out in accidental design along the shore of Lake Michigan. The rabbi had white, wavy hair, a powerful chest and a strong handshake. He was charismatic, and everyone loved him. Except Rosalind. She said she wanted to leave the synagogue. But surprisingly the rabbi left and a new rabbi was hired to take his place. Rosalind decided to stay after all. The new rabbi interested her.

In sharp contrast to his predecessor who had been the consummate father figure, Rabbi Dresner was not charismatic, dynamic or exciting. He was deliberate, proper and an intellectual. He didn't pinch little children's cheeks and he didn't chat it up with the congregants.

Rabbi Dresner was only in his midforties when he came to our synagogue but his dark eyes and full beard made him look older. His studied seriousness and cultivated weariness made him look older still. One felt that like the Lodges, he spoke only to God. Or perhaps that like Moses, God might have spoken to him. Rosalind loved him.

His sermons were 100-percent substance. He explained not only the importance of keeping *Shabbat*, but the reasons for doing so. He explained the importance of keeping kosher and the reasons behind that. Week after week, speaking about issues that were critical to Judaism, he lifted the veil of ignorance and revealed to the congregation the relevance of the Jewish religion. Rosalind loved it.

It was all very serious. Before he delivered his weekly sermon Rabbi Dresner would step up to the dais and look out at the congregation, waiting for silence, a condition not easily obtainable among Jews. Christians enter a church, sit down and join in the responsive reading. Jews enter a synagogue, sit down and embellish the responsive reading with a little responsive chatting with their friends. Defenders of this disarray tell me it's because Jews are so comfortable with God. Jews, God, we're all one big, happy family. But growing up among Christians, I preferred more orderly behavior. So did Rabbi Dresner.

Before speaking, Rabbi Dresner would stand at the dais, committed to waiting for silence. Complete silence. He might stand there for a minute waiting. Sometimes two minutes. Two minutes is a long time to stand and say nothing, all the time staring out at the congregation. The whispering would lessen, but still the rabbi would wait. Until finally it stopped. Silence at last. Never mind that you could hear a pin drop. By the time Rabbi Dresner spoke, you could hear a feather drop. When he spoke, dim memories of Jewish observances gave way to a new awareness of their beauty. Understanding and respect replaced skepticism. Rosalind was one of those who listened.

She read, too. She began with Rabbi Dresner's book about keeping kosher, the dietary laws that prohibit the eating of certain kinds of meat and fish. She also learned that we are not supposed to eat milk and meat at the same meal, an injunction that comes from the Bible and that she found particularly touching since its origins were to preclude the possibility of a young goat being cooked in the milk of its mother, one of many rules that convey compassion and sensitivity for others. Slowly, slowly, the religion of superstition became a religion of meaning.

Rabbi Dresner's handsome, young wife, Ruth, came over to our home to show Rosalind how to make the house kosher. Erect and purposeful, Ruth stood there with Rosalind washing our dishes in boiling water and then separating the dishes, utensils, pots, and pans that would be used for meat from those that would be used for dairy foods. To Rosalind's surprise, the new regimen that had seemed so intimidating began to feel quite comfortable, even comforting.

At the synagogue, Rabbi Dresner continued teaching about *Shabbat*, and slowly we transformed our Friday evenings into family gatherings where the children helped prepare a beautiful *Shabbat* dinner that was introduced with the lighting of the Sabbath candles and the traditional prayers asking for God's blessings.

So when Mike talked about Israel, the idea was not as preposterous to Rosalind as it might have been ten years earlier. In a way, the idea seemed like the continuation of everything Rabbi Dresner had been talking about. And who knows? Grandma Esther might have even liked the idea. And yet, there were thousands of Jews who were much more observant than we were and they weren't rushing off to Israel. What could she possibly be thinking? She sat silent and I remained separated from her by the space between people that even marriage cannot completely remove.

As far as I was concerned, Israel certainly had nothing to do with my life. In Oak Park, I had never heard the word Zionism. And like many Jews in the Midwest, as embarrassing as it is to admit today, as a teenager I knew practically nothing about the horrors of the Holocaust in those terrible days of World War II.

After the war I was a political science student at Northwestern so caught up in my studies about the dangers of Communism in Russia and China that I didn't even notice the news on May 14, 1948 when Israel became an independent nation again after two thousand years. I was so busy learning facts that I hadn't noticed a miracle.

It wasn't until 1967, almost twenty years later, that I ever thought about Israel and then for only a few days. It was the time of the Six Day War. Five Arab countries attacked Israel, and it seemed certain that Israel would be annihilated. The awesome danger, only twenty-two years after the Holocaust, sent waves of fear through Jewish communities all over the world. Money was raised to buy arms and supplies. Someone asked me for a contribution and I immediately wrote out a check, a conditioned reflex among Jews whenever there is an important cause. A week later the war ended in Israel's surprise victory. I didn't think about Israel much after that. Not until that day in Winnetka when Mike asked that absurd question. "Why don't we all move to Israel?"

I tried to break the silence. I turned to Mike. "Would you really do that?" I asked him.

Mike said he would. I didn't believe him. A moment of reflection and then he said it again. "I would do it." Again there was silence.

The mood was unnaturally solemn, disturbing. "Let's get back to reality," I said. I reached over and refilled the wineglasses. We returned to our small talk.

Nothing had changed.

Everything had changed.

Disturbing, elusive, something had entered our thoughts that day. Invaded our souls. Seized our imaginations. Something that defied logic.

Years later, talking to our Conservative rabbi from San Francisco, Sol White, I thought back to that conversation with Mike.

"Did you ever notice," Rabbi White said, "that the most important decisions of our lives are usually nonrational. Not irrational," he continued, "but nonrational."

"Nonrational?" I thought. That defied everything I had ever known. What was all that Midwest education about if not to teach me to think rationally with progress as the inevitable reward?

Rabbi White jabbed his fist into my shoulder to emphasize his point. He probably jabbed out of habit as well. White was a stocky, solidly built man who wore his nose flattened out against his face. He looked like a prizefighter, which is exactly what he was in college when he got his unsolicited nose job. He was a man of high energy, perhaps a prophet of sorts who constantly challenged the comfortable assumptions of his congregants. A man rooted in decency while acting out as contentious.

"Think about it," he said. "Is marriage rational? A commitment to spend the rest of your life with someone you hardly know? Usually we don't even know who *we* are.

"And what about twenty years later? Do you know whether you'll still be the same two people who fell in love, that you'll still be in love, that you'll have grown together rather than apart? Marriage a rational decision?" He paused. "Of course not. It can be wonderful. It can be a lot of things. But rational?" Another pause. "Forget it!"

He stepped back, maybe another habit from prize-fighting days. But he didn't stop talking.

"I don't say people shouldn't get married. It's just that a lot of the most important things we do are simply non-rational. We think there are reasons, but it's all in the heart. Sometimes only the groin."

I couldn't think of an answer and he wouldn't think of letting up.

"What about children?" he said. "Where is the logic in that? Sure they're a great joy. But you're signing up for a lifetime, not just of joy but often disappointments as well. Sometimes even heartbreak." He watched me, watched for a reaction. "Is that rational?"

That conversation always haunted me. Was he right, that our most important decisions defy logic? Could moving to Israel be one of those decisions? It certainly wasn't rational.

Yet I felt a sense of excitement. Mike had only mentioned the idea, a far-fetched idea at that. He hadn't made a big deal about it. So what was bothering me? It made no sense at all, and yet Mike's words evoked feelings I didn't even know lay within me.

They made me think about things people don't usually think about. They made me think about what I was doing with my life, made me think about whether my whole life was just a knee-jerk reaction to my past, behavior so internalized that I never questioned it. Made me wonder whether my life was a just a bunch of conditioned reflexes left over from childhood, from parents, from friends, from even the place where I grew up, Oak Park. They made me ask the kind of questions I didn't want to ask. Is this what I'm really all about? Is this how I want to use that precious gift of time called life?

When Mike and Rita left, Rosalind and I sat down and had another glass of wine. The kids were in bed, whispering to one another on their way to sleep. Flames sputtered up from the ashes, punctuating the quiet. We sat silently, each of us reluctant to talk about Mike's idea, uncomfortable that we hadn't dismissed it out of hand, trying to understand those amorphous feelings that seemed so strange, the attraction to an idea that seemed so far-fetched. After two thousand years of dispersion, the Jews had their own homeland again. For Rosalind, the idealism of being part of building a new country rekindled the idealism of the campus at Berkeley. I thought about the fact that this was happening in my lifetime. After years of reading about history, here was a chance to be part of history.

On the surface, I had everything a young man could want, and yet there was something about contentment that made me discontent. More than contentment, I needed a cause.

In my gut, I felt the same stirring of emotions I felt when I decided to run for Congress. I felt that and more, a strange attraction to the idea of moving to this strange country that I knew nothing about. A completely nonrational idea.

How could I ever explain that to anyone?

Chapter 5

You're Going to Do What?

The next day I tried explaining it to Dick Gottlieb, an old college friend who knew all about Israel. Dick was in the diamond business and traveled regularly to countries where diamonds were cut. Israel was one of those countries.

Dick greeted me warmly as I entered his office and slouched into a chair across from his desk. I asked him about his family. I asked him about his business. I asked him about anything else I could think of to avoid talking about the real reason I was there. He began shifting around in his chair and I realized I couldn't stall any longer.

"Dick," I said, "we're thinking about moving to Israel."

Dick didn't say anything. He just stared at me. Dick has blue eyes and his eyes seemed to bulge out as he stared at me. I had never before thought of him having bulging eyes. I began to wish I were somewhere else. I wished he would say something. He just kept bulging.

What he finally did say was, "Are you crazy, Yale?"

Dick was no Rabbi White. Dick was not given to introspection.

"Look," he said. "Israel's a great country. They're great people, but who can live with them? They're wonderful but they're all nuts. And what do you need it for?" Dick paused. I could see he suddenly thought of something. "By the way," he said, "you've been there, haven't you?"

It was a fair question. Embarrassing, but fair. Rational people like Dick tend to ask rational questions. Israel is more than seven thousand miles from Winnetka and obviously not the kind of place one moves to without first seeing the country. As quickly as he finished the question, he saw the answer in my face.

He was incredulous. "You're talking about moving to a country you've never been to?"

A terrible silence followed. I made one last effort to defend myself. "But I thought you love Israel!"

"I do love Israel," he said. "But that doesn't mean I'd live there. I've loved different women but that doesn't mean I married them."

I could feel it coming. An array of dismissive comments. Questions about my sanity. A tirade about my irresponsibility. I braced myself for the onslaught of expected indictments. For a moment I felt like the fictional Cyrano de Bergerac anticipating the excessive insults his enormous nose would elicit. Cyrano imagined comments like:

Aggressive: "I, sir, if that nose were mine, I'd have it amputated on the spot."

Friendly: "How do you drink with such a nose? You ought to have a cup made specially?"

Descriptive: "'Tis a rock—a crag—a cape—a cape? Say rather a peninsula."

And so on.

Similarly threatened, I fled into my own fantasy. "Dick, sir," I thought, imagining myself as a modern-day Cyrano. "Don't tell me I'm crazy. You might have said:

"Insulting: A desert your children need? A sandbox isn't big enough?

"Imploring: You'd leave your widowed father?

"Irreverent: Praying in English isn't good enough?

"Intrusive: A problem with your job?

"Insinuating: A problem with the government?

"Inquisitive: Have you gotten, maybe, some help?

"Irrelevant: What will people think?"

My self-esteem withered against his outburst that accused me of everything from being an irresponsible parent to an inconsiderate husband. He was relentless. "You have a wife and four children. Are you out of your mind?"

I tried to turn back his attacks. I tried to sound confident.

"We've moved before, you know. Don't you remember all the times I moved when I worked at ABC, from Chicago to New York and then back to Chicago and then San Francisco and then to the network in New York. It's not that I've never moved before."

"You're bragging about that?" Dick asked. "You may call that getting ahead but as far as I'm concerned that's already a pattern of irresponsibility. All that moving around. And now you want to move to Israel? You must have the world's shortest attention span!" He was almost shouting at me.

I kept slipping deeper into my chair as if to evade the onslaught. Dick didn't even stop to take a breath.

"And what are you going to do for a living? And you don't even know the language?" Finally a pause as he looked me over as if he had never seen me before. A long pause. And then, his final outburst of incredulity. "What the hell is going on with you?"

I didn't know myself what was going on with me. I was too young to be in midlife crisis. I was too old to be a pioneer, and I was too middle class to reject Winnetka. And yet more and more, the idea fascinated me.

"Look, Dick," I said. "What's life all about?" I tried to move the discussion into something more abstract, but Dick wouldn't let me go on. He wasn't interested in philosophy. He thought that by the time a man has four children, philosophy is a luxury and pragmatism a necessity. Finally he cut me short with a compromise.

"Listen, Yale," he said, "no one just picks up a whole family and moves halfway around the world. At least visit the country. See if you like it. Then you can talk about moving there."

That summer, we followed Dick's advice. Weaving our way through the crowds at O'Hare Airport and trying not to lose the four children whose ages then ranged from three to eleven, we made our way up the ramp to the TWA plane then connected with an El Al flight in Montreal. I still remember the feeling of excitement when for the first time I saw the Star of David proudly adorning the tail of the Boeing 747. Thirty years earlier, Jews wore the Star of David as a yellow patch on their ragged clothing as they were herded into concentration camps. For the first time in my life I began to feel an identity with the Jewish people, the ones who had been gassed and burned and the ones who had survived to rebuild their historic homeland. These were my people. I didn't know that back in Oak Park.

My first surprise came when I saw the pilot. Growing up in the American movie culture of the 1930s and 1940s, I knew that all pilots had blonde hair and straight teeth and had names like Randolph Scott and Jimmy Stewart. Movie pilots were Nordic. They wore dark jackets with brass buttons and a couple of gold stripes on their sleeves. Epaulets, too. As I boarded the plane in Montreal, for the first time I saw an El Al pilot. He was of medium build, wore a short-sleeve white shirt, and had black curly hair. He didn't look like Randolph Scott. He didn't look like Jimmy Stewart. I felt a sharp twinge of anxiety. Can this guy really fly a plane? I carried within me the same stereotypes of Jews that were prevalent among many Christians in those years, that Jewish men were small, dark, unattractive, and frail. I had seen enough Jews to know that wasn't so, and yet that was the image embedded in my mind.

It was in defiance of that image that American Jews were so quick to celebrate the occasional Jewish athlete, like boxer Barney Ross or football star Sid Luckman. By the time I flew to Israel, the image of the Jew had gone to the other extreme as a result of the Six Day War. After centuries of prejudice, fed by images of Jews as dark, deceitful, and devious, a new image had emerged of the Jew as the superhero. Of course, neither description was accurate.

The El Al plane landed in Israel ten hours later to the recorded music of *"Havenu Shalom Alechem,"* "Peace Be to You Who Come." We arrived like many tourists, knowing little about things Jewish and nothing at all about Israel.

We decided we would do most of our touring in the mornings before the summer heat became intense and the children would rise up in rebellion at being dragged from one tourist site to another. Our trade-off with them was that they could spend the afternoons at the hotel pool.

Intuitively, we spent two of our three weeks in Jerusalem. After all, Jerusalem had been the capital of the Jewish people since the days of King David 3,000 years earlier. So we thought we would begin at the beginning. For two weeks we roamed the city's streets, walked through narrow corridors and around corners, our feet pressing against the stones, the clay, and the bricks of streets that other visitors had trudged across centuries before us. Following their footsteps, we passed Roman columns that for two thousand years had lain prostrate in the heat, walked past the ruins of the Hurba Synagogue, past the crosses and carved inscriptions along the Via Dolorosa, the traditional path of Jesus on his way to the Crucifixion.

In the distance, we could see the gold-encased domes of the Russian Orthodox churches and metal crescents above Arab mosques. We walked through the restored streets of the old Jewish Quarter and passed its modest synagogues. We knew nothing, but could feel everything.

We walked silently to the Western Wall, the one remaining wall of the compound above which stood the Temple of the Jews built by King Solomon. We did know what that meant, that we were stepping 2,500 years back into Jewish history. I was surprised that within that past about which I knew so little, I, nonetheless, felt so completely at home. After so many years of formal studies, I was beginning to understand there may be meaning beyond knowledge.

As we walked, the heat waves shimmered against ancient sand-covered stone. In the Old City, Arab merchants beckoned us into their little stores and lustily showed off their endless array of carved olive-wood camels and brass trays. From a wooden rack, strands of brass bells glimmered like glittering suns. From the ceilings hung long dresses of more colors than could have been imagined in the coat of the Biblical Joseph. Behind the assortment of every conceivable souvenir essential to a tourist's memories of the Middle East walked painted camels patiently traversing canvases of sandy deserts. There were paintings, too, of the Jew, Jesus. Invariably he had blue eyes, an aquiline nose, and straight blond hair. His face radiated kindness. Born in Bethlehem among the dark-skinned, dark-haired people of the Mediterranean, he emerged in the paintings as decidedly Nordic.

We continued down David Street, blending into the rivulets of summer colors of shirts and blouses and dresses that flowed from the Jaffa Gate on through the crowded markets. It was early Friday afternoon. Jews shouldered by on their way to the Western Wall. Christians climbed the stairs of the Lutheran church and walked through the cavernous Church of the Holy Sepulchre. Thousands of Muslims were returning from their weekly prayer service at the gold-plated Dome of the Rock that for thirteen centuries has dominated the Jerusalem skyline.

The smells of honeyed pastry, falafel doing somersaults in vats of hot grease and the fresh corn bubbling up against one another in pots of boiling water created an ebb and flow of aromas. "Chai, chai," yelled an Arab boy as he commandeered his donkey through the throng of strangers already pressed shoulder to shoulder. Carcasses of freshly slain calves swayed on his cart. They hung head down except that their heads were no longer there. Laura, pushed to the side as they went by, turned white.

The warm, stiff fur of a donkey pressed against me as an Arab boy steered down the stone stairs the wheelbarrow of leather goods dragged along by his uncomplaining animal. David and Becca pulled back in a mixture of fear and fascination. There was a cacophony of excitement as the boy's high-pitched commands mixed with the seductive sobbing of muezzins calling Arabs to prayer, the rolling Rs of merchants chanting their bargains, the American accents of college girls asking the price in their newly learned Hebrew, "*comma zeh?*" and the answers in English from Arabs who for centuries had skillfully learned languages of conquerors, traders, and tourists.

The days swept by as we tried to absorb so many new experiences. The highlight for Becca and David was running from table to table at the hotel breakfasts to collect an assortment of jellies in plastic containers. That was their Israeli experience.

For Laura and Devorah it was Disneyland in Hebrew, camel rides and rides on donkeys and men in Arab streets puffing on nargillahs, others bent over game boards playing *shesh besh*, the Arab name for backgammon, young Jewish boys in man-sized black hats and oversized black jackets rushing to their studies and busloads of Christian tourists wearing bright plaid shirts and water bottles. Not the kind of sights the children were familiar with in Winnetka, although they did recognize the black-robed nuns. They had seen them before on the pages of one of their favorite books, *Madeline*. They had also seen the Franciscan friars in their full, brown robes before. In *Robin Hood*.

We tried to learn as much as we could through people we met. Advice was plentiful. Strangers urged us to settle in Israel. "Guns and tanks are not enough," someone told us. "We need more Jews." Others assured me the country needed my knowledge of television. I ran over to the educational TV station to see if there were any opportunities there. Yisroel Roi was as nice as he was discouraging. "This is not America," he reminded me in case I hadn't noticed. "In the States, you have three, four, sometimes seven television stations in one city. We have only one television station for the whole country and it's run by the government. And of course," he continued politely, "you have to be fluent in Hebrew."

So much for my television skills. Other strangers we met said that they would be willing to go into business with me. Too naïve to realize that their words would never match their deeds, I took encouragement from everything they said.

The question I asked again and again was how much money we would need to live in Israel. It was a tough question and we got a full range of answers. In those years few people lived the way a middle-class suburban family lives in the States, so their expectations were more modest than ours. People we met lived comfortably in their small apartments. Sometimes they would add a room by closing in a tiny terrace. Many times, parents helped their children buy an apartment, one of the mysteries of the Middle East because the same people could hardly make it through the month financially. Practically every Israeli lived "on overdraft," as they called it, always overdrawn at the bank. It was how they stretched their paychecks to cover their expenses. Not to worry, they would say.

Late one afternoon, the phone rang in our hotel room. An American couple who had moved to Israel with their children a few years earlier had heard about us and called to ask if we would like them to show us around Jerusalem. What's not to like, especially for someone like me who doesn't know one direction from another. "I would love it," I told Abraham Lazowick and thanked him profusely.

A few hours later, Abraham and Malka met Rosalind and me at the reception desk of the hotel and we began our tour of Jerusalem at night. There was no moon that night and few streetlights. As we drove along, I could see little more than outlines of buildings. As Abraham patiently steered us through the different parts of the city my eyes adjusted to the darkness. We drove more than an hour, past the Knesset, the Israeli parliament, past the military cemetery, through the upscale neighborhood of Beit Hakerem and over to the outdoor market opposite the makeshift dwellings that huddled close to one another, patched together with sheets of aluminum. Then we drove through the downtown area which was so small that I had hardly begun to see its small stores and cafes when it slipped into the darkness behind us. Next Abraham took us past the hotels, finally bringing the car to a stop as he reached the top of a hill.

"Let's get out," he said. It felt good to stretch, and as we stood there he pointed to a darkened apartment. "I think that place may be coming up for sale," he said. I looked up and saw a duplex that occupied the top floors of a four-story building facing the open area of the traffic circle. I had no idea where I was, but somehow I felt that something special had happened. Like Alice in Wonderland, I found everything becoming curiouser and curiouser.

As we stood there Abraham explained to us that in Hebrew a traffic circle is a *kikar*. He pointed up to a sign that said *Kikar* Wingate. "This is the highest spot in this old section of Talbia," he told me. "It was named after the British army officer, Charles Orde Wingate, who served in Palestine from 1936 to 1939. That's when the British ruled the country as a mandate of the League of Nations after World War I." I was getting my first history lesson in Israel. I soon learned that you can hardly stop anywhere in Israel without stepping into history.

Abraham told us all about Wingate, that he had been raised on the Bible by his missionary parents, that he had taught the Jews how to form special night squads to fight off Arab attacks, and that he believed there would be a Jewish state some day and that he himself would lead the Jewish army.

"Like many Christians," Abraham went on, "Wingate saw the return of the Jews to Israel as the precursor of the coming of the Messiah. As luck would have it, four years before Israel did become an independent country, Wingate died in an airplane crash in World War II."

I looked up again at the street sign that bore Wingate's name. The Jews had remembered him in a small way, placing his name over a little bit of earth on the top of that hill in the middle of Jerusalem. Then Abraham waved his arm in a half-circle indicating three stunning villas surrounding the *kikar*. "This area used to be called *Kikar* Salameh. That was its name before the '48 war when the Arabs still lived here. Salameh was a rich Arab contractor. He built those homes back in the 1930s. You know that old line about the golden rule, that he who has the gold makes the rules. Salameh decided that as long as he built the villas, he would name the traffic circle after himself. And he did. He put up a street sign with his name on it. So back then this was *Kikar* Salameh."

I looked up at the street sign again. *Kikar* Wingate. No more Salameh. Another lesson learned. Not only do the victors rewrite history, they write the street signs, as well.

Abraham went on with his history lesson. "What's really important is that where we're standing was the dividing line between the Biblical tribes of Benjamin and Judah. That will be remembered long after everyone's forgotten about Wingate and Salameh."

Clearly, Abraham was enjoying his role as a tour guide. As if I were some kind of mannequin, he gripped my shoulders with his hands and turned me to the right. "That's Balfour Street," he said, "where the prime minister lives. You know who Balfour was, don't you?" It was obvious I didn't, so he pushed on. "Balfour was the British foreign secretary in 1917 when the British were running Palestine. It was on his watch that the British issued what came to be known as the Balfour Declaration. What it said essentially is that His Majesty's government—how do you like that for an intimidating title?—His Majesty's government viewed with favor a national home for the Jewish people. Right here in Palestine. And just like that," he snapped his fingers when he said it, "the Zionist dream had international legitimacy." Abraham stopped to let me think about all that.

My head was spinning. I was standing right where history had happened from the days of the Bible to the present. It was almost too much to absorb. So much history inside such a small piece of land.

Abraham turned me around again. "You see down there?" he asked. "That's Marcus Street, named after the Jewish West Point graduate who came to Israel to fight in the War of Independence after having fought in the American army in World War II." He pointed to the right. "And that's where the President's House is." Then he turned me back to where he had started all the turning. "And that's the apartment I was pointing to, right in the middle of all this. Cecil Roth, the British art historian, lived there. I think his widow might want to sell it."

He could have stopped five historical facts earlier. I was sold. I leaned over to Rosalind and whispered, "I've got to see this."

We were there the next day, climbing fifty-one stone stairs to the third floor. Elevators were a luxury in Israel and were virtually unknown in older buildings like this one. By the time we got to the top, we tried pretending we weren't panting. Becca, only three years old, was the last one up, pushing her short chubby legs against each step, refusing to be left behind or let us help her.

I rang the bell and almost instantly a large English woman flung open the door. Her dramatic flourishes made her seem an even-larger presence. She motioned us in and we found ourselves standing inside a huge apartment suffused with sunlight and overflowing with brightly colored vases and museum-quality artifacts.

There was a separate dining room, as well, something almost unheard of in old Israeli apartments. A window from the dining room looked out toward the Old City. Jerusalem windows have shutters that are often lowered to keep out the heat of the sun. But the shutters were not lowered the day we visited. That's why I could see the outlines of the two bullet holes in the window frame, souvenirs from the Six Day War. I looked around to see if anyone was watching me. No one was, so I didn't bother telling Rosalind about my find. She would see it herself soon enough.

Every room was filled with artifacts. Tensely I guided Becca and David around them so they wouldn't break anything. In every room, art competed with kitsch. Paper angels dressed in wings of cotton hovered over the Roths' bed. Scotch tape affixed still others to the doors.

Beyond the master bedroom was a large curved balcony that overhung the bright flowers and grass of the *kikar* where we had stood the night before. My fantasy quickly took hold. I could imagine what it feels like to be the pope, standing suspended in space, addressing the venerating minions below.

"Careful!" I heard Rosalind call out. I spun around just in time to steady a tottering vase. David backed away awkwardly. Gathering the kids around me, I glanced back at the invisible crowds below. My fantasies would have to wait.

An inner staircase led us to a second floor across which was a huge roof garden that opened onto two smaller apartments that together made up the Roth complex. We were there little more than half an hour with more of my attention focused on the children not breaking anything than on the apartment itself. But that half-hour was enough time for me to see not only the apartment, but my name on the front door. I had to have it. This is where we would live in Jerusalem.

When I was only a youngster in Oak Park, my mother would look at me and say, "He may not be right, but he's fast." None of us changes. I was still making decisions fast and making plenty of mistakes, too. But I was pretty sure that this time I was making the right call.

I would like to say that Rosalind and I talked about it at length, but we didn't. I guess every couple has its own strange relationship. Rosalind's compliance was part of ours. I never thought about it much back then. She didn't complain and she always looked happy. But of course, that wasn't a healthy kind of relationship. I didn't understand that then. There were a lot of things I didn't understand.

We spent another two weeks in Israel traveling from Jerusalem to the Galilee and wilting under Israel's unrelenting summer heat as we tried to see everything. The images of Jerusalem burned into my memory forever. The sight of the sunburst that is the Muslim Dome of the Rock, the Russian Orthodox church's smaller domes shaped like onions and of course, the formidable Western Wall where Jews come to pray every hour of the day and night. Other impressions of our travels through Israel began to merge into a dizzying mélange of memories. Was that the Church of Saint Anne by the Lion's Gate? Was that ancient synagogue we saw at Capernaum in the Galilee? And is that where Jesus performed the miracle of the loaves or was that somewhere else around there? And what about Caesarea on the Mediterranean—were those Roman ruins or was some of that from the Crusaders?

For the children it was easier. They were not obsessed with learning the entire history of the Middle East in twenty-one days. What they liked best were the animals. They loved the surprise one day when they were looking out in the distance at the clumps of white wool lying strewn across the field when suddenly those clumps began to move and became hundreds of lambs bunched together in a huge field. Real lambs, not like the ones on the shelves in the third-floor toy department of Marshall Field's. And they never stopped talking about the day they saw an Arab pumping gas into a donkey. At least that's what they thought they saw because that's exactly what it looked like as we drove down a hill toward a gas station. Only as we came nearer did we see that three jerry cans were strapped to each side of the donkey's broad body and that the Arab was pumping gas into the cans, not into the animal. The realization was a great disappointment for them.

Another day, atop the Mount of Olives, they watched in amazement as an Arab with a bright red-and-white checkered kaffiyeh draped across his shoulders poked his cane against the folded-up legs of his camel while, as if in slow motion, the camel unfolded himself and rose up to an awesome height. Perched on the beast, a woman tourist clutched the handle of the saddle and laughed nervously as the camel swayed from side to side along the edge of the hilltop. Beyond her were the white headstones of the graves on the Mount of Olives and in the distance beyond them, the outline of the King David Hotel and the buildings of West Jerusalem glowing in the late afternoon sunlight.

The woman saw none of it. Her hands were locked in a stranglehold grip of the saddle. Her eyes were transfixed on the camel's head lest she accidentally look over the precipice. The children watched mesmerized. No camel or donkey had ever wandered across the neat lawns of Winnetka. This was better than television.

I tried to make the trip a Jewish experience for the children, but my ignorance kept getting in the way. Touring the Old City on Becca's third birthday, we stopped at a stone-encrusted building to get something to eat. Becca with her head full of curls was an instant attraction. When the women learned it was her birthday, they immediately brought out a huge tray of Arab pastry drenched in honey and cupcakes that they had thoughtfully attired in candles. As soon as we entered it was apparent that all those nice ladies were nuns. What's more, the place was called the

Sisters of Zion Hospice. The church was built above the limestone floors over which the Romans dragged Jesus and flagellated him before the Crucifixion. That's where we spent Becca's birthday, not exactly where a little Jewish girl should be on the Sabbath.

My attempts at Jewish ritual fared little better. At our synagogue in Highland Park I had learned about havdalah, the brief service that marks the end of *Shabbat*. Wherever observant Jews are, at home or in a synagogue, at the end of *Shabbat* they light a braided candle of various colors, sip from a glass of wine, and breathe in the scent of spices whose brisk aroma is supposed to revive one's spirits as darkness comes and *Shabbat* fades away for another week.

Staying at a kibbutz one Saturday, I gathered the children around me late in the afternoon within a beautiful setting of trees to perform the havdalah service. Practically all kibbutz members are secular, and many are hostile to religion, but no one would object to my praying. To infuse the children with their Jewish heritage, I filled a goblet with wine and recited the blessing. I passed the incense holder to them as each one sniffed deeply, and the little ones giggled as I read the appropriate prayer. Then I lit the braided candle and began to recite that prayer when I heard the know-it-all voice of a passing kibbutznik call out, "Shabbat isn't over yet," he said. "You don't make fire on Shabbat." He was right, of course. It wasn't yet nightfall. He wasn't religious, but at least he knew what to do. I was trying to teach my children and was already doing it wrong. "When is it easy to be a Jew?" goes the old expression.

It was becoming increasingly apparent that it was easier to take the boy out of Oak Park than to take Oak Park out of the boy. More familiar with my Christian background than my Jewish identity, I had a lot to learn.

At last, it was time to return to the United States. The

eleven-hour airplane trip with four children hadn't been easy. Nor was traveling with them for three weeks with all the suitcases we needed for the continuing changes of clothing as one kid got dirty and another got wet and we all got sweaty day after day. Besides that, it had been an expensive trip with three weeks of hotel rooms and meals for six every day, three times a day. But I didn't regret it for a minute. I was flying and probably would have made it home even without an airplane.

The kids slept all the way. Curled up and sprawled over one another in their adjacent tourist seats, they collapsed into cumulative exhaustion. I slumped into my seat and spent the flight thinking about all the fascinating people I had met and the different places we had seen. Finally, I closed my eyes and simply let my mind meander through all the memories. I had only one problem. When I returned, Dick Gottlieb would be there waiting to hear from me.

I waited a day to call him. Then I waited a couple of days more, rationalizing that I had so many things to take care of. Finally, I could stall no more. I called him. We agreed to meet on Friday.

"So?" he said. That was his greeting as I stepped into his office.

I faltered and started telling him about Israel.

He interrupted me. "I know all about Israel," he said. He pushed back into his chair and folded his arms. "So?" he said.

He obviously wasn't interested in how I spent my summer vacation.

I stumbled some more. "It's hard to explain, Dick." I stuttered around searching for the right words. "It's hard to explain. I felt at home there. I . . ."

"So?" he said.

By now, I was not only feeling defensive, I was feeling slightly hostile. "So, big shot," I threw out at him, "so all because of you, I spent five thousand dollars to find out something I knew before I left."

I waited for a reaction. Maybe a clap of thunder. No reaction.

"Rosalind and I talked it over," I said. "We're moving to Israel."

Dick stared at me and said nothing. And then more of nothing. Then finally, "You're crazy, Yale."

I don't remember saying goodbye, but I probably did. It's hard for people to understand things that aren't rational. The fact is I didn't understand it all myself. Why had Mike, who until recently was a stranger to me, suddenly entered my life and so greatly influenced it?

There's a stranger, too, in the Biblical story about Joseph whose father sends him to Shechem to look for his brothers. They are in the fields somewhere feeding the flocks. Out of nowhere, a man appears and asks Joseph where he is going. Joseph tells him he is looking for his brothers. The man tells Joseph he saw them and heard them say they were going to Dothan. So Joseph goes to Dothan and finds them there.

Now what if Joseph hadn't met that man? He had looked for his brothers all day long. What if he had just gone home, told his father that he tried, but that he couldn't find them anywhere? If that had happened, Joseph never would have been sold into slavery, wouldn't have become a ruler in Egypt second only to Pharaoh, and the whole story of the Exodus and the beginning of Jewish history might never have happened.

So, as I've learned, the rabbis ask who was this stranger, and why did he suddenly appear, and why did he initiate the conversation with Joseph? They conclude that perhaps he was not a man at all, but an angel and that directing Joseph to his brothers was an act of divine intervention.

I'm certainly no Joseph and, although I knew Mike less than a year, I hardly think he was a mysterious stranger. And yet . . . God does act in mysterious ways.

Who would have thought that the Jewish people's return to Israel, prayed for by so many righteous men for so many centuries, would finally happen because of the actions of a sectarian Jew who was a stranger to Judaism? He was a Viennese journalist named Theodor Herzl who reported on the French Jewish captain, Alfred Dreyfus, being convicted of treason on trumped-up charges that were driven by anti-Semitism.

That event changed Herzl's life. He became obsessed with the need to create a state for the Jews where they would not be subjected to such humiliation. Herzl, the nonreligious Jew, seized upon the nascent Zionist thinking of the day and molded it into a vital political movement that led to the rebirth of the Jewish state within only fifty years. Is that how the prayers of the righteous are answered, by a stranger to Judaism?

Maybe everything is nonrational.

I always feel guilty when I pray to God and ask his help. I think it's presumptuous that with everything else going on in the world, I should expect God to bother with me. Less so would I ever think that my sudden interest in moving to Israel was any part of some divine plan. And yet many people believe that not a sparrow falls, but that God knows it. I don't know what God knows. However it happened, I know that the idea of moving to Israel touched something deep inside me and that it felt right.

Years later, I learned that the Hebrew word for peace,

shalom, comes from the same root as *shalem*, which means complete or whole. I was still a little scared, but comfortable. Maybe more than I understood, I was *shalem*.

I asked Mike what he and Rita were going to do. Mike said that they were going to move, too.

Chapter 6

Packing Up a Life

There was no mysterious stranger or anyone else to help us move. And there were so many things to do.

I would have to sell our house. If I sold it before our moving date, would the new owners let me rent it until we left? And if I didn't sell it by the time we moved, what would I do then? I didn't want to be seven thousand miles away owning a house in Winnetka.

Meanwhile, we didn't have a place to move to in Israel. I was still negotiating long distance to buy that apartment I fell in love with in Jerusalem. And even if I succeeded, would we be able to move in there the day we arrived? And what if I didn't succeed? Where would we live then? How do I find a place to live in Israel while I'm still in Winnetka?

There were so many things to figure out, to work out, to coordinate. There were times when I felt like Eisenhower planning the invasion of Normandy. To cope, I fell back on an old trick of mine, breaking a big problem into little problems. I hoped that if I chipped away, one issue at a time, I would have everything in place by my D-Day. After all, how did Eisenhower do it?

I decided to begin at the end, to focus first on the departure date. That was an easy one. It would be after June when the kids finished school. On the other hand, the state-run classes in Israel where newcomers learn Hebrew begin in July. So the window quickly narrowed. We had a four-week period of leaving, between June and July.

Next question, how do we get to Israel? A distance of seven thousand miles is not exactly, as we say in the Midwest, down the road a piece. Obviously, we wouldn't be driving there. Flying seemed a logical answer, but that meant spending eleven hours in a cigar-shaped piece of metal within the tumult that is endemic to El Al coach flights where four hundred impatient Jews are in constant motion praying in the narrow aisles during the early morning hours, visiting one another along the aisles during the rest of the flight, eating the airline's meals, eating a few extra meals they brought along just in case, and running in and out of the bathrooms. There are those who say that Jews on El Al don't fly to Israel, they walk there. We had just made that trip, and I wasn't eager to do it again.

There was another problem with flying. It would be too fast. The more I thought about it, the more obvious was the answer. We would go by ship. The ocean voyage would be an upbeat way to begin with its swimming pools, shuffleboard, music, dancing, and eating in restaurants three times a day. The trip would take two weeks, ample time to segue into our new life, better than just dropping into a desert halfway around the world.

I called the travel agent, envisioning the music and fun of a playground at sea. I was quickly reminded that things are not always as they seem. This would not be the traditional Atlantic crossing to Europe on an exotic steamer such as the *Queen Mary*, *France*, or *Amsterdam*. The only ship sailing between New York and Israel was a Greek carrier, the *Queen*

Anna Maria. So Greek it was. I signed up and that's how we ultimately traveled, two weeks of swimming pools, restaurants, and dancing in the midst of old Greek widows on their way to Athens, all of them dressed in black. A bit funereal, but you can't have everything.

Because it was such a disruption to the children's lives to suddenly take them from one country to another, Rabbi Dresner suggested it would be easier if they learned some Hebrew first. But that meant changing schools, sending them to Solomon Schechter, where all the regular courses were taught plus Jewish subjects and where they could start learning the language. That would be a serious disruption at just the time we wanted to keep everything as steady as possible, but of course, the rabbi was right. It would certainly be easier if they arrived in Israel knowing some Hebrew. We had to do it. So the year before the kids left their friends at school to move to Israel, they left their friends at school to change schools. The beginning of the good-byes.

There still remained that most ominous of all problems, how do I support a family in Israel? The obvious answer, of course, was with difficulty. Even Israelis like to tell the old story of how you make a small fortune in Israel. Answer: Come there with a big one. I've been there, done that. It's not so funny.

Nor is Israel a place where it's easy to make money. It's hard enough just to make a living. The old Yiddish expression, *goldena medina*, the golden land, referred to the United States. It was never used to describe Israel.

I may have been idealistic enough to start life over in a new country, but I had no illusions it would be easy. So I brought along a lifetime of savings to help cushion the blow. From my years in television, I had squirreled away enough money to buy our Jerusalem apartment with enough left over to cover our living expenses for a few years until I made money in Israel, assuming that was, indeed, possible.

It was easier to plan ahead than to get ahead. My first problem was that the only thing I knew how to do couldn't be done in Israel. I learned that during our visit there, that my twenty-two years in broadcasting were worth nothing in a country where the government owned the one-and-only television station that all day long programmed nothing but talk shows where everybody spoke Hebrew, which I didn't speak at all.

So much for my career as a broadcaster.

What I had to do was glaringly obvious. Since I couldn't do the one thing I was qualified to do, be a broadcaster, I had to do the one thing I was completely unqualified to do, go into business for myself. The only problem was that I was exquisitely unprepared.

I read books, not balance sheets. While my friends studied Milton Friedman at the Wharton School of Business, I was studying Montesquieu at Northwestern's graduate school. Montesquieu didn't write much about business.

I didn't even know how to borrow money from a bank. Money was something I spent. I didn't know anything about raising money.

I did know something about producing television programs. And I knew something about selling them to advertisers. So I did the best I could. I decided I would make programs and sell them. Making and selling, that sounded easier than accounting and finance. My efforts were abetted by one of nature's most powerful forces, ignorance. I wasn't smart enough to know it couldn't be done.

The good news is that raising money turned out to be easy, even without a bank. Almost by accident, I found people who wanted to invest in my project. They were all people I knew. At first I thought their readiness to invest was motivated by their passion for Israel. Or maybe by their confidence in me. But neither premise made much sense. A passion for Israel would have been better served by a donation to Hadassah Hospital or the Hebrew University in Jerusalem. Confidence in me should have been confined to me as a person, certainly not as a businessman.

I finally figured it out, finally uncovered the real reason. Deep down, every Jew wants to be in show business.

Fifty years ago when New York taxi drivers were Jews, not Pakistanis, you could have a few laughs during your ride because every Jew is a frustrated stand-up comic. Maybe it's in the genes. Maybe it's because Jewish history is so steeped in suffering that a Jew has to laugh about life in order to live it. A coping mechanism. Don't psychiatrists say that comics are basically unhappy people?

That deep-seated attraction to show business is why there are so many frustrated millionaires. It's nice to be rich, but the fact is that being in pots and pans, for example, is essentially boring. But show business, that's fun. At least it looks like fun, which is why a Jewish businessman is quick to invest in a Broadway production even though he knows he could do better in almost anything else, even the racetrack.

This is the sociological insight that helped me set up in Israel a small company to produce television documentaries. True, Ben Yehuda Street in Jerusalem is not exactly Broadway. Not even off-Broadway. Not even off-off-Broadway. And documentaries are not feature films. But as they say in the ads promoting the New York State Lottery, "Hey, you never know." So investors were easy to come by.

It all began in the unlikeliest of places, a dental chair. Poking around among my gold crowns, silver fillings, and other repairs of forty-two years, Dr. Zigmund Porter chatted away. Dentists always do that, chat away, and always when you're sitting there with a mouthful of cotton.

"So you're going to Israel," Zig said. He tore away at my bleeding gums. "What are you going to do there?"

"Aaaahm starting a fillum bizhnuss," I answered through the cotton.

"What's that?" he asked as he pulled out endless wads of padding.

"Aaaaahm starting a . . ." The rest of my sentence drowned beneath a stream of mouthwash.

"Aaaah'll tell you latah," I gasped, trying not to swallow.

"It's all right," he said. "You can tell me now." His fingers reached in for an overlooked bit of cotton while his other hand pushed my head toward the white bowl.

"Spit it out," he said.

I spat it out and then sat back and took a deep breath. Zig's thumb pressed my lower lip down so he could survey his work. "Not bad," he said. The thumb and my lip returned to their usual places. "Tell me more," he said.

More? I thought. With his fingers, the instruments, and the cotton going in and out of my mouth, I hadn't been able to tell him anything. More? Suddenly I was Alice in Wonderland at the tea party with the March Hare when he insisted she take more tea. "I've had nothing yet, so I can't take more," Alice said.

Zig's words brought me back to the dental chair. "You're starting a film company," he said, reminding me where I left off. "So what does that mean?"

"Not a whole lot," I told him. "You know how in Hollywood everyone with a quarter for a public phone thinks he's a producer? Well, it's something like that. I'll open a small office, get a phone, a secretary, and zap—I'll be a film producer. Not feature films or anything fancy. Just documentaries. I can do that."

"Sounds great," he said, starting to work on me again. "After all those years at the network, it'll be a piece of cake for you."

"Not necessari . . ." I stopped talking. His drill had missed my tongue, but did cut off the last syllable. Zig drilled away, spotless in his white gown. His red curly hair seemed incongruous above the intense look of his blue eyes. His eyes follow the movements of the narrow metal instrument that he kept turning and twisting around between my teeth.

At last he stopped, just for a moment. He stepped back to get a better look at his work. I seized the opportunity to breathe. There was even time for a few words. "It's nothing special," I said. "All a producer needs is an idea and an investor. Then zap, he's in show business. So that's what I'm going to do."

"Show business," Zig said.

"Documentaries," I said. "Not really show business."

"Documentaries," Zig said.

"I think I'll like it," I said. "I've spent a lot of years watching other guys make the shows. Now I'll see if I can do it."

"Documentaries," Zig said.

"Look, Zig," I said, "it's not a big deal. It doesn't take the kind of skill you have. And it's not even that important. After all, at the end of the day, you make people healthy. I'm just going to entertain them."

"Show business," Zig said.

I was beginning to get the idea. Dentistry may be fine, but it's not fun. Show business is fun, especially to people who aren't in show business.

"You're putting together some investors?" Zig said.

"I'm putting together some investors," I said.

"How many guys? How much each?"

I gave him a figure.

"I'm in," Zig said.

"But it's risky," I said.

Zig leaned forward and pushed his thumb against my upper lip so he could take one last peek. "Don't worry about it," Zig said.

I was lucky. My sociological insight was right on the button. Jews do like show business. Even if it's only documentaries. Insofar as Zig was concerned, it was apparent that all that glitters is not a gold crown. But show business, that's something else. Zig sent me on my way with an ice pack pressed to my cheek and a check inside my pocket.

It wasn't long before Bob Weiss, a friend from Northwestern, came into the deal and brought in a friend of his. Don Nathanson, the head of a Chicago advertising agency, came into the deal, too. Don is a natural enthusiast, so he was enthusiastic about my plans. Another close friend, Arnold Thaler, who likes to take a gamble now and then, also joined our group. Arnold knew there were better gambles, but not many better friendships. So he was there for me.

Outside the synagogue one Saturday, another investor suddenly appeared. "I hear you're moving to Israel," Joe Perlman said. Joe was old enough to be my father. I started walking and Joe walked alongside me. He put his left arm around my shoulder. His right arm hung by his side. It was artificial.

"That's right," I said. "I'm moving to Israel."

"What are you going to do?" he said.

"I'm going to start a film business," I said.

I was beginning to feel like Benjamin in the movie, *The Graduate*. I was waiting for him to tell me about plastics.

"I'm going to produce documentaries," I said.

"Maybe I should invest with you," Joe said.

"Maybe so," I said.

I tried to stay calm. Joe was a multimillionaire. I had dated his daughter. No matter how late I brought her home, Joe was always in the living room waiting for us. If he didn't trust me with his daughter, how could he possibly trust me with his money?

"Come over this afternoon, and we'll talk about it," Joe said.

I was immediately drenched with guilt.

"But, Joe," I said, "this is *Shabbat*. We're not supposed to do business on *Shabbat*."

"We won't do business," Joe said. "We'll just talk."

That afternoon, Joe and I walked along the shore of Lake Michigan. Joe asked questions, a lot of them. He was a businessman, a real one. His questions soon became an intense interrogation. Joe probed my plans more aggressively than Zig probed my gums.

As we walked, my *Shabbat* guilt drifted away within the haze of the autumn sun. I didn't have to know about business to know that behind all those questions lay the prospect of money. What I didn't know was that fate, maybe God himself, would later punish me for my *Shabbat* negotiations. At the moment, such thoughts were the furthest thing from my mind. The sun was shining over Lake Michigan and over my dreams.

After a long time and a lot of questions, Joe was ready to invest. Not only that, he volunteered to bring in two other investors, his friend, Jerry Margulies, as well as Joe's inseparable son-in-law, Ray Pololsky.

I had no idea that raising money could be so easy. I also had no idea about a lot of things.

A few weeks later, I received a letter from my friend, Burt Harris, who had started several businesses in his career. "You'll probably find," Burt wrote, "that little by little, your partners will drop away." I was so excited about my easy success that I paid no attention to Burt's warning. I never dreamed that within a few months I'd be recalling his words. But at the time, I wasn't smart enough to worry. I had too many other things on my mind

I was still negotiating long distance for the apartment in Jerusalem. I met with Mrs. Roth's New York lawyer. I wrote to Mrs. Roth's Jerusalem lawyer. I was trying to get her to lower the price. Everyone I'd met in Israel told me the apartment was overpriced by at least 50 percent. I was certain she would come down, at least a little bit, but she didn't. At the same time, I had a feeling that my new Israeli friends were wrong and that Mrs. Roth was right, that a duplex apartment located on that hilltop in the most-prestigious area of Jerusalem was worth what she was asking.

Meanwhile, summer gave way to autumn, and autumn gave way to winter, and we were still at an impasse. Then it was spring, and it was getting close to the date when we were to sail. At that point, Mrs. Roth agreed to lower the price by five thousand dollars, a quixotic victory for me, little more than a fig leaf to cover up my embarrassment at paying top dollar. I gratefully took the deal. We could move in July 1. The ship would arrive in Haifa June 25. No matter. We would spend a few days in a hotel and wait, impatiently. But at least we had a place to go.

Now my problem was to be sure I didn't end up owning two houses on opposite sides of the Atlantic. It was time to sell the Winnetka house. I decided that rather than use a real-estate agent, I would simply sell it myself. I learned how to do that during my peripatetic years with ABC Television. As a matter of fact, I had bought and sold three homes already. My parents had owned only one home in their entire lives, spending twenty years looking for just the right one.

"That's my son," my mother had said a decade earlier when I told her that I was moving from San Francisco to New York only five months after having moved into a home in suburban Burlingame. "Buys a house, sells a house. That's my son." It reminded me of another of her expressions: "You can't choose your relatives." That's the kind of son she had, what could she do?

The fact is, selling a home didn't strike me as so complicated.

"What do realtors do?" I asked myself. "They put an ad in the paper." I decided I could write an ad as well as they could, that I didn't mind spending a little more money to make it a longer ad, and was even willing to run the ad weekly rather than occasionally to really get the word out. Whatever the advertising cost me would be a fraction of what their commission would be. What else do they do? I thought. They walk people through the house and tell them how wonderful it is. I figured I could do that, too. I could probably even do it better not only because I knew the house better, but because I was more passionate about it and was more motivated.

So that's what I did. I only had two worries: What if I sell the house, but the buyer insists on moving in before we set sail? Second worry: What if we set sail and I still haven't sold the house? Problems like these can't just be broken down into smaller problems. They are what they are—terrifying. So I moved to my ultimate backup position when facing problems. I turned to denial. I figured I would do my best and somehow everything would work out. I did, and it did. Never deny the value of denial.

Next I had to get rid of all those possessions we couldn't possibly take with us. It was amazing how much we had accumulated, as if there was a law of physics that garages, basements, and attics are vacuums that must be filled.

Everything we owned had to be touched, handled, decided about, and put somewhere.

There was that box of Laura's skirts and blouses that were to be hand-me-downs for Devorah. But when the time came, they didn't look right on her. We put them back in the box because there might be a third child some day. By the time the third child was born, we had hand-me-downs from Devorah as well, but the third child had the temerity to be David, so all those girls' outfits were useless. By the time Becca was born, we didn't even remember we had all those boxes.

There was the double stroller that we had pushed down the sidewalks to Central Park when we lived in New York with Laura and Devorah bunched together until Laura, like the Energizer Bunny, would inevitably jump out and dash ahead on foot. The memories remained, but the stroller had to go. We gave it to a young couple down the block who didn't mind its few scratches and would soon have memories of their own.

Some decisions were easier than others. David, just turning six, would finally fit into the winter jacket we had bought on sale two years earlier, but winters aren't cold in Israel. So much for that bargain. And it certainly didn't make sense to take that old tricycle with the twisted wheel. We wouldn't need the rusting lawn mower either, not in an apartment. Ditto for the wheelbarrow. There were appliances, too, like the television set that had been replaced but that we never threw out because it still worked, and the dishes from my mother that we would use someday but that someday never came, and an old three-wheeler we had saved for the next child but was never used because a friend gave us a better one that her children had outgrown. Every year, we had given things away and yet we still had so much, as if things had a life of their own and were committed to procreating when you weren't looking.

Now, of course, there could be no excuses. Get rid of it or take it. Kitchen gadgets were tossed together for the garage sale. But what about my favorite sweaters, worn out at the elbows, but still comfortable to wear? Out.

Some memories I was delighted to abandon. Gladly I gave away my old blue suit with the large checked pattern. The first day I wore it to work at ABC, oblivious to its garish pattern and oversized shoulder pads, I was sitting in a sales meeting when my colleague, Marshall Karp, looked me over with exaggerated slowness. "Yale," he finally said, "you forgot your saxophone." Out with the suit, happily.

And there were all those books read long ago and too heavy to take, but how can you throw away a book? No choice. Quickly I added them to the pile before I could change my mind.

But nothing is just a thing, and everything contains a memory. No need for that crib anymore, but four children began their lives in that crib. How can you throw away memories like those? But out it goes, and you do it quickly so you don't let in the tears. There's the worn-out teddy bear that Becca loved. Okay, that one we keep, but she still feels bad about abandoning all her other stuffed friends.

Devorah asks if she can keep her old baby blanket. The very fact that she is looking up at me and asking breaks my heart. Sure, Devorah, a little blanket doesn't take up much room. And giving in is easier than condemning her to discussing it for hours with a psychiatrist someday. On the other hand, what about her four-poster bed? For the money spent shipping it, I can buy a new bed in Israel, but trying to explain that to a ten-year-old girl whose four-poster bed is where she first heard her favorite fairy tales and where she felt her first stirrings of becoming a young woman.

For the children it was hard parting with so many treasures but even more difficult was leaving friends behind. I tried to make that a little easier by sharing with them my own excitement. I tried to convey a sense of adventure, like in all the stories I had read to them over so many years— Hansel and Gretel venturing into the forest, Dorothy leaving Kansas. Of course, there were witches in those stories, but I didn't talk about witches, and I didn't think there would be wars. I told the children we would be like the early settlers in America, helping build a new country.

If they harbored fears, they never spoke of them, and I wasn't good at hearing things that weren't said. Nor were we like the modern family, discussing everything with the children. We didn't hold family conferences and we didn't take votes. The grown-ups made the decisions and the children went along.

Moving to Israel as we did would be much harder for a modern family where mom, dad, and the children would discuss the entire matter as equals. In that case, at least one child would refuse to go, and another would throw a tantrum. So mom and dad would wait a few years until the first child graduated from grammar school and the other finished high school. Of course by then, there would be other problems. How can you take the children away from their old grandparents, especially Grandpa Joe who has only a couple of years to live? So they would wait a few more years, but by then the first child is married. Now the situation is reversed, and the parents say, "How can I leave my grandchild?" And so it goes. The fact remains that in any generation, no matter how the decision is made, no time is the right time and any time is painful.

Only years later did I fully understood that no dream, no matter how exciting, can compensate for transforming a child's life into memories encased in loss, the abandonment of all things small and precious that make up life, a child's own bed, blankets, toys, stuffed animals, all that is reassuring. And yet a funny thing happened after we got to Israel. The kids liked being Israelis. As they got older and became rebellious as most teenagers do, they had no trouble finding fault with me for a lot of the things, but it's interesting to look back and realize that moving to Israel was not one of them. I'm sure that like all of us they carried hidden fears, yet they were more resilient than we could have ever imagined.

For the moment, all that lay in the future. Each of us was consumed racing the weeks and months as summer grew closer. And then on a Sunday in May, I hammered into the lawn a sign that said, "Garage Sale," and put our way of life on display in the driveway for everyone to see.

Six-year-old David sat in front of it all, propped up in an old aluminum beach chair, wearing a white polo shirt and blue jeans, his short, stocky legs spread wide, his hands gripping the arms of the chair as he stared out with a steady gaze at the people milling about. He looked like a caricature of a small-town sheriff keeping law and order.

The lawn mower and wheelbarrow went fast. So did my rusty rake. I sold a bunch of books to a neighbor, if you can call twenty-five cents a book selling. Someone else found a bargain in an old living-room chair I never liked, so there was one more thing I didn't have to worry about. Just getting rid of things was as important as the money. We asked Goodwill Industries to take away whatever was left, not sure who was performing the greater favor, they or we?

Soon it was June, and the day when we would leave our home for the last time. A page off the calendar and the last page off a life I had known since birth. There was no turning back. We wouldn't let ourselves think of turning back. This was everything we had worked toward. But even so, good-byes are never easy.

I backed the dark-blue Volvo station wagon out of the garage so we could begin loading it. Becca, now four, in a yellow sweatshirt and blue corduroys was a bundle of curls running around everyone and trying to stay out of the way as we carried out twenty-two suitcases. She already had her little pretend suitcase stuffed with her most favorite possessions, as long as they were small, and an array of games to play along the way. David dragged out a real suitcase as best he could, while Laura and Devorah were miniadults helping me get everything into the car.

It was early Sunday morning. Only a few churchgoers were out already. From down the block, Charlie Schaff saw us and ambled over to help. Dave Shapiro came from next door. Dave was balding, but fit, and was always amused that whenever Laura and Devorah would see him jogging in circles around his house, they would fall in step behind him creating the sight of an improbable trio. Dave brought over some rope and he, Charlie, and I started pushing suitcases onto the roof rack to keep free as much space as possible for the children inside. Our plan was to drive to New York and take the Volvo with us on the ship.

We adjusted and readjusted the suitcases until they fit together as tightly as the pieces of a jigsaw puzzle. We bound the bags to the roof rack and to one another until nothing short of a hurricane could blast them loose. Over all that, we fastened a heavy green tarpaulin, satisfied at last that nothing would fall off. I was concerned about what it would be like to negotiate highway turns at seventy miles an hour with a narrow station wagon piled high with its own sail, but I felt I would simply deal with it when the time came. Working hard to get all the luggage together kept us busy, Charlie, David and me. We made a point of being busy.

Finally, the bags were in place, and that was that. Except for the awkward good-byes. We muttered a bunch of jumbled words. It was a time before men were allowed to have feelings, let alone show them. Men didn't embrace in the 1970s, certainly not in Winnetka. So we did what men usually do when they don't know what to do. We jabbed at each other, punching the other guy's arm and his chest. There were small attempts at humor and a few irreverent remarks as we tried to express or maybe cover up our feelings of loss at leaving one another. And then Charlie and Dave turned away. They glanced back just once and tossed me a wave as if to say, well, that's the way life is. What's to get emotional about?

I went back into our brick home one last time to be sure the water and gas were turned off. I knew they were, but I wanted to go back anyway. Everything was immaculate. We had made a point of leaving the house spotless for the new owners. Spotless and empty. No more children's pictures on the mantle. No more favorite chair where I used to stretch out my legs and lose myself in a good book. Only walls and memories.

I gazed at the corner where we huddled that winter day with Mike and Rita. A Christian family had bought our house and next year there would be a Christmas tree in that corner. Changing. Everything changing. I walked out and closed the door. Out of habit, I turned the handle to make sure it was locked. It was locked, and we were outside.

The children were hovering around the car impatiently as I came out. I lifted the heavy rear door of the station wagon and they all scrambled in. On the left side, David and Becca sat facing each other. On the right side, the two older girls laid down on their backs with their legs bent up and over the suitcases stacked inside. They looked like astronauts ready for launch. Watching for stray fingers and heads, I closed the heavy door behind them. Bang. Twenty-two suitcases and four children all accounted for.

I turned around and saw Charlie and Dave in the distance, awkwardly watching me. They had been good neighbors, exchanging small talk when I raked leaves in autumn, catching a lift with one another while rushing to the commuter train. I tossed them a feeble wave. Their eyes looked sad. I pulled the car door open quickly and jumped in. Rosalind was already in, turned toward the children, pushing at the suitcases to make sure the astronauts were all right.

Carefully, I backed down the driveway for the last time, turned into our elm-shaded street, and headed for Israel.

Chapter 7

Saying Good-bye

I drove slowly at first, trying to get the feel of the station wagon now that it was piled high with suitcases and a tarpaulin that caught the wind as we picked up speed. Cautiously, I eased it onto Edens Highway heading south. We were on our way to New York to meet our ship but first I had to say good-bye to my mother. It was a short drive. She is buried in the Memorial Park Cemetery just twenty minutes north of Winnetka, a convenient place, she pointed out to Rosalind one day, because the cemetery was right across the street from Saks. Rosalind could do her shopping and stop by for a visit.

Mother's grave lies perhaps a hundred yards from a narrow pond where without causing a ripple, four swans glide by like question marks passing the endless graves. They hardly disturb the water, and the cemetery doesn't disturb them. They're focused on their own lives, oblivious of the death around them. Like the rest of us.

I steered along a dirt road that runs next to the pond. Stopping the car, I raised up the heavy door that sealed the back of the station wagon. Becca and David bounced out from behind the suitcases, eager to run around and excited at the unexpected adventure of running along the side of the pond to keep up with the swans.

I wandered past the rows of familiar headstones with their familiar names that were like street signs in a small town guiding me to my mother. I stood at the foot of her grave, feeling disbelief that she could actually be lying there. In my mind, she was always active and doing something. How could there be an end to all that doing? I thought about how cold she must be.

It's strange standing by a grave, to be so close to someone you were always so close to and yet be separated. It is not good to think too much at a grave. I knew my words would not be heard and yet I felt that somehow she would, indeed, hear, if not my voice then perhaps my heart. After all, how could I leave without saying good-bye?

I started to talk to her, just a few words at first, and it felt good. I told her I was taking my family to Israel, and at once I could hear her response, "Now that's an asinine idea." Asinine was one of her favorite words of dismissal. And yet despite her obvious rebuke—I had expected that— it was easier to say good-bye to my mother than to other people. Not because she wasn't living, but because I knew that despite her protests, she would understand. She would call it asinine, but on some very deep level she would probably think it was okay. People are complicated.

Of course, she would never admit it was okay. On the contrary, if she had lived, she would have complained about it endlessly. Something like "Millions of people risk their lives to come to America, my son decides to leave." Or some variation. "Two hundred million people are happy in the United States. My son can't stand to be happy." And then inevitably the comment that would bring closure to every family discussion. "In our family, nobody's normal."

There was no doubt she could say that about me.

Certainly, there was nothing normal about moving to Israel. I had learned a lot of things from my mother, but Zionism was not one of them. Even her religiosity was tenuous. Certainly erratic. She was like many Jews of her generation who, coming to America as small children, wanted to be Americans, period. Jewish traditions existed as little more than amorphous memories from childhood.

Unlike Orthodox Jewish women who light Sabbath candles in their home every week, my mother lit them as the spirit moved her. Sometimes twice in one month. Sometimes not at all for several months. But when she did light them, I loved watching the magic of her movements as the first candle began to glow and then the second rounded out the aura of light. The candles stood erect in two ornate silver candlesticks that had belonged to her mother in Russia.

After they were lit, she would make the traditional gesture she had probably seen as a child, extending her hands over the candles and then in three motions sweeping toward her the invisible spirit of the Sabbath. Next she would cover her eyes with her hands and pray silently. I never knew what she was praying. I imagine she was sharing with God her feelings and her fears, perhaps giving thanks and asking for help, too, with some problem or other. I doubt if she said the traditional prayers. I don't think she knew them. But I liked standing next to her when she lit the candles, transfixed by the movement of her gestures and the mystery of the flickering lights. I felt close to her, standing there, but it was a far cry from growing up Jewish.

That's why I was so surprised, years later in Israel, when our neighbor, Naomi Cohen, said that my mother was the reason I had moved to Israel. My immediate response—I couldn't believe I was using those same words—was: "That's really asinine."

The fact is that I didn't know myself why I was turning my life upside down and, worse than that, turning upside down the lives of Rosalind and the children. And yet I always felt comfortable with the decision though I couldn't explain why.

It took me a long time to figure out that feelings and thinking don't have much to do with each other. How can you explain why you love a certain person? There are some things, maybe the most important things, that you just feel. They're not something you can explain. So I never did do a very good job answering the inevitable question about why I was moving to Israel.

Of course, most people are polite. During the year I was getting ready to move, I would run into friends I hadn't seen for a while and would tell them the news. They would say something like, "How interesting!"

"How interesting" bought them time to sort out their real feelings. They couldn't just blurt out, "You're doing *what?*" So instead, there would be a tentative smile followed by the inevitable question, "Tell me, what made you decide to move to Israel?" Freely translated that meant, "What are you running away from?" Some people were more direct, as in "What did your wife say?" laying out an image of my taking her and the children by force, perhaps with a gun to their heads. Other questions were more delicate and conveyed compassion, "What about the children?" The complete sentence would have been "What about the children, poor things?" Christian friends seemed to respond differently, in a tone of awe, expecting to hear about a moment of religious revelation.

But until Naomi Cohen, no one ever blamed it on my mother.

Naomi lived directly across the hall from us in Israel. Her father had been a prominent Orthodox rabbi in the

United States, her husband was a prominent rabbi in Israel, and Naomi was an intelligent woman in her own right. When Naomi spoke, people listened.

She was only forty at the time, but with her heavy-rimmed dark glasses set against a firm nose and dressing in dark colors she looked older, like one of those women staring out from a faded black-and-white photo pasted inside a picture album from the Old Country. She had a disconcerting habit of bending forward and looking up at you when she spoke. But she was smart and honest and had common sense.

When Naomi said, "it's all because of your mother," I began to laugh but Naomi started me thinking about my mother differently than I ever had before. My mother had been a social worker in Chicago. In the heat of the city's intolerable summers and during its brutal winters, she traveled on elevated trains and on buses to visit her clients. I don't think I ever saw her cry more than two or three times in her life. One of those times was when she told us about waiting so long for a bus on a winter day and being so terribly cold. I wish she had talked more about her work. I could sense that she loved it and did her best to help people living in poverty.

She could see beyond the obvious. One day, she told us that the woman she worked for complained about an Italian family that used part of their relief money to buy wine instead of food. "She doesn't understand," my mother told us, "that wine is a part of their customs, that in a way it's as important as food." I could feel her frustration.

I was just a kid at the time, but now that I'm older I wish I had heard more of her stories. Now that I am older, I understand there were other jobs she could have had and there must have been a reason she chose social work. She never lectured us, but her values were in the air we breathed. She knew little about the rules of Judaism and yet she lived them. She probably knew that you're supposed to love your neighbor as yourself but she also knew that whether you love him or not, you had better show up when he needs help. She knew there were things you were supposed to do, like feeding the hungry, comforting the mourner, visiting the sick. Maybe those kinds of things are prayers themselves, maybe more important than prayers.

The Hebrew word is *tikun*, the act of helping mend the world, working with God to make the world a little bit better. It's an important Jewish concept. That's why many Jewish country clubs won't accept members without verifying that an applicant's charitable giving is at the appropriate level. That's why if a wealthy Jew doesn't help support a synagogue or a hospital or a school, people who know him, instead of being impressed with his wealth, will dismiss him saying, "He's still a bum."

I've seen that with my own eyes. That's why so many socialist and utopian organizations whose agendas embrace everything from helping the starving to the issue of global warming attract Jews. It's because many Jews, even Jews like my mother who don't know much about Judaism, carry within them that internalized religious injunction to make the world a little bit better.

So maybe Naomi was right. Maybe I was acting out something I saw in my own home. Doing it my own way. As asinine as it was.

Standing in front of my mother's grave, I looked around for a small stone. It's a tradition. You're supposed to leave a stone at the head of the grave, a token that you were there. That much I knew. It was easier to find the stone than to find the words to explain my feelings. I tried to tell her how I felt. The graveside seemed safe, a place where I could try to understand my feelings and share them.

Some of those feelings were romantic, a chance I thought to be part of history. The Jews are back in their homeland after two thousand years, and I could be a small part of that return. That was exciting to think about. I told my mother about other feelings, too, like being a part of that strange people who have survived in spite of genocide, in spite of intermarriage, in spite of acculturation, a people who in a sense were outside of history.

That's how Yaacov Herzog described the Jewish people in his debate with the world-famous historian, Arnold Toynbee, who as recently as the 1950s dismissed the Jews as irrelevant to history. The word he used was *fossils*.

Yaacov Herzog, the Israeli ambassador to Canada, debated Toynbee about that charge. Some fossil, Herzog argued. Herzog's very presence as a representative of Israel was his most persuasive argument. But he went on. Perhaps by history's rules, Herzog said, the Jews do not exist, but look around. They are in their own country, with Jerusalem as its capital, the same Jerusalem that King David made the capital of the Jewish people more than three thousand years earlier. And he reminded Toynbee about the Biblical story of the pagan prophet Balaam who was sent out by King Balaak to curse the Jews and instead ended up blessing them, telling the king they are a people that dwells alone. In other words, a people outside of history.

The very thought embarrassed me. Educated people don't think that way. Educated people look for logic. That's what Toynbee was doing. Romantic causes are not logical. History is not a place for romantics. And yet, Israel was there. And I was going to be part of it.

So maybe mother was right, that I'm not normal. I'm not even sure what normal is anymore. I'm beginning to think there is wisdom beyond knowledge. Intuition perhaps. Maybe something mystically internalized. Or sensory. I don't know, but I think that somewhere within that mystery may be the reason for my journey.

In any case, I had the feeling that mother would have understood all that. I had the feeling she might have approved what I was doing, even if it was asinine.

Maybe that's why I was smiling as I left the cemetery.

Back in the station wagon, the children dutifully folded themselves into their assigned positions. Rosalind slid in beside me. The drive was a little longer this time. To say good-bye to my father. I drove back to the highway and then turned off at Cicero Avenue to begin the thirty-mile-per-hour monotony of passing Chicago's dreary storefronts that were lawyers' offices and real estate offices, a place to put a couple of desks and try to make a living. Past pizza parlors and barbershops at a time when men got haircuts instead of having hair styled. In the distance, a red neon Pegasus pranced through the sky, the sign of the Mobil gas stations. There were drugstores, too, most of them owned by Walgreens. We drove south and west toward the apartment in Oak Park where my mother and dad had moved after selling their house. He lived there now with his new wife.

My mother had always said that after she died, some little blonde would come along and snatch my father away. He was a good-looking man with gray eyes and graying hair that added a distinguished air to his presence. He was a dentist who had the aura a surgeon might hope for. But he was naïve, and my mother knew exactly what she was talking about. "Some little blondie will tickle him under the chin," she would say, "and that will be that."

Which is almost exactly what happened. After years as a dutiful Jewish husband, my dad met an attractive Christian woman, a friend of the neighbors. A couple of months after my mother died, the two couples went out together and Lenora—that was her name—put her hand on my dad's hand in a consoling fashion and, as they say, the rest was history.

Lenora was probably ten years younger than my dad. She was blonde, at least when he met her, and attractive. She looked like Zsa Zsa Gabor, the Hungarian darling of the gossip columnists known for her beautiful skin, curvaceous figure, and honed capacity for pleasing men, several of whom she married. Lenora had done that, too. No matter. My dad was a happy pushover. Lenora was the antithesis of my serious, introspective mother. She was outgoing and fun, like my dad. And she was gentile. He loved it, and his few years with her were probably among his happiest. Life works out in funny ways.

When we arrived the children ran up the stairs they were so accustomed to, and my dad opened the door, eager to see them. Rosalind and I followed, and the awkward moments began. It was less than two years since my mother died, and now my dad was facing loss again, the son he idolized and four grandchildren. I hadn't thought about it that way. I had thought that now that my dad was remarried, it wasn't as if he was being abandoned. I had thought it would be all right to leave. Not a big problem. We all see things differently.

We sat down at the kitchen table as we had so many times before with my mother and visited just as if this were like any other visit. And made small talk, saying words that covered up the words we were afraid to say.

"What are you and Lenora doing this afternoon?" I asked. ("Even though we're leaving, I care about you deeply.")

"Maybe we'll go for a little drive," dad answered. ("Don't worry. Everything will be all right.")

"I'll phone when we get to New York," I said. ("It won't be so bad. We'll stay in touch.") I looked at my father. The muscles of his cheek rippled, a familiar habit as he clenched his teeth and held in check his feelings.

"That'll be nice," he said. ("I hope we'll hear from you often.")

David was fidgeting with his food. "Why isn't David eating?" he said. ("Will the children be all right?")

"He had a big breakfast," I said. ("They'll be just fine. Don't worry.")

And so we ate the food for which we had no appetite, made small talk without conviction, and hoped that somehow each would understand what the other could not say.

Finally we could leave. David and Becca jumped into my father's arms and gave him big hugs. We all embraced, and I felt the bristled texture of Dad's face against mine, a feeling I remembered and loved from my earliest childhood.

We left the apartment and huddled the children down the stairs. There was no sound of the door closing. Without looking back, 1 knew dad was still in the hallway, still watching us go down the stairs, then from the window of his apartment watching us walk down the path to the car, watching every last second we were in sight as if by never letting us out of sight he might hold onto to us forever and that somehow we wouldn't leave after all. I didn't look back. I kept my eyes forward, kept walking, sad at the thought of leaving him and angry at his dependency on me, so much anger caused by the simple act of his loving us.

I was angry at myself, too. It was my dream, but my dad was the one paying the price for it.

Once again I raised the heavy back door of the Volvo as the four children tumbled in and over one another to claim their small piece of the floor. "Only one more stop," I called out to them, "and then it's full speed ahead to New York!" I tried to keep up the sense of adventure. I wanted them to be excited about the future. I didn't want them to feel sad as they left their grandfather for a long, long time.

The last good-bye was to a past I had never known, but

which was as real to me as Oak Park. I steered the station wagon through the traffic and into the southbound highway. We were on our way to Hamlet, Indiana. It was out of the way a bit, but it was a pilgrimage I had to make, the town where my mother grew up. I had been there once before as a youngster, but remembered almost nothing about it, and yet I knew everything about it. Hamlet, Indiana, was the only part of her life that my mother ever shared with me. I could feel its loneliness in her stories. I could feel its raw strength, for I knew the Midwest. I understood its people because I had heard all about them, all the stories of good small-town Christian neighbors of my mother's early years. I liked that town and I liked the people who lived there and, though I never lived there, I knew its past was a part of my past.

It's funny how things change. When I was younger, I'd look ahead to see what I would become. As I grew older, I began looking back to see where I came from. As I drove on, the Indiana Turnpike unfolded before me, bringing me to some of those beginnings.

After a couple of hours I turned off the highway and onto a back road that led me to the red brick building I wanted to see. I had seen it many times before in old photos. It was easy to find. There aren't many big buildings in Hamlet.

I got out of the car and walked toward it alone, walking slowly through the tall weeds and grasses that fell back listlessly before me. I walked through the brush and across pebbles and stones that scuffed my shoes. Abandoned so many years ago, the red brick building seemed weary just standing there, like a tombstone rising above a long-forgotten grave.

I climbed the cement stairs that led to its locked doors and looked up at the words chiseled into the stone above the entrance: Hamlet High School—1900.

In the old photos, young men and women stood in four rows below those words, posing proudly at their moment of graduation. Some of the girls smiled, just a little. Some of the boys stood with arms folded across their chests, straining for a look of maturity, their faces lined with seriousness. They were all so young, their faces smooth, their vision confident. My mother's face was among them. My mother looked sad.

Life wasn't easy for her in Hamlet. Her father was an immigrant there, one of some two million Jews who fled Russia at the turn of the century. How he ever found Hamlet, Indiana, is a mystery, but that's where he settled in 1902. He even bought a small piece of land that pretended to be a farm. It didn't seem to matter to him that he knew nothing about farming or that he never intended to be a farmer. Maybe in Russia someone told him that when you come to America, you should buy land. So that's what he did. He bought a cow, too. Then he went off to Chicago during the week and became a leather cutter in a factory, leaving my grandmother in charge of the farm.

My grandmother was a small, plump woman who didn't know any English. When she bought vegetables in town, she used Yiddish words for things like onions and potatoes. The German grocer quickly learned the Yiddish words for onions and potatoes, but my grandmother never learned one word of English.

She didn't know anything about cows, either. As a matter of fact, she was terrified of the cow. So at the age of ten, my mother had to learn how to milk a cow, had to take care of her younger sister and brother, and in effect, became the mother of her mother. Small wonder she looks so grim in the yellowing photos I still have of her.

The Christian neighbors were protective of my mother. One was a classmate named Paul Luken who always felt a special affection for her and who wrote to my mother every year at Christmas time until the year he died. Another was Jim Short, son of the town banker. When I drove through the few blocks that made up the entire town, I saw the Short name in several places. The family was still doing well.

The last name I remembered was Nellie Schuster, daughter of a German farming family. She and her older brothers made special efforts to help my mother, sometimes taking her along to school with their horse and buggy and helping with chores on the farm. I knew that Nellie's married name was Buck. I had no idea where to find her, but in a town so small, I knew that everyone had to know everyone else and that I would find her. And I did. Someone pointed out a faded farmhouse down the way. I got out of the car and saw a white-haired lady in a thin cotton dress sitting, just sitting, in an old rocking chair surrounded by silence. I walked toward her, climbed the few stairs to the porch where she sat, and held out my hand. Quietly, I said to her, "I'm Frieda Poll's son."

She looked at me carefully. Her skin was uncommonly smooth for her age. Her eyes were tired, but steady.

"Frieda's gone now," she said. She spoke to me as if we had already been engaged in conversation, as if nothing was more natural than my standing there talking to her. As if we alone existed in the world.

"Most of them are gone," she said. "My husband, too. And a daughter."

"I'm sorry," I said.

Another daughter and her husband were sitting on the grass nearby with their baby. They greeted me and then went on with their own talking. They were visiting Nellie, being around, the way young people often visit old people. Being around.

"A person gets weary from too much living," Nellie said. "The body aches a lot."

Nellie drifted off into thought. I didn't say anything.

"I remember Sarah, too," Nellie said, recalling my mother's younger sister.

"She's gone now, too," I said.

"I'm ready," Nellie said. "I've had enough."

"I'm glad I got to see you," I said. Nellie rocked a little and didn't say anything.

"Can I take your picture?" I asked. "I'd like to have a picture of you."

Nellie nodded. I adjusted the camera lens and looked at her through it. Nellie smiled for the first time, ever so slightly. Almost imperceptibly, her body settled into a pose. For a moment, Nellie was a young girl again. I snapped the shutter.

I put the camera down and gently clasped her hands. I thanked her for spending time with me. I walked away, turning to look back just for a moment. Nellie was crying.

Chapter 8

Leaving America

*S*lowly I drove back to the highway. I was emotionally drained. I felt empty inside. But at last, the
difficult good-byes were behind me. At least that's
what I thought. New York would be easier, seeing old
friends, enjoying warm memories, and then the magic of
the ocean voyage.

I fell into the rhythm of the highway, taking my place
among the other cars speeding ahead, following the road
through Indiana. We'd sleep in a motel that night. After
that, Ohio, Pennsylvania, New Jersey, and then at last,
Manhattan.

I looked up at the rearview mirror and saw the rectangle
image of the children clapping their hands to the rhythm of
their singing. The droning rubber tires against the asphalt
accompanied their song. As I drove on, the fields of June
slid past. The sight of the open farmland eased the tension
within me. Slowly my body drifted into peaceful weariness.
We were doing it.

They had been good years, those early ones, filled with
big dreams and little children, years that started in San

Francisco. On a weekend, Rosalind and I would join other couples for a picnic in Golden Gate Park.

Jack McConnell was one of our friends, a young ad man with a wide smile, an adoring wife, and an impressive new job managing the Hills Brothers coffee account. Another was Kurt Melchior, a lawyer whose family had fled the Nazis. Kurt was already a bright young star on Montgomery Street, the city's financial hub, happy to have left Germany behind. Married to a Swedish-American girl, he was happy to have left his Judaism behind, too. Ted Rosenak was a buddy from Northwestern married to Jeanne, a young artist from the Bay Area. Ted and Jeanne were so poor starting out that one night in their tiny apartment on Telegraph Hill, their daughter, Jessica, was bitten by a rat. The tourists who came by to admire the beauty of Telegraph Hill didn't know there were rats there.

None of us had much money in those days, but it didn't seem to matter. We knew that some day we would be successful and have much more. Nothing to worry about.

We would each bring a basket of food, lay out the fried chicken and potato salad across a red-and-black plaid blanket, open a bottle of wine, watch the children play in the grass, and, as a professor of mine used to say, think deep thoughts together.

Only seventeen years earlier, the United States had dropped atomic bombs on Hiroshima and Nagasaki, and we would sometimes talk about whether we were doing the right thing bringing children into the world. In the skies over nearby Nevada, the government was testing new atomic weapons. Many of us feared that the poisonous fallout would drift down over California's grazing land and contaminate the children's milk. The government said there was no problem, the same thing they said years later when they tested Agent Orange. Governments do things like that, reassure people. Years later, they admit they made a mistake. Governments do that, too, make mistakes.

Stretched out across the blankets, juggling our babies as we chatted, we managed to solve most of the world problems. When you're in your thirties, you have more knowledge than self-doubt, so that was easy. But eventually we'd become bored with our brilliance and would happily retreat to the comfort of small talk, gossip, and our personal dreams and let the world take care of itself. We would talk about the kind of homes we would like to have someday and where we would like to live. We would admit to our ambitions and our fantasies, not always certain where one ended and the other began.

And we would speculate about all sorts of improbable things like whether two-year-old Laura and our friends' son, who were busy running in circles chasing two geese looking for leftovers, would possibly marry someday, and we would laugh about whether we could still be friends if we were in-laws.

Whatever problems we had never seemed serious in those days. We took for granted that, somehow or other, we would work them out. Rolling onto my back as we talked, I pushed out my arms against the prickly grass and stretched hard so I could feel the muscles pulling all the way down from my chest to my legs. I closed my eyes to feel more intensely the warmth of the sun. It felt good, and I knew I would live forever.

As time passed, almost imperceptibly, things changed. The original starter apartment we loved soon seemed too small. I was earning more money, and we could afford more. It was easy to adapt, and before long, the excitement of that starter apartment evolved into the excess of a large suburban home. We didn't go on picnics anymore. Instead, there were cocktail parties. Maybe I imagined it, but not infrequently,

I seemed to hear loneliness behind the laughter. We met new people, but now it seemed that an introduction was quickly followed by an assessment, how-do-you-do had become what-can-you-do-for-me, and all the time everyone was smiling.

Cocktail parties gave way to dinner parties and then to corporate affairs. A friend who worked at CBS complained to me one day that his wife wasn't supportive, that often he had to go to those events alone. She wasn't a good corporate wife, he told me.

It didn't seem we had changed that much. We were still nice people, all of us. And yet something was wrong. We had all done well. If there was any doubt, all we had to do was open any glossy magazine and see our own reflection in the ads, the beautiful couples with the beautiful children getting into beautiful cars outside their beautiful homes. We had everything, but increasingly everything seemed to be nothing. I looked at my friends and saw myself. I wasn't happy with what I saw. Maybe that's why Mike's wild idea didn't seem so wild, after all. It was a chance to be young again and idealistic and even naïve. There are worse things.

Our little family bounced along inside the Volvo as I drove on, while the children alternated between games and spats. I tried to break the monotony of the long drive.

"Look at the cows," I called out. The children obediently pressed their faces against the windows and looked at the cows.

"Look at the horses," I called out fifteen minutes later. The children lurched toward the windows to see the horses.

But after the first few times, all the cows and the horses began to look alike, and the children drifted into benign disinterest.

"How about word games?" I asked gamely. Word games got us through another thirty miles. I finally realized they were better left to their own devices, that they had their own books, games, songs, and thoughts and didn't need a father playing master of ceremonies. The fact is that they were good sports about the trip and good companions, too, much better than I had been at their age.

I still remember the many times when as a child I rode with my own parents, constantly nagging them with the recurring question, "How much longer?" Our children spared me that. They were obviously more self-sufficient than I had been or perhaps simply resigned to their fate— three days of driving.

A modest motel room along the turnpike revived everyone's spirits. The children rolled themselves out from the array of luggage like divers from a decompression chamber, slowly working their cramped bodies and limbs into more normal shapes. Quickly they returned to their original vitality and more, bursting with pent-up energy. After the confines of the station wagon, the motel room was like a playground.

David and Becca turned the beds into trampolines, careening from one to another and then onto the couch.

Laura and Devorah were the first to uncover the mysteries of the bathroom with its array of small presents, plastic containers shaped like perfume bottles with their miniature treasures of shampoo, conditioner, and even body cream. Bars of scented soaps were individually wrapped like special gifts.

The best treat of all was the television set in each room, so big that it covered almost the entire top of the dresser. With television, there was the prospect of more to look at than just cows and horses. For the moment, this was better than home. The children, all four of them, piled into the same bed to watch. Devorah and Laura quickly took over the remote-control unit while the little kids gratefully watched whatever appeared on the screen. Everyone was happy.

The next morning, we made coffee in the room, gave the children muffins we had bought the night before, and were on the highway by dawn. Better to take a snack now and break up the drive with breakfast later than have nothing to look forward to. The Volvo sped eastward, the green tarpaulin flapping its edges in the wind but still bound tightly over the fourteen suitcases on the roof rack. Inside the children were once again wedged against the remaining eight. The Lego company couldn't have done it better. As the car hummed along the highway, Laura and Devorah were already drifting back into sleep while Becca and David sat with their eyes half-shut sucking up choco-late milk through small straws, a gift the motel manager surprised them with just as we were leaving. Looking out the window, they saw life as a rerun, more horses and cows.

It seemed that even the morning light wasn't fully awake. It still lay snuggling against the sensuous curves of distant hills. Rust-red barns peered out from the rich darkness of the soil. In the distance, the fields seemed to stretch out and yawn, rousing themselves for another day.

I stopped more frequently the second day, at roadside stands so the children could check out arrays of tourist trinkets and at a farmhouse where a friendly sign in the image of a rooster announced they served breakfast all day. The children met other children along the way and stared at them the way kids often do when they're uncertain how they are supposed to act away from home or, as in our case, when they didn't even have a home.

Early that afternoon, I tried to lift the children's spirits by telling them we were already halfway there. Toward the end of the day, I promised them that by the next evening, we'd be in New York.

That night was David's sixth birthday.

Back home, whenever a child had a birthday, Rosalind made a cookie castle. She made the frame of the castle out of cardboard and covered the walls with vanilla wafers pasted on with melted sugar. The cookie-wafer walls were dotted with green-and-yellow- and orange-and-red-colored candies. Upside down cones, the kind used for ice cream, formed the imposing towers of the castle. The year before, Becca didn't get her birthday castle. That was when we were visiting Israel and she turned three at the Convent of the Sisters of Zion. They were very nice, the sisters, but they didn't make cookie castles.

This year, it was David's turn without the castle. They don't make sugar cookie castles at Howard Johnson, either. That's where we stayed on the Pennsylvania Turnpike our second night on the road.

I did the best I could. I called over the waitress, a young country girl with freckles, and told her what an important day it was. She was one of five children, she told me, and the youngest one was also a boy who just turned six. Miraculously, she found some birthday candles and with great care soon reappeared holding a huge tray with a cupcake for each of us. Six candles balanced precariously atop each one. By the time we lit them, the cupcakes looked like miniature conflagrations. When they were all ablaze, David's eyes looked as big as the cupcakes. Just as loud as we could, we all sang "Happy Birthday."

With David the center of attention, Becca pushed her chair closer to mine. Her navy-blue sweatshirt framed her tiny chest and was tucked into her blue jeans. Her brown curls were soft like the curls the angels wear in Renaissance paintings. And then, as they always did when she was preparing to ask a serious question, her eyebrows came close together in two furry arches. She shoved her small hands deep into her jeans pockets and looked up at me.

"Daddy," she asked, "where do I live now?"

I fumbled for an answer.

"You always live with us, Becca, wherever we go."

That didn't sound right. I tried for something more reassuring.

"We're on our way to a new home," I said. "You and David will have a wonderful new room."

I wrapped my hands around her narrow shoulders and pressed my cheek against hers. I knew that my words were not enough. I hoped that maybe from the warmth of my body, from the way I held her tight, she would feel the reassurance she was looking for. I tried, and it helped a little, but I could still feel the fears that swirled about her like falling leaves on a dark autumn day.

I glanced over at the other children and wondered what their fears were. On the surface, there was none. They were talking about what they would do on the ship and the fancy dining rooms they would soon be eating in—we had shown them big color pictures from the cruise line's brochures—and that they'd swim in a swimming pool on a ship that was already floating in water and that there would be orchestras playing music every night. And yet beneath the excitement, each child clung to secret apprehensions. It seems that each of us is that way, that each of us has a small secret place for hiding things from others, sometimes hiding them from ourselves, a space where things are hidden because we want to keep them there or because we don't want to keep them there but are afraid to let them out, afraid someone else might not understand. Sometimes it's that way with the people we love the most. Often with the people we love the most.

My exhaustion that night overcame all my other feelings

and I slept soundly, grateful for the weariness that erased all my other feelings. Or at least covered them up.

We reached Manhattan early the next day. As I pulled into the hotel driveway and one by one the children appeared from the recesses of the luggage, I felt we must look like the Joad family in the movie, *The Grapes of Wrath*.

I tried to appear nonchalant as the bellboy wrestled the twenty-two suitcases onto three different brass carts. I looked away as if I were surveying the hotel lobby as he piled on top of the stacks of luggage all the souvenirs of our drive that the children decided they couldn't part with, plus the stuffed animals and other reminders of home they insisted on taking in the car, as well as the final accumulation of sweaters and jackets that began the trip tightly packed inside suitcases but that, after a couple of nights of packing and unpacking, mysteriously escaped into the confusion of collectibles strewn through the few air pockets of the station wagon.

There isn't much that New York bellboys haven't seen, but I have a hunch that our array of children and luggage may have given our bellboy a new story to regale his friends with. I was grateful that against all logic he managed to fit everything inside the two rooms. I tipped our bellboy well, very well, not so much out of decency as out of guilt.

We went out that night with old friends from ABC. The next day we visited neighbors we had known when we lived in Westchester. That evening, the day before we were to sail, still more friends from New York crowded into our two hotel rooms to say good-bye.

They wanted to hear all about our plans and I was eager to share everything with them, to tell them about our new apartment and the people we had met in Israel and how much everyone loved children there.

I was caught up in my own enthusiasm. But slowly I

realized that for some our leaving was not a personal journey, but a rejection of their way of life and therefore a rejection of them. No one said it but I could sense it, like an apparition unacknowledged. Some expressed concern over our welfare. Their faces looked like they were making a condolence call. But most of the farewells were warm and encouraging. We left one another with clumsy hugs among the men while the women planted wet kisses on the children. One by one, our friends made their way to the door within a swirl of good-luck wishes and assurances we would always stay in touch. No matter what.

At last, it was morning, June 25, the day we were set to sail. I found my original bellboy. I didn't want to undergo the surveillance of someone new. Better organized this time than the day we arrived, we assembled on the main floor, counting faces and suitcases.

But the lobby was not the Fifty-seventh Street pier. I still had a ways to go. I looked over the suitcases, the four impatient children, the stroller and the assortment of stuffed animals, and plotted my next move. I would take the luggage and family to the pier in shifts.

Fortunately in the 1970s, most New York taxis were the roomy, box-shaped Checker cabs of blessed memory, a means of transportation from an earlier civilization rarely remembered among modern New Yorkers who think it is normal to sit in a taxi on a sunken backseat that is little higher than the floor, with legs pulled back and knees pressed tight against the cabby's section, all the time separated from the driver by a plastic partition not dissimilar from the kinds used in pick-up trucks that cart stray dogs to the pound.

The Checker I hailed was big enough for more than half the luggage. All the driver and I had to do was meticulously fit the bags piece by piece into the huge trunk, pile another three suitcases atop one another on the seat next to him, and push the rest, another half-dozen suitcases, onto the backseat, leaving just enough room for me to squeeze in. The driver was good humored about the whole thing. He was a New York cabby. Nothing could faze him. And best of all, he spoke English. The 1970s were not the worst of times.

Depositing all that on the pier, the driver and I returned to retrieve the rest of the luggage and the family, and soon we were all reassembled on the pier facing the huge dark shape of the Greek liner, *Queen Anna Maria*, our new home for at least a couple of weeks. Its gangplank reached out to the pier waiting for us to step into our future.

I had envisioned a festive farewell in our cabin before the sailing, like the one I had when I sailed to Europe as a young bachelor almost twenty years earlier. Friends from ABC had tumbled into my small tourist cabin, bringing champagne and snacks. The cabin came with a roommate, a young man from India, who joined us in toasting farewells. Jim Weiller was there, the tall, dark-haired actor I had hired to host our reruns of Hopalong Cassidy. His wife, Jean, too, one of the most beautiful women I have ever seen, tall with white skin like cream, her body elegant in its bearing. Today they are divorced and Jim is one of the many actors no one ever heard of. But when we were in our twenties we believed that marriage was "till death do us part," and that "till divorce do us part" wasn't even a possibility, let alone that it would happen to so many of us.

Gordon Kunz was there, too, as tall as Jim, but with a head of full blond hair styled into a pompadour that added a couple more inches to his height. He looked even taller next to his tiny wife. Divorce was something that would never happen to Gordon. He had grown up within a solid, old-fashioned German-American ethic of what is today called family values, but which in those days you didn't need phrases for. Family values, marriage, and rearing kids, that's what Gordon was all about.

I remember dark-haired, sensuous Maria sitting on my lap as we all drank champagne together. Funny how life is. I don't remember her last name, but I never forgot her. My loyal secretary, Anita Gingrich, was there too, Anita dressed with the propriety of the fifties in a modest dress and hose, the waves of her blonde hair pulled back tight.

Everyone crowded into the small cabin, cheerfully toasting farewells, recalling absurd anecdotes, and sharing stories about our antics in television, like the night I was working late at WABC-TV when the phone rang and a frantic director, calling camera shots on a network program that was live coast to coast, asked if he was supposed to run the commercial of one of our big advertisers in the next break.

I hadn't the slightest idea. I couldn't even recall what show was on the air just then. And I certainly had no authority. But it was obvious that at the same time he was busy directing the show live, he was frantically dialing every phone number he could think of so someone would tell him what to do next. But I was the only one around. The clock was ticking, and something had to be done.

"What should I do?" he called out to me. I had no idea.

"What do you think you should do?" I shot back.

"I think we should run it," he said. "But I don't have the authority."

"Run it," I said. And he did.

That carefree spirit was gone by the time we sailed to Israel. Two years earlier, in 1970, Palestinian terrorists had hijacked three commercial airliners and blew them up. A few weeks before our departure date, there was a bomb threat aboard the *Queen Elizabeth* while sailing across the Atlantic. Nothing happened, but suddenly everyone was alert to the frightening possibilities. I had planned a farewell party for a few friends who were coming to the ship but as soon as I arrived at the pier I saw the sign.

"No visitors," it said.

People were arriving to say good-bye to relatives and friends, but they weren't allowed into the cabin area. Instead we were all directed to a barren warehouse near the dock that would be used as a waiting room prior to boarding. It was large, cold and depressing. Scratched-up folding tables leaned against the barren walls. I grabbed a big one, creaked open its metal legs and commandeered a small area that would be our space.

On my second trip to the pier with the family and the last of the luggage, I had persuaded the Checker driver to stop at a liquor store so I could buy champagne and cans of salty nuts for our farewell celebration. I did my best to distribute the bottles and the nuts across the paint-splotched tabletop to make it look festive. I stepped back to study the effect. Nothing helped. The table won. In that setting, the display looked pathetic, the champagne bottles forlorn.

I kept looking around. A few friends had said they would come to see us off. Not only that, but at the last minute, my dad had called. He and his wife had gone to Boston to visit her son. As long as he was that close to New York, he decided he would surprise us for one last good-bye at the ship. A good-bye to me and to his grandchildren.

The call left me with mixed feelings, most of them feelings of guilt. It had been hard enough to say good-bye once. I didn't want to go through that again. It had been hard enough convincing myself that because he was remarried, it was all right to leave him, all right to take his four grandchildren so far away. And now I had to go through all that again. I was angry at his dependency. I was angry at myself for feeling shackled by his needs. I was angry at myself for making him pay the price for what I wanted to do with my life. I was angry that whatever a person does affects the lives of others, often hurts the lives of others, too often the lives of the people he loves most.

And then I saw him. He walked toward us slowly, looking handsome and, despite a slight limp that had come with age, trying to look jaunty. He waved and smiled, but his face was drawn, and the stiffness of his walk reminded me of the pain that had settled into his knees. The woman who replaced my mother, Lenora, walked next to him, erect, glamorous, and exaggerated like the movie stars of the black-and-white films of the 1930s.

At his other side, another surprise, my loyal cousin, Ann, who lived in New York and had also come to say good-bye. Cousin Ann who had sent me the chocolate Easter bunnies when I was young. Cousin Ann, several lovers later, smartly if inexpensively tailored, and holding tight to my father's arm, a generation in passing.

The kids were excited to see "Papa Roe," and they all ran up to him, Becca and David grabbing him tight. Soon a few other friends joined us, and we all made Styrofoam toasts. It was so sad, and it was nice.

Foghorns bellowed out from the ship announcing it was time to board. Visitors started to leave, and passengers pushed closer together toward the gangplank. I walked a short way with my father, slowly because of his knees. I walked with him and felt a closeness to him. I was grateful for that feeling. I wished I had felt it more often. I tried to take that feeling and hold on to it and keep it, but feelings are intangible and memory inexact. I held on to that feeling for only a moment or maybe a little more.

There were good-byes, a quick embrace and once again I felt the bristle of his face against my own, that inexplicable feeling of reassurance I felt as a child. Then I turned with the family toward the gangplank. People pressed against us on all sides. Rosalind and I drew the children close to us and at the same time I turned to look back at my father until his face disappeared among the hundreds of faces calling out their good-byes. I was sure he was waving, and I waved back hoping he would see me. I waved for several minutes.

At last I turned away. The children pushed in close beside us as I moved away from the railing. I began to search for our cabin.

It was all over now.

It was all beginning.

Mike and Rita also left Chicago that summer. Just a few weeks earlier. We were on our way to Biblical Canaan. That same month, they moved to New Canaan. In Connecticut.

True story.

Chapter 9

Israel at Last

*D*uring the twenty-one days at sea, it was as if life held its breath. All that was familiar lay behind us. All that lay before us was unknown. For the first time, my body permitted itself to acknowledge the emotional strain of leaving. And the physical strain, as well. Every muscle was taut. Climbing up ladders, carrying things down from shelves, and climbing back up to reach deep into those shelves and find still more things, running down to the basement and up again over and over to bring everything out of there, bending down to pack the boxes, bending down to lift boxes, carrying boxes out of different rooms, carting some things off to the garage and carrying other things to special piles marked for different destinations, it was so much that if I had thought about it, I wouldn't have even considered it. But I was on an adrenaline rush of excitement, and at the time, everything seemed effortless. At the time. When I finally stopped, the adrenaline stopped, too, and my body came crashing down.

As I walked along the ship's deck our first morning at sea, savoring the warmth of the sun, I could feel the tension seeping out of my body. I strolled slowly along the wooden planks, just meandering through time. I hadn't the energy to do more than meander. Even my thoughts were numb.

I breathed deeply and could taste the air. It's strange how one small thing can carry your thoughts far away. Suddenly, I was nine again, that summer in Colorado, pushing down the rusting iron handle of the pump and leaning over to catch the ice-cold water that was so crisp you could bite it. That's what the cold air felt like as I walked along the deck.

The sight of the deck hand polishing brass railings or a steward rushing to the kitchen would briefly catch my attention, and then I would drift back into my nirvana. Now and then I'd feel the spray of the ocean splash against my face. I kept walking along the deck. The pressures of leaving were behind me, the problems of our new lives unknown. Everything was good.

Deck chairs were lined up outside the cabins and after a while I stepped over to lie down on one, my toes pushing out to stretch the muscles of my legs, my head tilted back to catch the sunlight that like the gentle fingers of a lover caressed my closed eyes.

For the children, the voyage was a grab bag of new experiences. Meals served by waiters, not by mommy. And not just regular meals, but plates and platters and trays of fancy appetizers and meat and turkey, selections without end, and best of all, an assortment of desserts beyond anything they could have ever imagined. So many desserts in one place and at one time.

Wherever they turned, something was going on. There was a room with music and another with books and magazines and another with board games and another where people were exercising and another where people were dancing. How come they weren't going to work every day, they wondered, the way adults are supposed to? Outside on the deck, they saw grown-ups playing something with long sticks and big pieces of wood that looked like hockey pucks, but were bigger. The grown-ups said that was called shuffleboard. There were swimming pools too, three of them, with slides that sent children twisting and turning into the water while the real water of the ocean splashed nearby. No wonder Pops wanted to go to Israel!

Evenings, after everyone was asleep, I would stand on the deck against the smooth wooden railing and watch the ocean liner glide along a path of moonlight. On the last night of our voyage, I stood there with Rosalind and the children while, as if by magic, there emerged from the darkness ever so slowly the sight of the Carmel mountain range where three thousand years earlier a Jew named Elijah implored his people to reject their pagan deity. "If the Lord is God, follow him," he called out to them. And there we were three thousand years later completely ignorant of Elijah or his life or his ideas and yet following his God to the very hills from which Elijah had preached.

No exotic sunrise greeted us. Perhaps such scenes exist only in paintings. There was only the churning of the ocean, the repetition of its rhythm and then, as has occurred more than a million times before our brief moment in time, the gentle fading of the night. As quiet as a whisper, the darkness disappears within a soft haze to reveal a grey etching of hills that rise and dip against the horizon, sharing the rhythm of the sea itself. Slowly dawn emerges from the void, erasing those charcoal streaks sketched against the heaven until at last we see the hills themselves.

It is there, in the distance. Israel.

Laura is excited. She looks up at me.

"Who's meeting us?" she says.

"No one," I say.

She looks away for a moment, looks back at me, and says nothing, trying to fathom what she could not believe.

There was always someone to meet us wherever we went. Family. Friends. I could see the apprehension in her eyes and her first realization that from now on everything would be different. We had told the children that many times, told them how many things would be different. They heard our words, and they understood what we were saying, and they nodded in acceptance. But deep down they never believed that so much would change. That night was the beginning of their believing.

A loudspeaker broke the tension. All passengers down below to the nightclub. No entertainment this time. No band, no party. That same space where we had enjoyed so many good times during the two weeks at sea was suddenly changed into a stern assembly hall. In an air of excitement, passengers, all sorts of people who had sailed with us on that Greek liner, crowded around crew members who sat behind long tables dispensing forms and papers to read so we would know what to do next.

Devout Christians were there, fulfilling a lifelong dream to walk in the footsteps of Jesus. A young anthropology student was there trying to fill out the forms without leaving the line. There were college girls on summer vacations and at least three couples honeymooning on our Greek ship of all places. They were easy to spot, always arm in arm or hand in hand. It was fun to see them. There were a few families like ours, though not many. I met one of the fathers. He said his name was Pesach Schindler and that he was going to Israel to build a Conservative congregation. He was a nice man. All sorts of people were there, but no Greek widows. They had all disembarked in Athens.

There were a lot of young men on board. Many wore

young beards, torn jeans, and red bandanas. Some even wore earrings, a novelty at the time. They wanted to make clear that they didn't believe in middle-class conformity. They looked askance at the Orthodox Jews on the ship with their black beards and dark suits and wide-brim dark hats.

The rebellion of the sixties with its enthusiasm for taking drugs and burning bras had drifted into the seventies. While many young dropouts still sought out the Haight-Asbury district of San Francisco in search of pot, others went to Israel in search of pot and spirituality. Their parents were grateful for that. It was less embarrassing explaining that your son was in Israel than telling people he was at Haight-Asbury. To the boys, it didn't matter. They had no trouble finding pot in Israel. And some found religion, too. Often the religion found them, even went looking for them.

Orthodox Jews from a new yeshiva, *Aish HaTorah*, would go to the Western Wall Friday nights and invite young men there to come back with them for *Shabbat* dinner. An hour after standing as strangers at the Wall, the boys would be surrounded by new friends midst the chanting of prayers and psalms at a festive *Shabbat* dinner with its bounty of food and the warmth of wine, in a spirit of camaraderie and bonding. No judgmental parents here, no family conflicts. Instead, a warmth they wished they had felt in their own homes. It seemed to exist there in Israel with those embracing Orthodox Jews.

Some of those rebellious young men stayed on and studied at the yeshiva and became Orthodox Jews themselves, trading in their torn blue jeans for new black coats and wide-brim black hats like those worn by the founders of the group's sect two hundred years earlier in Poland. They studied Talmud and kept kosher and prayed three times a day and sent their parents into shock. "Where did we go wrong?" the parents would say. "We send our son to Israel, and he ends up being religious. Why can't he just be like us?"

As they say, God acts in strange ways.

We got in line along the tables and, surrounded by hundreds of tourists, showed our passports, filled out still more forms, and finally received our printed documents. For all that effort, we at least were staying on in Israel. Everyone else went through all that just for a visit.

A tiny old man was the next person to check us through. As he handed us our papers, he suddenly pulled them back and slid off the paper clip, returning it to its glass bowl to be used again. I smiled to myself at his penurious ways. "It's only a paper clip," I thought. I never forgot that old man because within a couple of years at a bank or in a government office, I was doing the same thing, retrieving a paper clip no longer in use or bending down to pick up a rubber band I had dropped. Everything was in short supply in Israel. Scarcity can change your habits quickly, even habits of a lifetime.

Paper products were particularly scarce. At children's birthdays, I made a point of helping unwrap the presents so I could carefully smooth out and put away the paper, especially if it was from the United States. What little wrapping paper there was in Israel had the same texture as the wax paper used for food. I learned all this quickly once we lived there and long regretted my dismissive attitude toward the old man with his paper clip.

We continued down the line past the paper-clip man. At the end of the table another man, this one with a receding hairline covered by glasses pushed back onto his head, looked up at me with a smile. I sensed he was a fellow American, as indeed he was. He was a representative of the Americans and Canadians in Israel and had moved to

Israel a decade earlier. He welcomed us and asked us one question.

"Do you need any money?"

I was shocked. I had never seen a stranger offer someone money without even being asked. And then I realized what was happening. There's a long tradition in Jewish communities around the world to provide money for those in need. For centuries, Jews have raised money to buy dowries for indigent brides, to buy graves for Jews who die alone in poverty, and to give interest-free loans to people in need. The American-Canadian organization wanted to make sure that any Jew moving to Israel who needed financial help would get that help.

Even so, from our appearance, it certainly didn't seem we would need help. And then I understood what he was doing. He asked everyone moving to Israel if he needed help rather than single out someone and risk embarrassing him. The Talmud teaches that you should never humiliate another human being. It says that just as the color drains from a person's face when he dies, so does embarrassment often drain the color from a person's face when he is humiliated, and therefore in a sense, humiliating a person is like killing him. I had never realized before how much tradition influences the most cursory relations between Jews.

I was a stranger in a strange land, but didn't feel like a stranger at all.

"Mr. Roe, Mr. Roe." The words from the loudspeaker snapped me out of my reverie. "Come to the Information Desk."

What now? I thought. We had just received all our papers. Everything was in order. I made my way through the people milling around to find out who was looking for me.

"I'm Mr. Roe," I told the lady at the desk.

She looked up. "Rafi Bar Am is looking for you."

Who the hell is Rafi Bar Am? I thought. The name was exotic like a character of intrigue who might appear in a Graham Greene novel. The woman nodded in the direction of a tall, young man with dark, curly hair. He was striding toward me. A delightfully arrogant black moustache set off his gleaming white teeth.

"Mr. Roe?" he said, stretching out his hand to greet me. "Welcome to Israel. I've come to take you through customs."

"Rafi Bar Am?" I asked tentatively.

A small smile of embarrassment flickered below his moustache. "That's my Israeli name," he said. "I'm Fred Greenberg from Chicago."

I looked at him closely, sensing something familiar behind the moustache. Slowly the memories slipped into place. I had seen that face somewhere before.

"I used to monitor a television class you taught," he said.

That was it. I did remember the face. "But you never enrolled," I teased him, pleased with myself that I had remembered such an arcane detail.

"You're right," he said. "But you were okay anyway."

By that time the kids had gathered around me, sharing my own amazement that there was someone I knew there, that perhaps this meant that all Israelis spoke English. I quickly introduced Rafi, or Fred, or whoever he was supposed to be, to the rest of the family.

"Walter called me in Israel and asked me to meet you," he said. "Walter Schwimmer, my stepfather. My wife and I came here three years ago."

My thoughts dug twenty years deep into my memories. Walter Schwimmer. I had met him the first week of my first job in television when I was making forty-five dollars a week.

Walter was thirty years my senior, an intimidating presence with his tight Oriental eyes and thinning white hair. In those early days of television when everyone was flailing around for programming, Walter came up with the idea of producing "Championship Bridge" and "Championship Bowling" and a whole array of other improbable shows that made him a lot of money. I hadn't seen or thought about Walter since then.

If he had been there, I would have kissed him for what he did. Not off the ship yet, knowing no one in Israel, I was suddenly blessed by the appearance of the young man he sent me who was ready to take us by the hand and bring us into the Promised Land. Only later when I better understood the incomprehensible maze that was Israeli bureaucracy did I fully appreciate how deftly Rafi guided us through the final machinations of disembarking and even managed to reunite us with our station wagon. Nor did I know at the time that he'd driven a hundred miles to meet us. In retrospect, I could have kissed Rafi, too.

Soon it was like old times with the whole family, the Volvo, and the twenty-two pieces of luggage all together again. Everything else would be new times, I realized, as I looked up and down the narrow street across from the ocean liner, squinting against the intense sunlight that bounced off white plaster walls. I tried to concentrate on Rafi's instructions, but was immediately distracted by the sight of a wrinkled old Arab in an outsized galabia steering a donkey loaded down with firewood along the side of the road. An endless stream of old autos, practically all of them white, impatiently weaved past him. The autos honked at the Arab and at everyone else in sight, my first introduction to Israelis who drive with their foot on the accelerator and their hand on the horn.

"Where are you headed?" snapped me back to attention.

"The Dan Carmel," I told Rafi. "I bought an apartment

in Jerusalem, but we don't own it until July first. So we'll have to stay here a few days."

"No problem," Rafi said with a wave of his hand. It didn't take me long to realize that in Israel, "no problem" is the answer to everything. I heard it so often that I quickly learned how to say it in Hebrew, "*ain bahyah!*" That arrogant self-confidence grew out of the victory in the War of Independence in 1948 against overwhelming odds, the victory in the Six Day War against overwhelming odds, and the achievement in less than twenty-five years of exporting to Europe flowers and tomatoes grown in the middle of the desert and building housing and cities in spite of a stifling bureaucracy that arose from a convoluted combination of laws still on the books from the Ottoman Empire, the post-World War I British Mandate, and the heavy socialism brought to the country by immigrants from the Soviet Union. The Israelis had become so accustomed to doing the impossible that everything was possible. No problem.

There is even a story of Ben-Gurion preparing to announce Israel's statehood in 1948 when an aide who had just heard the news rushed up to him in desperation.

"B. G.," he said, "you can't declare independence. We're surrounded by seventy million Arabs. It's completely unrealistic."

"Young man," Ben-Gurion is reputed to have answered, "this is no time for realism."

No problem.

In any case, finding the Dan Carmel was certainly no problem, at least for Rafi. For me, who in today's world of euphemisms would be called geographically challenged, it was more complicated even though all I had to do was follow him. There was no way we could all drive together in the Volvo. We couldn't even squeeze in one more toy let alone a young man more than six feet tall.

"I'll get a taxi," Rafi said, thrusting out his arm at the traffic. A dented car suddenly twisted away from the road and pulled next to us. It looked like all the other white cars driving by except that there was a sign on top of the roof. It said Taxi. In English yet. My kind of sign.

"I'll take the family with me," Rafi said, "and you follow."

He opened the door and shooed everyone in. I slid behind the wheel of the Volvo, ready to follow him and fearful of what would happen if I lost sight of his taxi. I certainly didn't know how to ask directions in Hebrew and had trouble following them even in English.

The taxi started up, and I aimed the Volvo in its direction. The street was two lanes, but that was no deterrent to the intrepid Israeli driver who had briefly been behind me and was now squeezing by on my left between my car and the oncoming cars. I quickly learned that driving like that was not unusual.

In the middle of the road, an Arab woman wearing a black caftan with red brocade, and effortlessly balancing on her head a basket of woven branches filled with purple grapes she was selling, weaved her way through the lines of traffic. A couple of tall Israeli soldiers in rumpled uniforms and with rifles slung casually over their shoulders crossed the middle of the road going the other way. In Israel, it often seems that people's faith in God is attested to more completely by the complacency of their jaywalking than by any formal religious act. Straining to keep the taxi in sight, I did my best to justify their faith by not running over the woman or the soldiers.

Out of habit, I reached over to the radio and pushed the first button. It was programmed for CBS. I thought I might catch the network news, expecting to hear the musical introduction, "See the USA in your Chevrolet." Instead,

I found myself in the middle of a Muslim prayer service. The constricted sound of the high-pitched ululations was different from anything I had ever heard, a sound that is virtually impossible for any Westerner to replicate unless he is being strangled.

The strange jagged rhythms crashed against my senses as one car after another cut in between Rafi and me. Momentarily I would lose sight of him and then spot him again as one of the cars that had cut in between us pulled out again to cut in front of still another car. Straining to keep up with him, I was relieved each time I saw the little yellow taxi sign on top of his white car.

After about ten minutes, his taxi turned and I followed it. The congestion of the narrow road drifted behind us as we followed a corkscrew path up the Carmel hillside. Rafi's taxi was right in front of me now, and I relaxed back into my seat as only an occasional car wended its way down toward us. For the first time I had a chance to look out from the hillside and for that moment felt I was back in San Francisco. The waters of the bay of Haifa churned into circles of blue. Along the sides of the hill, sunlight bounced off the white and pink houses along the way.

The rear lights of Rafi's taxi suddenly glowed red as the car slowed down to turn left into a large driveway. The sign of the Dan Carmel Hotel loomed above it. With relief, I pulled up behind the taxi as the kids raced over. They seemed unusually happy to see me. Apparently they were worried I might get lost, an apprehension nourished over years of driving with me.

As the children grabbed on to me in their excitement, I realized that one of them was missing. I looked up, and there on the hotel steps all alone sat six-year-old David, his face a pastel green. I had seen that color before. Even in Winnetka, we could hardly drive a mile without David getting sick.

Now in Haifa, between the excitement, his pent-up fears and the winding roads, he looked worse than usual. I picked him up and went over to Rafi who was pulling our luggage out of both cars. Hastily, I thanked him and told him I had better get the family into the hotel quickly before David got sick over everybody. I apologized for not being able to stop and have coffee with him and quickly made arrangements to see him later that day. That done, it was a race to the reception desk to get David into our rooms.

"Your rooms will not be ready for an hour," the manager announced. The words were English, the tone imperious.

"My son doesn't feel well," I said.

"I'm sorry, sir," he said. "Perhaps . . ."

"He is turning green," I said.

"You'll simply have to . . ."

"I think it would be better if he throws up in the room," I said, "instead of in your lobby."

"Perhaps rooms 342 and 343" the manager said, reaching for the keys.

I grabbed them and whisked David toward the elevator. Rosalind and the rest of the children raced along behind me. The bellboy completed the procession, trying to steer the brass luggage cart piled so high with suitcases that he had to peer around it from the side to see where he was going.

"Good show," I whispered to David as I carried him into the elevator. "You got us a room." David was not amused and still green.

That was the beginning of our new life in Israel.

Chapter 10

Home, New Home

Haifa was the beginning of everything we had ever known, every expected, ever experienced being turned on its head. For six days, we lived in that port city in northern Israel, waiting until July 1 when we would get possession of our apartment in Jerusalem. For six days, Haifa was our Israel.

We wandered everywhere, wending our way through sidewalks crowded with Arabs and Jews. Strange aromas pinched our noses as we passed shanks of lamb rotating on skewers and falafel, fried balls of chickpeas, tumbling through a huge pot of boiling oil. An Arab boy in a bright red shirt was spooning them out of the oil and stuffing them into pita bread already filled with finely chopped tomatoes and lettuce. One more motion and he covered it all with more chickpeas beaten into a thick spread called hummus. Customers pushed paper money across his wooden table and seized the pitas as quickly as he could make them.

It was always hot, and we were always thirsty. No problem. Wherever we were, there was a kiosk nearby where we could buy fresh orange juice squeezed right before our eyes. Its brisk scent of citrus retained its pungency despite the inevitable presence of falafel nearby.

The five of us crowded around an orange-juice man. Seeing us, he eyed his other customers, seized their glasses as quickly as they emptied them, sprayed them with water, and then quickly wiped the edge of his thumb against the rims to wipe away lipstick and other leftover marks. One more spray and he filled the glasses with fresh orange juice. The taste was wonderful. Only weeks away from supersanitized Winnetka, we already were displaying man's incredible ability to adapt.

We heard the sounds of Hebrew and couldn't understand the words. We couldn't understand the Arabic, either, but in no time at all we could tell the difference. The Arabic sounded more constricted, as if the speaker was being choked. At least that's how it sounded to people like us who all their lives had heard only the flat speech of the Midwest.

We heard another language, too. We couldn't understand that, either, but we recognized it immediately. Yiddish.

I turned toward the speaker and did a double take. He was a dark-skinned Arab with wrinkled jowls and a red-and-white checkered kaffiyeh draped over his head. He was gesticulating his way down the street in intense conversation with a heavyset man in faded work shirt and baggy black pants, a Jew.

That was the first of endless anomalies I would see in Israel, Jews and Arabs at war with one another one year and then a few months later, sitting in cafes and drinking coffee together at small tables where ashtrays overflowed onto flower-patterned oilcloths. I saw Jews and Arabs working together in the *souk*, and I saw Jews and Arabs teaching together at Haifa University. I began to learn how different from the headlines are the vagaries of everyday life.

We immersed ourselves in this new adventure, walking

the streets of Haifa the first couple of days and then taking our first journey by car, driving along the winding roads of northern Israel across a landscape of green hills and vast fields that give the illusion of that small country stretching out forever. I knew that Israel was no bigger than Rhode Island but, as if to be perverse, it never seemed to admit it.

Nor did the illusion of endless space change the following day when we drove almost half the coastline of Israel. Going south from Haifa, we stopped to have a picnic lunch among the Roman ruins of Caesarea, continued south through Tel Aviv, and ended our journey at the bottom of Israel in the ancient port city of Jaffa where a couple of thousand years earlier Jonah set sail, was tossed overboard by his shipmates, and found himself inside the belly of a big fish.

In a matter of hours, we had touched Arab, Roman, and even Biblical history. It was almost too much to absorb, made no less improbable at the end of the day as we watched the huge ball of a blazing sun slip into the Mediterranean and extinguish itself within its dark waters. If I had made that journey without stopping, the trip would have taken only a couple of hours. And I'm not a fast driver.

It's even a shorter distance crossing the country from west to east. I quickly learned that if I drove from Tel Aviv on the shores of the Mediterranean and headed straight east, I could cover the width of the country in about an hour and a half.

Any more than that and I'd be in Jordan.

Israel doesn't seem that small when you read about it in the newspapers. From the papers, you'd think that Israel is as big as the United States.

And so the perception is that it's no big deal if Israel returns the Sinai to Egypt. And Israel should give back the entire West Bank, too. Why not? Somehow it feels no more serious than the United States lopping off Arizona, there would be so much left. Of course Israel is not the United States, and giving back the entire West Bank means that at its narrowest point Israel would be only nine miles wide. I'm basically a peacenik and believe in compromise. Yet the fact is that there's not a lot of slicing and dicing you can do with Rhode Island.

We didn't think about all that those first few days. We were so busy seeing our new country that before we knew it, it was July 1. At last, we could move into our new home.

We got up early that morning. The movers were scheduled to be at the apartment at eleven o'clock. For the last time, we loaded the suitcases into the station wagon, the kids took their assigned positions, and with a feeling of trepidation we began the journey.

It was exciting, to be sure. At the same time, there was a creeping tension that filled the pit of our stomachs. It was one thing to come to Israel and live in a hotel and sightsee every day. To actually move into your own apartment, that was serious.

The drive to Jerusalem did nothing to assuage our anxiety. It was something like the chaos I had seen on the streets of Haifa, only at seventy miles an hour. We drove south toward Tel Aviv and then turned east toward Jerusalem on a two-lane highway. Two lanes, not on each side, but two lanes altogether. And mysteriously, there was a third lane as well, invisible to me, but not to the other drivers. It was the space between the two lanes.

Driving along, I would see my rearview mirror fill with an image closer than tailgating. Just as suddenly, that vision would disappear into a swish of white blur that swept past my side window. At the same time, I would see another car suddenly veer out from the path of the oncoming traffic, pull into that nonexistent middle lane, and race directly toward the car that just passed me. My teeth clenched tight. The muscles of my back clenched tight. I leaned against the steering wheel and braced myself for the inevitable crash. Strangely, it didn't happen. At least not on that particular trip.

I pressed on, determined to get to Jerusalem no matter what. I would learn later—I had a hint of it already—that in Israel, reckless driving was a way of life and, unfortunately, of death with the loss of lives on the highways far exceeding the loss of life to terrorism.

In the United States, close to half the highway deaths are due to drunken driving. In Israel, heavy drinking is rare. Or maybe just different. In Israel, drivers are drunk with arrogance and impatience. "Let the other guy worry," my good friend, Gadi Danzig, cried out merrily one day as he raced through a four-way stop while I pushed back into the upholstery as far as possible to protect myself against impending doom. We were spared that day, though sadly, Gadi was killed a few years later filming from a helicopter in the Philippines, probably a victim of the pilot's same it-can't-happen-to-me attitude.

As I came closer to Jerusalem, almost imperceptibly the interminable flatness of the highway began to rise and then turn and then dissolve into tighter turns and then into steep curves, higher and higher. David girded his loins. The rest of us held our breath hoping he would not spoil the moment. Up and up we went until we could feel our ears pop.

Moving to Israel is called "making *aliyah*," the Hebrew word for ascent. It refers to the spiritual ascent to Jerusalem. It could just as well refer to the literal ascent you make to enter that holy city.

Not everyone who has tried that ascent has made it. The rusted hulks of armored cars destroyed during the 1948 battle for Jerusalem still lie scattered along the winding roadside, grim reminders that there was a time when you couldn't get to Jerusalem, when an Arab blockade kept food and medicines from reaching its inhabitants. The Israelis leave those burned-out hulks there so that no one forgets what it means to live in Israel, as though decades of precarious existence for the Jewish people were not reminder enough.

I drove on past barren rocks that had lain within that earth for centuries, past hills fought over by Jews, Christians, Muslims, and countless other peoples who no longer exist, whose names are but brief paragraphs in history books. Sometimes no more than a sentence.

Higher and higher we climbed until the road gently guided us into that city that was known in the Middle Ages as the center of the world. No one thinks that way today, and yet you have to wonder why one terror attack in Israel that kills a half-dozen people is major news from the *New York Times* to the BBC while thousands massacred in Africa and Asia are barely noticed. Reading the newspapers, there are times when one might, indeed, feel that Jerusalem is the center of the world.

Our first glimpse of the city was a disappointment. It didn't look like the center of anything. No Israeli version of a Parthenon or Colosseum rose up in the distance to stir our spirits. We saw no ancient ruins as we entered, no Crusader arches or Roman columns. Jews praying at the Western Wall or Arabs going up to the Dome of the Rock were far from our view. Instead, we were greeted by laundry hanging limp from the small balconies of dilapidated stone buildings.

And yet we could feel the change. Something inexplicable. There was not the excitement of New York. Nor the magic of beauty holding its breath in Paris. Nothing at all—and yet everything. We could feel it, a city that is not just another city. A city that is a journey beyond reason, an ascent. *Aliyah*.

I drove on through the Rehavia district, wended my way through a narrow main street where black smoke poured out of lumbering buses, and then with a turn to the right and another to the left, soon eased the car against the curb of a large traffic circle. There it was at last, our new home, a duplex on top of a hill.

I looked up and once again saw the sign that Abraham had pointed out when we visited the previous year, *Kikar Wingate*, memorializing the British officer who didn't live long enough to fulfill his dream of leading a Jewish army. And as for Constantin Salameh who built three of the large homes that stood there, few remembered him at all. One of those large houses, the one he named for himself, is the Belgian Consulate. The Belgian flag hangs brightly above it, but I saw no sign there that recalled Salameh.

Once again, I looked up at our apartment. For a moment, I held my breath. How small would the rooms look now that all furniture was gone? Would it have that same sense of importance without the intimidating presence of Mrs. Roth with her large rouged features that burst out from under a huge bouffant? Had I acted too impulsively? Once again, I thought of my parents who had spent twenty years looking for the house they would finally buy. I spent thirty minutes finding this one. Well, what was done was done. I could only hope for the best.

The children didn't share my apprehension. They were excited. I watched them race ahead to see who could run up the fifty-one stairs fastest. I followed them to the fourth floor where they stood clustered outside the door. I took the key that Mrs. Roth had sent me and bent down to find the keyhole. One turn and we were in.

The kids ran ahead to see where everything was and to

fight over who would get which bedroom. Rosalind and I walked in tentatively and looked around and then looked at each other. It wasn't quite the same place we had spent so many hours talking about during the past year. Not even close. I was right, that without the furniture our memory of how large the apartment was disappeared into a black hole of self-deception. What we saw was less than we remembered.

The art treasures that had adorned the rooms were no longer there, of course. I hadn't realized to what extent they made the apartment look so special. What did remain were dirt, dust, and scraps of paper strewn across the floors. What remained were loose wires and fragments of dangling plaster hanging limp from raw holes ripped open to remove the sconces. The torn-up openings looked like gaping jaws, wide open in a state of shock, still spitting out the plaster fragments. I didn't know people tore up their walls to remove their lamps. Whenever I sold a house in the United States, I left behind whatever was attached to the walls, even washing machines and clothes dryers. It seemed that in Israel, the custom was different. Selling a home meant exactly that and nothing more. Everything that could be removed was removed. The rectangles of grime that outlined where the frames of priceless paintings had once hung, those remained.

I tried to hide my disappointment. I began to walk through the rooms to get my bearings. The door where we entered led directly into the living room, which in turn led into the dining room. What was unusual was that the dining room wasn't near the kitchen. To serve there, you had to carry the food all the way across the living room. So maybe it wasn't a dining room after all. But it wasn't closed off and there was no bathroom connected to it, so it couldn't be a bedroom. We came full circle. It must be a separate dining room after all, even if there is no such thing in Israel.

The master bedroom was as I had remembered it. Most of all, I remembered the romantic balcony that looked down on the *kikar*, the traffic circle, below. Across was a small bedroom that Becca and David could share.

I climbed the narrow interior staircase to remind myself what the upstairs looked like. There was one room there that could be my office. Instead of living above the store as the early immigrants to America did, we would live below the store.

That room led out onto a large roof garden. An assortment of clay jugs had been abandoned there, some still spouting dusty cacti. And then across the way were the two small apartments I remembered. They would be perfect for the girls' rooms. I began to feel more hopeful. Once we cleaned up the rooms and put in our own furniture, everything would be fine.

I turned around and saw the sweeping view of the Old City. There, looking east, was the sight that had captivated me the first time I stood there, the distant spires and domes that stretched toward the heavens as if seeking to bring God down to earth. That was an easier task, no doubt, than trying to bring man up to God.

The mysticism that is Jerusalem overcame my apprehension about the apartment. More hopeful now, I turned back to go down the seventeen stairs of the inner staircase, that itself was fifty-one stairs above the ground. A lot of stairs, but that's the way it was. In the 1930s, neither Constantin Salameh or anyone else in Jerusalem built their houses with elevators, nor was there any way we could put one in now.

Life without an elevator was only one of the compromises we had to make. There were others, too. Not only was the separate dining room separated from the kitchen, but the kitchen itself was no larger than you'd find in a studio apartment. Rosalind was a gourmet chef who in less than an hour could lay out an exotic dinner. How could I have let this happen? We looked at the kitchen again and looked at each other. No matter, somehow we would manage. Seven thousand miles from the country we still thought of as home, we didn't have much choice.

We sat down together on the dusty floor trying to think everything through, trying also to ignore the children who were yelling and screaming and making all sorts of noise. What about those two bedrooms for Laura and Devorah on the other side of the roof garden? They were literally detached from the main apartment. On a rainy day, the girls would get drenched running across the roof to get into the house for breakfast. Well, no matter, they wouldn't melt.

And then there was the issue of the stairs again, a long and difficult climb when you're carrying shopping bags full of food for a family of six. We tried to put a positive spin on the stair situation. We would think of it as our own private StairMaster.

The fact is that in spite of all our misgivings, most of them justified, it was a wonderful apartment with terraces and balconies and extraordinary views and light pouring in all day long. There was almost a sense of magic about it. In a way, it was like falling in love. When you fall in love, you overlook all the things that are wrong.

Suddenly I remembered the time. I had been so consumed with the apartment that I had forgotten that the movers were due at eleven. It was already ten-thirty. Soon we would be reunited with our eight rooms of Winnetka possessions crammed into two huge containers that we had sent by ship shortly before we left.

By now, the children had exhausted themselves from running up and down the stairs and in and out of all the rooms. They happily joined us on the bedroom terrace where we looked toward the main street hoping to see a moving van plodding our way, as if looking for it could actually will its appearance.

We didn't mind waiting because it was fun for the six of us to sit out there and talk over all our plans. The Jerusalem air was crisp, and the sun felt warm against our faces as we tried to figure out where each child would sleep, where each piece of furniture would go, and whether it was possible to fit into the kitchen a small table for snacking.

Meanwhile, eleven o'clock came and went, and we were beginning to get hungry. Talk about the kitchen added an edge to our appetites. By one o'clock, we had all pretty well agreed on which bedroom would be right for each of the children, and they themselves were caught up in their thoughts about just how their rooms would look. As time went on, we all thought less about decorating and more about eating. No one wanted to leave and miss the excitement of the movers coming, but by two o'clock we were ready to compromise. Food was more important than furniture.

Rosalind tried to lift everyone's spirits. "Let's have our first picnic in Israel," she said, "right on our own terrace under the sun." We had already spotted a tiny grocery store right across the traffic circle. The thought of such an unusual picnic generated a resounding response, and within minutes, Rosalind and the children were on their way to pick up bread and cheese and anything else that looked good. My job was to stay home and wait for the movers.

I didn't want the family to feel my impatience. I waited until the door closed behind them before I started working the phone to find out what had happened to our furniture.

As soon as someone answered, I talked to him in the only language I knew, English. He must know English, I reassured myself. After all, if they take shipments from overseas, they must know English.

"I'm in Jerusalem," I told the man at the other end of the phone. I spoke slowly to make it easier for him. "I'm in Jerusalem," I repeated and then told him my name and the numbers on the shipping document. I reminded him that our things were supposed to arrive at eleven that morning.

"No problem," the man said. I still wasn't sure he understood English. I wasn't sure he understood what I'd just told him. Maybe he always answered someone speaking English with the words "No problem." But clearly, there was a problem. And worse than that, it was my problem.

"No problem," he repeated.

"But there is a problem," I said. "The furniture was supposed to be here three hours ago."

"*Zeh b'derech*," he said in Hebrew. I didn't know what that meant, but I could tell from the tone of his voice that I was supposed to feel reassured. I learned later that *zeh b'derech* means "it's on the way." It's the standard answer whenever you phone about your taxi or pizza or—as I quickly learned—your furniture.

"*Zeh b'derech.*" The Israelis live outside of time. Nothing is on time. And there is no concept of some future time such as "it will be there in ten minutes, or a half an hour, or next month." It has been more than three millennia since Moses received the Ten Commandments. Against that vast sweep of time, the Israelis don't seem to see anything as particularly urgent. Especially not our furniture.

At least I knew where it was. It wasn't still in the middle of an ocean. It wasn't in a warehouse. It was on the way.

Our picnic lunch on the terrace made us all feel better and thinking about food took our thoughts away from thinking about furniture. But we couldn't eat forever. As the afternoon gave way to evening, we thought about nothing but the furniture. I phoned again. Several times, naïvely thinking that my calls would make a difference. The answer was always the same, it's on the way. With waning patience, my politeness gave way to insistence and insistence to hostility and hostility to disbelief. The answer never changed.

The mood of the rest of the family matched my own. Everyone was grumbling. Thirty-three-hundred years earlier when Moses led the Jewish people through the desert to the land that would be Israel, the Jews never stopped complaining. There wasn't enough food, there wasn't enough water, and come to think of it, everything was better in Egypt. More than three thousand years later I faced the same kind of insurrection. My own children had turned on me. They didn't have enough food, they didn't have enough Coca-Cola, and life was better in Winnetka.

The worst part was that there was nothing I could do about it This was our first day in our new home in Jerusalem when I wanted everything to be wonderful. It wasn't.

Becca and David finally fell asleep on beds made from suitcases we pushed together. Devorah and Laura stayed awake into the evening, still wanting to wait with us even as the hour grew late. We stayed out on the terrace and watched the soft light of Jerusalem fade into shadows and the shadows fade into a blackness that looked like velvet. We waited in that darkness that was broken by only a few scattered streetlights. And then at last, sneaking through the quiet of the evening, was the muffled sound of a heavy motor chewing up the silence. A few minutes later, there were the sounds of voices we couldn't understand. I looked at my watch. It was eleven o'clock, just as they had promised. Except it was P.M., not A.M.

A new expression came to mind, one I had learned

shortly after our arrival in Israel, an expression enhanced
with the kind of gestures no one ever sees in Winnetka.
When all else fails, you stand there with your arms out-
stretched and your palms wide open facing toward heaven.
You raise your shoulders, and you sigh. And then you say it.
"This is the Middle East!"

Years later, I heard an anecdote with the same line, the
story of a killer scorpion who asks an alligator to let him
ride on his back across the river. The alligator turns his
head, looks back at him, and says, "Are you crazy? If I let you
ride on my back you'll sting me and I'll die." "Don't be
ridiculous," the scorpion says. "If I sting you in the middle
of the river and you die, I'll drown." The alligator thinks
about that. "Okay," he says and motions the scorpion to
climb onto his back. And with that the crocodile pushes off
from the muddy shore and starts to swim. And swim.
When he is about halfway across the river, he suddenly
feels a terrible pain. He turns his head and looks back at the
scorpion still sitting there. "You stung me," he says. "I'm
going to die." The scorpion looks at him, thinking about
what he has just heard. "You're right," he says. "But if I die,
you'll drown," the alligator says. "You're right," the scorpion
says again. "How could you do such a thing?" the alligator
says. The scorpion shrugs. "This is the Middle East," he says.

I had already figured that out—without an alligator.

Looking down from our balcony, I saw the outlines of
two containers. A half-dozen Arabs were scurrying around
them in the blackness. I ran downstairs to meet them, trying
to ignore the fact that they were twelve hours late. I greeted
one of them, even smiled, and pointed to the apartment that
was ours. Busy taking furniture out of the containers, he
hardly looked at me. It was obvious he had no interest in
small talk, things like where the furniture goes. And could-
n't possibly understand me anyway.

My eyes scanned the boxes that were beginning to fill the sidewalk. Three of them were marked "This side up." They were on the sidewalk with that side down. It hadn't occurred to me that writing directions on a box in English was pointless if none of the workers understood English. Another lesson learned too late.

Arabs, like many of the Jews from the Mediterranean area, are often of medium height and small boned with narrow hips. Our movers in Winnetka were just the opposite. They were the size of the guys who play professional football. Each weighed more than two hundred pounds. They wore white, starched uniforms that sported their company's corporate logo. With great effort, huffing and puffing, two of them would pick up a heavy sofa and weave through the house and down the stairs and then with all their strength, lift it into the container.

Our Arabs did not look like the movers from Winnetka. They were half the size, wore old shirts and baggy pants, and lifted everything soundlessly. I watched as one small Arab, and then another, tossed a rope around a heavy chair that weighed almost as much as he did, squatted down, tied the ends of the rope around his forehead, and rose up on his haunches to begin the journey up the fifty-one stairs. I watched with amazement. I watched with guilt. I felt guiltier still for those who had finally made it up all those stairs with a chair or a desk and were ready to set it down when I had to motion to them that there was an inner staircase, too. I pointed upward toward what would be the girls' rooms. Another seventeen stairs, if you don't mind.

Everything was happening so quickly, one Arab after another gasping his way to the top, standing there panting, waiting for me to point in one direction or another to indicate where he could, at last, put down his burden. One Arab after another resolutely climbing upward with living-room chairs, a kitchen table, boxes of lamps, more chairs, more boxes, and never complaining.

Then they began arriving in twos with dressers and bookcases and heavy wooden tables, each piece precariously balanced on the back of the man in front who was staggering under the load while right behind him, almost hidden from view by the huge piece of furniture, was a second man supporting the bulk of the weight, his head and shoulders barely visible, his skinny legs and narrow ankles inside leather slippers struggling for a grip against the marble-smooth stairs. Unlike the men of Mayflower Movers, these Arabs did not flaunt their testosterone amid grunts and groans to give testimony to their accomplishments. There was not a sound from the Arabs, just the relentless thrusting ahead. Stoicism by men who never heard of Stoics, an acceptance of fate that empowers them with endurance. That night, I had my first insight into what the Crusaders had been up against.

Watching the arrival of one piece of heavy furniture after another, I suddenly remembered our most important piece of furniture, a fifty-year-old Steinway grand piano. A premonition of problems flashed through my mind. I rushed down the stairs, leaning into the railing so as to not plunge into any of the movers straining upward. My feet barely touched the steps as they slid over the marble in a race against time, a race that was in all likelihood already lost, a likelihood I wasn't prepared to accept.

At ground level, I dashed past the large metal doors of the entrance and around the obstacle course of boxes, crates, and containers that littered the sidewalk already furnished with all our possessions, which for some inexplicable reason had been taken out of the crates and left to stand exposed to the night air until one by one each would be at last rescued and carried upstairs.

And then I saw it, at the very end of that long array of torn-up crates and endangered furniture. There through the darkness was the outline of the piano crate. Excitement surged through me and just as quickly gave way to fear. The crate was already open, its wooden sides spread out like limbs bent backward in pain, perhaps imploring the Creator about its fate. Twenty feet away, I saw the piano itself, its legs removed, lying on its side. On the cement sidewalk.

For a moment, I thought I had arrived in the nick of time. Not so. A few nicks preceded me and a few scratches as well on a piano we had treated as a shrine. The Arabs had thrown some thick rags around it to help them pull it along the sidewalk and closer to the apartment entrance. For the first time since we left America, I lost it. I started screaming like an Old City fish peddler.

"You can't do this," I shouted. I shouted a lot of other things, too, becoming frustrated as I realized they didn't understand even one word of those well-chosen expletives. And yet the sound of my voice said it all, with or without the words. For the first time, the movers stopped moving. They stood still and stared at me. It was like a scene from *High Noon*, a face-off.

In the old Westerns I used to see as a kid, the cowboys would make themselves understood to the Indians by means of some bastardized English. They would have said something like, "You gettum paper. You puttum paper under piano."

But as I thought about it, the cowboys never had to deal with a Steinway. The only pianos in the cowboy movies were those uprights that adorned the local saloons.

I snapped out of my reverie. Why am I having these crazy thoughts? I thought.

"Paper," I yelled. "Paper, cardboard, anything!" They had to understand one of those words.

The Arabs stared at me blankly. No, they didn't have to understand one of those words.

I twisted around looking for something I could grab to show them what I was talking about. Show and tell, I thought. If it works in school, it ought to work here.

I pantomimed heavy lifting. "Up," I yelled. "Up! We have to pick it up!"

I looked at them. They looked at me, but their heads were shaking, "No." So were their forefingers, wagging from side to side accompanied by a kisslike sound made by the tongue pressing against the roof of the mouth. It was obvious that meant no, also.

I tried to be more visually articulate. Instead of looking like a madman, pretending to lift up the night air, I stepped over to the body of the piano which still lay on its side, without legs, and pantomimed lifting the piano. "Up," I grunted.

Again the kissing sound. Again forefingers waving back and forth. We were at an impasse. You don't have to know the language to know you're at an impasse. And then I saw one of those fingers point past me. It pointed to the staircase fifty feet away. I got the idea. Lifting was for stairs. That's where they would lift. Until then, pushing. Along the sidewalk. Scratching all the way.

I was desperate. Then I got another idea. A dolly. There must be a dolly somewhere. Maybe there was. Maybe somewhere in Israel. But not there, not on the sidewalk, on this dark Jerusalem night. I looked at the piano, its shiny ebony gloss reflecting the streetlight. I suppressed all thoughts about what the other side of that ebony looked like by now.

And then another thought. Bending down, I pressed my shoulder against the side of the piano, grabbed it as best I could with my two hands, and pushed it toward the grass.

The Arabs watched transfixed, apparently waiting for me to toss a rope over the piano, wrap the ends around my forehead, and carry it upstairs. That was the furthest thing from my mind. What I was trying to do was push the piano off the cement and onto the grass without getting a hernia. Meanwhile, I was still on the sidewalk. I pushed again. The sound of scratching vibrated through my ears and down my spine. I was making things worse, but I kept on. Just a little bit more. I leaned forward and again pushed against the piano and then joyfully felt the resistance of the grassy surface. One more move and it would be completely off the sidewalk. Not a solution, but it was better than the alternative.

I looked at the Arabs, and I could see they were beginning to get the idea. With a wave of my hand, I tossed out a "let's go, guys" gesture and pushed again. Suddenly, two Arabs moved into place right alongside me pushing the piano across the grass and toward the stairs. If someone had taken the photo, we would have been the poster children for brotherhood.

Better at pushing than lifting, at the stairs I stepped back to see what would happen next. A piano, even with the legs removed, is not exactly the kind of furniture a mover can throw a rope over and hoist onto his back. I knew that. So did the foreman. With a quick gesture that was like a saber slashing through the air, he motioned three Arabs to get into position, one in front of the piano to hopefully steer it safely past the stucco walls at each landing, and another two behind it to lift. Their bony shoulders pushed upward against the ebony, their thin sandals pushed hard against the marble as step by step they strained upward. Up fifty-one stairs they went, then eased the piano through the entrance to the living room, put its wooden legs back into place, and turned it upright. The men of Mayflower would have stopped to congratulate themselves at this point, sit down, catch their breath, and drink a Coke. Maybe even a beer in celebration. Our Arab movers simply finished their task, wiped their hairy arms against their foreheads, and went back to work. Their only concession to the strain of the work was to accept a glass of water from me.

For hours they continued the work, hauling up 306 cartons of furniture, dishes, clothing, and assorted capitalistic necessities from Mixmasters to water picks until at last they finished, disappearing into darkness that was rapidly disappearing into daybreak. I slipped them some extra money for all their hard work, no longer angry that they were twelve hours late. I was just grateful that, at last, we had everything with us. I was even more grateful that the move was finished.

I looked across the living room. Becca and David were curled up on the suitcases asleep, oblivious of all that had happened. Limp from the tension and exhausted by the experience, Rosalind, Laura, Devorah, and I sought out the mattresses scattered over the floor. We lay down and closed our eyes, a roomful of exhausted immigrants strewn across the disorder.

It was our first night in Jerusalem.

Chapter 11

Life with the Israelis

We woke up within a scene of total disarray. Every inch of space available after the movers brought up tables, dressers, lamps, chairs, and the rest of our furniture was now filled with 306 boxes stuffed with dishes, toys, silverware, glasses, clothing, and everything else we owned. Using a black Magic Marker, I had meticulously written the contents of each box right on the top. I lacked the imagination to write the same thing on the bottom. That would have helped. More than two hundred boxes had been unceremoniously set down, upside down.

Just to move across the living room, I had to make hairpin turns around this box and past that dresser and then pull in my stomach so I could slide sideways between a pillar of piled-up boxes that was barely inches away from the king-size bed that should have been left in the master bedroom but that in all the confusion ended up in the living room.

Clearly this chaos was beyond organization. Our only choice was to methodically empty each box one at a time and move each piece of furniture to its proper place one at a time, however long it would take. It was something like pick-up-sticks for grown-ups.

It took us a week to find a place for everything. We made up job assignments as we went along. Becca's job was to empty the boxes. David and Devorah were the movers, at one point struggling to hold up an end of the heavy sofa while I held up the other end and guided it into its proper place in the living room. Laura worked with Rosalind in the kitchen deciding where to put the "good" dishes and where to put the everyday dishes, selecting which cabinets would be for pots and pans and which for condiments. Everything we owned had to be individually handled— towels into the bathroom, jackets into the closets, ironing board into a closet, the mirror into the master bedroom.

We didn't know one person in Jerusalem and yet, Israel being Israel, from out of nowhere people appeared. Lee Berlman who had moved to Israel from Chicago years before heard that another family from the Midwest just moved in, so she came over to help. She introduced herself, welcomed us to Israel, and spent the entire day in the kitchen with Rosalind, washing and drying every dish we owned. From across the hall, Naomi Cohen knocked on the door to welcome us, bringing over several platters of food, which we accepted gratefully.

Another knock on the door, and there was a neighbor from downstairs who introduced herself as Miriam Blumenthal. She had come to Israel from Czechoslovakia. Her husband, Pinchas, was part of the Israeli army that fought the Arabs in Jerusalem in the 1948 War of Independence. When the war was over, one of the commanders told Pinchas to move into the apartment where they now live. It was vacant at the time. The Arab family that used to live in that house that Salameh built fled the country during the war. Like thousands of other Arabs, he thought he would soon return when the Jews were driven into the sea. But that didn't happen, and he didn't come back. Pinchas has lived there ever since.

Miriam was a large woman whose stern appearance was made sterner still by the way she wore her gray hair pulled back into a tight bun. She was a literature teacher and came to invite us in for coffee and cookies. The children were nearby, so I introduced them, one by one. Becca was the last to step forward. "Becca," I said, "this is Mrs. Blumenthal." Becca stretched out her tiny hand, looked up at that imposing figure, and bravely whispered, "How do you do, Mrs. Blumenthal?"

"My name," Mrs. Blumenthal announced as she bent down to take her hand, "is Miriam."

Becca stood transfixed. In Winnetka, children didn't call grown-ups by their first names. We didn't do that in Oak Park, either, when I was Becca's age. Our school principal was the tall, erect, and proper Mr. Albertson. I would have no more thought of calling Mr. Albertson by his first name than jumping out a window. As a matter of fact, it never occurred to me he might have a first name. Not Mr. Albertson.

But in Israel, I quickly learned, everyone is on a first-name basis. It all began with the early *halutzim,* pioneers, the egalitarian idealists who came to what was then called Palestine. They thought, as the saying went, that they were returning a people without a land to a land without people. Like the English settlers who came to America and didn't pay much attention to the fact that Indians were already there, the Jewish pioneers didn't seem to think much about the fact that there were Arabs around.

There was one big difference, though, between the Jews and the English. The Jews who came to Israel had an historical connection to the land that went back three millennia. They felt they were coming home. Nonetheless, the Arabs living there thought it was their home.

Those early idealists labored to make things grow in the country's barren soil and built simple housing in small communes that they called kibbutzim. Like the bohemians of Paris and the hippies of San Francisco, they eagerly threw off the shackles of convention while sharing work, dangers, and lovers. The kind of life where, of course, everyone would be on a first-name basis. That's why years later, even the intimidating Mrs. Blumenthal was just Miriam.

Every day people we had never met would somehow appear in our lives. There were only a couple of million Jews in Israel in those days. Just outside Israel were more than seventy million Arabs. People seemed to appreciate anyone who would come there voluntarily to share in that life. Immediately, we were part of the family.

Of course, with family comes familiarity, something we learned that very evening.

After unpacking and throwing out boxes all day, we were completely exhausted. Worse yet, the living room looked as crowded as when we first began. All our efforts had made hardly a dent in our starting figure of more than three hundred boxes. Although it was only eight o'clock, one by one, each of us retreated into any place where one could lie down, a bed that had been set up or a living-room chair or a sofa without pillows, but at least without pots and pans on it, any place at all where we could possibly sleep that night. The floor and the furniture were littered with the crumbs of sandwiches and snacks from our sudden benefactors, but when the only thing that matters is sleep, no one cares about crumbs. We closed our eyes and lay there silently, waiting to retreat into slumber.

That's when the doorbell rang.

I didn't move. I only knew the few people we met that day. I couldn't imagine that anyone would ring our bell at ten o'clock at night. For a moment, I waited. I just lay there. It was like a scene from a 1930s movie when the doorbell rang and the lady of the house opened the door to find herself facing a bright-eyed Western Union boy delivering a telegram. She would never just take the telegram, rip it open, and read it. Instead, she would hold the envelope up to the light in an effort to discern who could have possibly sent it and the news that would have demanded the urgency of a telegram, all the time creating an unnecessary sense of fear and apprehension about the unknown. She never just opened it.

That's how I was. Instead of jumping up and answering the doorbell, I just lay there wondering who would possibly come to our home at that hour. I lay there in silence. Finally, I broke through my stupor and jumped up. I opened the door and found standing there a wisp of a man whose small eyes peered out with intensity from the black-rimmed glasses that balanced precariously on his nose.

I didn't know him and he didn't know me, and it didn't matter because he wasn't looking for me. He was looking for Rabbi Cohen from across the hall. Rabbi Cohen's father had died the day before we moved in, and the man came to pay a condolence call.

Apparently all Americans look alike because instead of the man assuming that since I lived there I would understand Hebrew, he immediately spoke to me in his haphazard English. "Nobody answers from Rabbi Cohen," he said. "Maybe you know where he is to?"

"Matter of fact, I do," I told him. Naomi, the rabbi's wife, had left me a note with the information just in case anyone did ask. "He's at his mother's house. Fifteen HaNavim Street."

"Where is that?" he said.

I was the last person he should ask. I didn't even know where the supermarket was. "I don't know," I told him, "but I have a street map."

I motioned him in, ran into the kitchen, and pulled open the drawer where I had put the English-language maps I had bought in the States.

I brought out the one of Jerusalem and spread it across the table where he was standing. We both leaned over the map, finger to finger, tracing the streets on the map. There it was, HaNavim Street, not far away.

Straightening up, the man thanked me, gave me a big smile, and looked me over carefully. Then he looked over the apartment, the walls, the ceilings, the furniture, even the boxes.

"You have a nice apartment," he said.

"Thank you," I said.

"Do you own it?" he said.

"Yes," I said.

The man turned to leave. I was closing the door behind him when he paused slightly, turned around, and looked back into the apartment. "Tell me," he said, "how much did you pay for it?"

Not the kind of thing a stranger would ask in Winnetka, I thought. And then I realized the problem was mine. I had left Winnetka physically. The trick would be whether I could leave it psychologically. I had to come to terms with the fact that I had become part of a family. So if I own an apartment, isn't it natural that somebody in the family would want to know what it cost?

In any case, I wasn't enough of an Israeli yet to tell him. I just smiled and using one of my new Israeli phrases wished him *lylah tov*, good night.

I was impatient to settle in. After four weeks of motel

rooms on the highway, closet-size rooms on the ship, and motel-in-the-sky rooms in our Haifa hotel, I was eager to get our apartment together and retreat into normalcy. So the next day I kept scrubbing out cabinets and shelves, and putting things away. I was amazed at how many things make up a life, from stuffed animals to a stuffed sofa, from cups and saucers to beds and mattresses. Even a simple can opener.

I was good at manual labor, but couldn't do much else. Hundreds of stores sell do-it-yourself items for men who do it themselves. I wasn't one of those men. I knew nothing about plumbing and wiring and fixing. My only skill was as an unskilled laborer. What I needed were real workers. A lot of them.

I asked the neighbors. I asked the grocer. I even asked the mailman. I didn't have the patience to spend a week checking references or conducting interviews, and I didn't know enough Hebrew to do it anyway. I just wanted to get things fixed and over with, so I hired anyone who was willing to work immediately.

Quickly I assembled my own ingathering of Jews plus a few Arabs and assorted other nationals who attacked their work in a mélange of words, some Hebrew, some English, some Arabic, occasional French and Russian, and still other sounds I couldn't even guess at. I never did know what the Armenians were saying. I had never even seen an Armenian before. I didn't know if they had their own language or whether they spoke something else. In any case, it didn't matter because so many different languages were being spoken that I hardly understood anyone. Worse than that, I had the feeling that the men who were working together didn't understand one another. It was like instant United Nations, but no problem. When somebody's words were greeted by a stare of incomprehension, the speaker immediately resorted to a few swirling gestures until the listener's eyes lit up with understanding. It worked. It was amazing.

The electrician was a Hungarian with a clubfoot who balanced himself fearlessly atop a rickety ladder as he closed up wires that, like twisted fingers, groped through holes in the wall, still searching for the sconces they had once known.

My two Armenians were the painters. They would squat down side by side, hunched over two cans of paint that they stirred with thin wooden sticks in search of the perfect color. The older one wore a wide-brim hat that almost covered his eyes. His job was to sporadically squeeze paint from different tubes into both cans as they stirred. Squat, squirt, and stir, the rhythm interrupted only occasionally when the man who squirted reached deep into the pocket of his stained white coverall, pulled out a small bottle of brandy and took a comforting swig.

Meanwhile his partner concentrated on stirring, his own paint-splattered fedora pushed back on his head, a cigarette flattened between his lips as the glob of fire at the tip quickly transformed it into a precariously long ash. He never flicked off the ash. It just grew longer and longer. Observing him, I felt the tension I had known as a child while watching the man on the high wire at the circus, gripped by the fear he might fall. The man never did.

It seemed that the ash would never fall. The Armenian kept stirring, crouching over the can, blending the occasional squirts from his partner's tube into his own can of color. As if in a trance, I stared at him, mesmerized by the rhythm of his movements. He took a few more deep drags of his cigarette, daringly extending the length of the ash until the inevitable happened. The ash collapsed into space, falling right into the can of stirred paint. The Armenian barely noticed. He just kept stirring as the paint grew a shade darker.

"Ruined!" I cried out. I pointed to my right. "That wall will be darker than the other!" His partner heard my voice, saw my consternation, and understood nothing. But he, too, had seen the ash drop. His face showed no emotion. Instead, he took another sip of brandy. It was clear it was not the first time this had happened. The painter was experienced. With the precision that experience brings, he squirted the tube once again, another blotch fell into the paint can, there was more stirring, and then before my eyes I recognized a blend of color that had offset the ash and returned the paint to its original shade. The wonders of the Middle East!

At last the men stood up, walked over to the bedroom and began to paint, the older one in a perpetual liquor-induced state of languor, his partner adrift in cigarette smoke. I stood back and watched. Against all logic, the walls started to look good, their color a subtle beige, the subtlety perhaps a function of the ash. Maybe liquor is good. I remembered the old story about someone complaining to Abraham Lincoln that his first successful general in the Civil War, Ulysses S. Grant, was a drunkard. "Find out what he drinks," Lincoln supposedly said, "and give it to all the generals." Maybe they should give it to all house painters, as well.

Painting was one thing. Finding someone to stain the inner staircase was not as easy. The steps were pinewood, more like something out of the American West than the Middle East. I ran back to the paint store where I was quickly becoming the owner's number-one customer.

"Stain!" I called out to him, gesticulating. Fortunately, he understood English. It's hard to gesticulate stain.

"No problem," he said.

I waved my right hand up and down, holding an imaginary paintbrush. "A man to do the work!" I said.

"No problem. I have a friend," he said.

"Send him over," I said. "Twenty-one Balfour Street."

It was eerie. I was home only a quarter of an hour when the doorbell rang. I opened the door and found myself facing a weary-looking, one-eyed Arab holding a can of floor stain. Actually, the man had two eyes, but one of them was glass. He didn't have to tell me why he was there. It was obvious. If he stained with only one eye, this must be my man.

I looked back into the room where the clubfooted Hungarian was hanging off his ladder and the Armenian was hung over. I had the feeling that our new home was beginning to look like a hospital ward.

Next came the Turks. Five of them and two huge waxing machines. Building on my success at finding the Arab with the glass eye, I found them, too, through the paint store. Their job was to clean and polish the floors. In Israel, most floors are made of marble, not the fancy kind they use on Roman statues, but marble, nonetheless. Our floors were a special kind of marble, marble overlaid with decades of grime.

Within minutes of their arrival, I heard the horrendous sound of metal against marble as a parade of mechanized Turks marched across the living room, two polishing in one direction and two polishing in the other while a fifth cho-reographed the performance. The whole apartment began to vibrate. In my entire life, I had never heard a sound like that. Apparently, neither had the man who lived directly below us.

The next sound I heard was a loud knocking at the door. That's how I met still another neighbor, the artist from downstairs. I hadn't seen him before. He wasn't one of those who had come over to introduce himself and offer help. But he was there now, banging on my door. I opened it and reached out my hand to greet him. Ignoring the gesture, he swept right past me, searching out the source of the noise.

"What's going on here?" he shouted in perfect English. My luck, I thought. Someone finally speaks good English, and instead of talking to me, he's yelling at me. He was angry. Maybe very angry.

"You're upsetting my wife," he shouted, trying to make himself heard over the racket of the machines. The Turks didn't hear him. Nor did it matter. They wouldn't have understood him anyway. The racket continued. So did his yelling.

"My wife!" he shouted. "She's right below all this. She can't take all that blasting." I had no trouble hearing him. His mouth was inches away from my left ear.

"It'll only take half an hour," I yelled back over the noise, "and then it'll be done forever."

His eyes grew larger, and his eyebrows reached up toward his hairline. "Now!" he demanded. "You've got to stop this right now! My wife has emotional problems!"

I backed up a couple of steps trying to figure out what to do. If I didn't finish the job then, I never would. If I kept going, I'd have two neighbors, not just one, with emotional problems. Meanwhile, the man was yelling at the Turks, crowding as close as he could to them without getting run over. I decided to give up. I walked over to the closest machine and snapped off the motor. I motioned to the Turk with the other machine to turn off his. Our neighbor turned and stomped out of the apartment and down the stairs to comfort his wife. I still didn't know his name. He hadn't bothered to introduce himself. But I knew where he lived, right downstairs. And I knew he would hate me forever.

I reached into my pocket, gave the boss of the Turks a big wad of shekels, and motioned to them that they could leave. As they backed out of the apartment with their big machines, I looked up and saw all four children hanging over the railing, staring at me from the top of the half-stained stairs. I could see the "what's going on?" look in their eyes, I knew how to answer them if not in Hebrew words, at least in Hebrew body language. I shrugged my shoulders, tilted my chin slightly upward, and stretched out my arms with both palms facing heavenward. Which means, of course, "What can I do?"

At that point, I should have quit winner, or loser, as the case may have been, but ever since we moved in I was bothered by the large rectangular entrance to the dining room. Instead of differentiating the dining room from the living room, it made the dining room look like an extension of the living room, at which point the living room didn't look like a living room at all. It looked more like a warehouse. That's when I had my Eureka moment. An arch, I thought. After all, this is the Middle East. The city is filled with arches. Roman arches, Crusader arches, Arabic arches. Everybody must know how to build an arch.

But where to find someone? There was no such thing as the phone book's Yellow Pages in Israel. And I decided that I had to find a better source of manpower than the guy at the paint store. That's when Rosalind came up with her idea. She remembered seeing a lanky, toothless Arab plastering a garden wall a couple of blocks away. She figured that if he could plaster a wall, he could plaster together an arch. We had been in Israel only a couple of weeks and were already stereotyping, confident that every Arab could build an arch.

Rosalind ran down the street to find her man. One block and then another and then there he was, still plastering in the sun. She came up behind him quietly and tapped him on the shoulder.

In her beginner's Hebrew, she tried to say, "Can you

build an arch for us?" She had already learned that the word for rainbow was *keshet*, but she seemed to recall that the word also meant arch or bridge or something like that, so she took a chance and said *keshet*. For sure he couldn't build a rainbow, but there was a chance he could build an arch if he knew what she meant.

Maybe he understood her. Maybe he didn't. But there weren't a lot of attractive, fair-skinned, blue-eyed women in Israel, so he did what any man would do. He nodded yes to whatever she was talking about and followed her home.

I shook hands with him when he entered the apartment. His hands were hard and calloused. His teeth were missing, but nothing fazed me anymore. As long as he could build an arch, I didn't care what he looked like.

I led him over to the entrance to the dining room. I stretched out my arm and gestured upward, sketching an arch against the air. He looked at Rosalind. She also pointed to the entrance to the dining room and with an upward sweep of her hand created another imaginary arch. The Arab pushed back his shiny black hair, smiled at her, and nodded. He seemed to have gotten the idea. An arch. At the entrance to the dining room.

He gestured that he would return, or least that's what we thought he gestured as he quickly disappeared down the stairs. Much to our surprise, he was back within an hour weighed down with what was apparently everything he needed, a black rubber bucket encrusted in dried cement drippings, scraps of splintered wood that looked like they were left over from the Crucifixion, a bag of sand, and a trowel. And most important, a wooden frame in the shape of an arch. That would be his model. I felt some anxiety when I noticed that his model was smaller than our dining-room entrance, but I figured he must know what he's doing. We always believe what we want to believe.

Carefully, he kneeled down, placed the wooden frame on the floor in front of him, and hammered on to it his fractured pieces of wood. Slowly, slowly, the frame got bigger and bigger, large enough to be propped up next to the sides of the dining-room entrance.

After a couple of hours of hammering and plastering, he carefully raised his creation to a standing position and maneuvered it into place. Of course, it was not a perfect fit, but that worried him not at all. He would simply plaster the sides of the dining-room entrance to make the space between them smaller. He stepped back to survey his work, the arch on its frame precariously erect, but not yet affixed to anything. He would be back the next day to take care of that.

The doorbell rang at eight the next morning, the normal time the Israeli workday begins, and he almost leaped into the room in his enthusiasm. He grabbed his black rubber bucket and began a regimen of pouring in powdered plaster, running into the bathroom to fill the pail with water, stirring vigorously, and then smearing the plaster up and down each side of the entrance to the dining room. Into the bathroom, out of the bathroom, more stirring and more smearing until at last the space between his wooden frame and the sides of the dining room entrance narrowed until they were almost actually touching.

It was a big job, and he was still working on it the next day and the day after that and then, much to my amazement, the rectangular entrance to the dining room did evolve into the shape of an arch. Even more surprising, the smaller entrance—created more by the need to make his wooden arch fit—made the dining room itself look more inviting.

There was only one problem. The man had created an arch, but it was an unusual-looking arch, an arch that wavered. Quite simply, the man couldn't plaster straight.

While the hard-drinking Armenian painted to perfection, the cold-sober Arab could not control the width of his arch. It dipped and bent as it moved. It began five inches wide, morphed into five-and-a-half inches a little higher up, and grew to almost six inches wide before it started its turn. Then stretching above us from left to right, it stayed six inches for a while, but before reaching the midpoint it narrowed back to five and a half as it continued its meanderings over our heads and down to the floor at the right.

I stepped back and studied the effect. I changed my position to see if perhaps from different angles the variations were imperceptible. It didn't help. They were perceptible, whatever the angle. Glaringly perceptible. For some strange reason, I found myself thinking about Buckminster Fuller, the father of the geodesic dome. I wondered whether I would someday be thought of as the father of the undulating arch.

It was obvious this was no way to fix a house. But I had never fixed a house before, so I didn't know the right way. And I didn't have the patience or the money to learn how to do it right. I just wanted to settle in, no matter what. So I settled.

All this time, our other workmen were working away, my original Arabs, a few more Arabs, the Armenians and the Hungarian. Until the afternoon when I heard shrieking from upstairs. In a second, I realized there was a fight going on and that camaraderie had given way to history. I jumped up and dashed over to the inside staircase. Just as quickly, I saw a look of dread on the face of the one-eyed Arab. He had just finished putting on another coat of stain. I got the idea, turned, and raced out the door and up the outside stairs.

I yanked open the door of the second floor to see most of the workers out on the roof deck. The chain-smoking Armenian had grabbed the shirt of one of the Arabs and was screaming at him. I watched horrified, but at the same time fascinated, as I realized that in spite of all the shouting, the cigarette never dropped from the Armenian's lips. A second later, one of the other Arabs pulled out a knife and lunged into the fray. By this time, the Arab with the arch, who had apparently run up the stairs right after me, jumped in between them and grabbed the Arab with the knife. Everybody was shouting, men were pushing this way and that across the roof deck, and a knife was flashing ominously above everyone's heads.

The children had run out of their rooms to see what was going on. The night before, they had complained they couldn't see their favorite television programs in Israel. Now they were watching a live performance better than TV. Without thinking, I stepped into the middle of the maniacs and tried to push them apart. It was obvious that I did it without thinking because the slightest iota of thought would have dissuaded me in a second. The knife was now frozen in space above my head as the Hungarian joined in, struggling to hold back the Arab's arm. At the same time, the Arab with the arch was pulling the other Arab away from the Armenian until at last the antagonists were separated. The violence receded into an onslaught of expletives. You don't have to know a language to understand an expletive. And any missed nuance of the cursing was graphically underscored by the hand gestures.

By the time every curse word and movement of fingers was exhausted, the workers quieted down into a sullen truce. I decided that was enough drama for one day and managed to get each one to understand he could go home early. It was my first taste of violence in the Middle East. Unfortunately, it would not be my last.

Meanwhile, for better or worse, we were managing to settle in. We had finally emptied most of the boxes and cartons and found places to put most of our things. We had put down the rugs and figured out what we thought were the right places for the different pieces of furniture. There were hopeful signs that we were transforming what had looked like a warehouse into a real home.

Dust still covered everything, not all the plaster was completely dry, and there were still dozens of boxes filled with the odds and ends of life that were hardly necessary but were always there, a candy dish, an award, an objet d'art, a quilt for a cold night, and endless other items that had not yet been assigned a drawer or a shelf. But we were getting there.

We hadn't been in our apartment one whole week when once again the doorbell rang, introducing us this time not to new neighbors or new workmen, but to the last people in the world we would expect to see.

Tourists.

I opened the door to see a woman I had never seen before in my entire life. She introduced herself.

"I'm a friend of your sister," she said, obviously sensing my puzzlement.

I thought I knew all my sister's friends, but I certainly didn't know that lady.

She pushed her head beyond the door to look over the room. I opened the door wider to make it easier for her. She smiled at me and mumbled her name. I was still looking at her, and she was still looking around the room.

"Well, come in," I said, trying to get the door to open over the drop cloth the painter was still using. She stepped in and continued looking.

"Funny," I said, "I'm surprised we haven't met before." She finally looked at me instead of the apartment. She smiled. "I'm a new friend of your sister," she said.

I didn't say anything.

"I met her at a bridge game," she said. "A week ago. She said she had a brother in Israel."

"How is she?" I said.

"She looked fine," the woman said. "I guess she's just fine."

She shifted her weight to take in a better view. Workmen were still hanging from stepladders, painting, wiring fixtures, and nailing molding atop doorjambs. The woman shifted her weight to the other hip and leaned back to make a better assessment.

"Look, Henry," she said. I hadn't seen Henry before. He was still outside the door. Henry came in, nodded at me. "Over there, Henry," she said, pointing to the stairs where the one-eyed Arab was putting down still another coat of stain. "They have an inner staircase, too. Just like *Fiddler on the Roof*, one staircase going up and one staircase going down."

"And one staircase just for show," Henry said, completing the lyric for her.

"I hope you enjoy your visit," I said.

She took the hint and tugged at Henry's jacket. "We were just in the neighborhood and wanted to say hi."

"Thank you very much," I said, easing the door shut. It was almost closed when I heard her call back to me. "Oh," she said, "your sister sends regards."

"Thank you," I said to the closed door.

By Friday, the workers were gone, all of them. The staircase was dark brown. The arch was finished, more or less, and we had cleaned the rooms as best we could. There were still cartons in the dining room waiting to be unpacked and even more in the living room. But there was some semblance of order, and it was easy to walk through the rooms.

As the sky began to slip away into dusk, we set a small lamp on one of the boxes and put another on a carton to give us more light. We pushed another carton over to the side to make room for a table we had already unpacked. From a box of linens, we dug out a white tablecloth and carefully spread it over the table. We pulled out the good dishes and silverware from another box and two candlesticks that had been packed with them so we could have our *Shabbat* dinner.

By sundown, we had all showered and changed into the nicest clothes we could find and then gathered together at the table. Rosalind's hair glistened in the candlelight as she recited the traditional *Shabbat* prayer. Beyond that light, the rest of the room seemed to fade into oblivion.

The children gathered around me. I placed my hands on the heads of the two older girls, Laura and Devorah, and then on the heads of David and Becca. Their hair was still wet from their showers, and some of the *Shabbat* clothes were a little wrinkled, but everyone seemed to glow in the shared excitement.

I recited a blessing for the children.

"May the God of our fathers bless you. May he who has brought us to this day make you a blessing to Israel and to all mankind." After that I filled the silver cup with wine and chanted the *Shabbat Kiddish* prayer. Then we sat down, and over two loaves of the traditional challah bread, I gave thanks for the food.

There are people who say that the *Shechinah*, the divine spirit, hovers over Jerusalem. That evening, as the lights of the candles flickered and I looked across the table at the faces of our children, I could feel the *Shechinah* in our new home. In Jerusalem.

Chapter 12

Habla Hebrew Here

*I*t was the first day at school. Not for the children, but for Rosalind and me. This was the beginning of the summer session of *ulpan*, the crash course in Hebrew that Israel offers free to all immigrants.

At seven-thirty in the morning, the kids were already lined up at the door—Laura, Devorah, David, and Becca—ready to see us off.

For years, it had been the other way around. We saw the kids off. But it was quickly becoming obvious that nothing would ever be the way it was.

Clinging to routine as much as possible to preserve some continuity in my life, I was reluctant to race through breakfast, my favorite meal. Freshly squeezed orange juice, crisp Israeli bread, scrambled eggs. It was as good as it gets. Rosalind sat opposite me finishing her coffee. Notebooks and workbooks were stacked next to her.

"Go to school," Laura said.

The kids' classes didn't start for another month. They had nothing to do but send us on our way, wash the dishes, and roll around the floor or whatever children do during those endless days called summer.

I scooped up our books and looked at those expectant faces waiting to see the strange phenomenon of *Eema* and Pops going off to school. *Eema* is what they now called Rosalind, the Hebrew word for mother. They had learned the word for father, too, but they didn't call me that. I was Pops, a sign that my high-energy American style had not yet morphed into the image of an Israeli. Or their sense that it never would.

I put on a cheerful smile and waved good-bye. They stood lined up, waving back. I all but expected one of them to call out, "Careful crossing streets!"

We trotted down the fifty-one stairs and jumped into the car. Nothing is far in Jerusalem if I could manage not to get lost. I aimed the car in the direction of the school and hoped for the best, driving through our neighborhood of orderly apartment buildings and then south where the street widened into a black road. Through the windshield, I saw a bunker that had been manned by enemy soldiers just five years earlier when Jordan controlled the West Bank. The Six Day War changed all that, and now the bunker, just a couple of miles from where we lived, was painted a bright yellow to make it look less threatening.

The road rolled on through a stretch of scraggly land. Beleaguered strands of brush poked up through it here and there, as if looking for the sheep and goats that so recently grazed there. The harsh sunlight ricocheted off the barren land, blurring the square-shouldered shapes of sand-colored buildings in the distance.

There were few street signs in those days and fewer numbers on doorways, so I felt great relief when a large 10 came into view, the address of our *ulpan*. I pulled over to the curb and came to a stop. There were a few other cars there. Only a few. Most people, I quickly learned, took the bus.

I faced a cavernous stone building. As I climbed the stairs, I could hear the crunching sounds of my shoes scraping against the sand-splattered steps.

I pushed hard against a scarred wooden door and was greeted by a little old woman, about the same age I am today when I still delude myself that I'm young. She motioned to me briskly. She vibrated with energy. Her broad smile made me feel she had been standing there waiting just for me. Again the brisk motion and a few words we didn't understand, but we got the idea. We were supposed to keep moving down the hall. I didn't yet know anything about my second language, Hebrew, but I was quickly learning a third language that I could see would be even more valuable. Sign language. It held out the promise of hope.

Another woman hurried toward us in small, staccato steps. She greeted us in Hebrew. I had no idea what she was saying, but at least she said it warmly. She held out a form for us to take.

"How come nobody here speaks English?" I whispered to Rosalind. I was like all Americans expecting everyone in the world to speak English and resentful if they didn't. Rosalind answered me in her own sign language, the kind of look wives reserve for recalcitrant husbands. I answered her with an impatient look of my own and thrust the form into her hands.

"You fill it in," I said.

That's when I heard some wonderful sounds. English.

"It's just a short test," someone said. I turned around to see my benefactor, an attractive girl not yet thirty, with bobbed red hair and green eyes, the first of many encounters with Israelis who looked so different from the anti-Semitic caricatures.

"Just fill it out," she said. "Some people who study here

can read. Some know a few words. Some know more. This is how we find out what class you should be in."

"I can save you a lot of time," I said. "We don't know anything."

"Fill it out anyway," she said.

It was my first confrontation with a native Israeli. She was pleasant, but firm. The Bible says it better—stiff necked.

I took the form back from Rosalind and sidled up to a table where a few other people were filling out their forms. My hands were sweaty. I glanced around. It's strange how the mind works, but from the recesses of memory, I thought of the first thing every kid learns at school: when all else fails, peek at the paper next to you. I peeked to my left, but the woman was leaning over her form. I peeked to the right, but all I could see was a man signing his name at the bottom of the page. I peeked at my own paper. I understood absolutely nothing. I signed my name at the bottom and left the rest blank. I turned it in and was assigned to the first grade. Because we were grown-ups, there was no kindergarten.

The classroom was a collection of rickety chairs and old desks that had long suffered the scratches and ink stains inflicted by bored students trying to get through an interminable hour. Facing the students' seats was a large desk of plain wood that too bore the scars of wear. Behind it, a smudge of erased chalk marks that swirled across the blackboard.

The light in the room struggled in through the dust of tall windows. The heat came in with less effort. That day would be the beginning of five weeks of days, five days every week, five hours every day in a barren classroom in July when the desert heat kept the temperature inside the same as outside. There was no air conditioning. For Jerusalemites who during the War of Independence didn't have enough food to eat, sweating was not an imposition. Air conditioning was like elevators, not a high priority compared to all the other things the country needed.

Awkwardly, we students drifted into vacant chairs. Many of us already recognized one another from the hour spent filling out papers and asking questions and being directed to various rooms. In that brief time, like molecules responding to an invisible law of nature, we took seats in groups of three or four, each unit formed in grateful response to the sound of a familiar language.

Inside the classroom, the teacher spoke only Hebrew to us immigrants. The rest was our problem.

It was hard to think of myself as an immigrant. That was something my grandparents had been, people whose foreign accents embarrassed me when I was trying to grow up American. And now I, who so recently thought of himself as a prospective member of the United States Congress, was an immigrant. Suddenly, I had compassion for every foreign cabdriver I had ever encountered back in the States, from Carlos to Mohammed.

Within a few days, we learned about one another. A young man from Moscow sat next to an elderly woman from Kiev. A Catholic boy from Venezuela who had come to the Holy Land to study for the priesthood sat next to a dark, sensuous Jewish girl from Chile. Everyone had a different story, a Jew from Iran, another from Turkey, and several Americans including an athletic black man who wore tennis shorts every day.

Each of us uncovered fragments of the lives of others whose experiences were so different from our own. With revolutionary fervor, a vivacious Irish girl, her eyes flashing with intensity, told of her adventures with the Irish Republican Army. We leaned over to better hear the frail voice of a young girl from Finland who came to Israel on her pathway to Jesus. And there was a frail Jewish lady, close to eighty, who had returned home to Poland after the Holocaust and twenty-five years later come to Israel still looking for home.

Some of the students were fleeing the Russians, some were fleeing their past. Some were social idealists, and some were social cases. There were eighteen of us from different backgrounds with different pasts. The one thing we had in common was our ignorance of Hebrew.

Neither our reasons for coming to Israel nor our ignorance of the language was of interest to our teacher. All she cared about was teaching Hebrew. A long, leggy young woman who every day came to class wearing long, leggy slacks, she pranced across the room in a ballet of pantomime, trying to teach us a language without explaining the language. The idea was to remember the sounds she made and connect them to things she was pointing at or the actions she was miming.

Her blonde hair was pulled back tight, emphasizing a long, aquiline nose and face that were as mobile as her body. She twisted that body, flailed her arms, arched her eyebrows, wiggled her nose, and emitted a burst of strange sounds as she choreographed herself across the room. I felt I was in the middle of Twenty Questions starring Barbra Streisand.

Convoluting herself into a figure eight, she aimed her long forefinger into the air, pointing in one direction and then another and still another crying out, "*Zeh! Zeh! Zeh!*" We listened in silence.

For just a second, her look revealed vulnerability, perhaps even disappointment. Then she tried again. Another pirouette as she spun through the air yelling "*Zeh, zeh, zeh,*" pointing at everything in sight, thrusting her finger forward as if it were a saber, pulling it back, thrusting it forward again toward another object and back again like a deranged count of Monte Cristo.

"*Zeh, zeh, zeh!*" she cried out.

I was so fascinated by her performance that I forgot it was supposed to mean something. She wouldn't stop. She aimed her finger at the desk, at books nearby, at the blackboard, at her sandals, at her desk, at my desk. "*Zeh, zeh, zeh!*"

"I've got it," I called out, shoving my elbow into Rosalind's arm. "This!" I cried out. I was so excited that like the first-grader I was, I jumped up with the answer and started pointing at everything just as she had. "This, this, this," I exclaimed.

The Russian woman called out from the back of the room, "This, this, this." She was supposed to be learning Hebrew, but I had confused her into learning English. Realizing what I had done, I switched to my new language, Hebrew. "*Zeh, zeh, zeh,*" I repeated, virtually out of control with excitement as I pointed to everything in sight. A chorus of "*Zehs*" from the other students echoed mine. I sat down, beaming at my accomplishment, unaware that I would never again match the majesty of that moment.

By the time the first class was over, I had learned another word, *vah*, which means "and." *Zeh* and *vah*. I was suddenly empowered. I left my schoolroom that day with a new sense of confidence. Later that afternoon, I rushed to the grocery store, eager to show off my burgeoning vocabulary. Once I had the attention of the owner, I motioned for him to follow me around as I pointed from one thing to another declaring, "*Zeh, vah zeh, vah zeh,*" and so on. I was on my way. And more importantly, I had improved the prospects of having food in the house.

I didn't do as well with my Hebrew a few days later when I drove to the Jaffa Gate, the entrance to a maze of narrow streets, crowded outdoor markets and shops within ancient caves that make up the Old City. I hardly noticed two young Arab boys walking toward me as I parked the car.

I was still in awe at the very sight of those walls and the idea that they had stood there for five hundred years since the Arabs of the Ottoman Empire built them. They were supposed to ward off enemy attacks, but just five years earlier had failed to keep out the Israelis as they had failed so many other times during those five centuries. But for me, so new to the country, none of that history mattered. I was still overwhelmed at the idea that so much history was so casually integrated into the everyday life and that I could drive up to all that history, park close by, and proceed with my errands.

As the Arab boys drew closer, it was obvious they weren't just passing by. They were walking over to talk to me. A new problem. My Hebrew vocabulary had quadrupled since my conquest of *zeh* and *vah* a few days earlier. I now knew eight words in Hebrew. But my Arabic was worse, eight words worse.

The boys approached me, their wide smiles framing teeth that were brown except for those that were missing. Their bodies were burnished by the sun. Cheerfully, they called out to me in what was obviously Arabic. After all, they were Arabs, so of course they were speaking Arabic. But as they continued speaking, I recognized a few sounds I had heard in my class. What I was hearing was Hebrew. It hadn't occurred to me that an Arab living in Israel could speak Hebrew. I was still an outsider, an immigrant who didn't speak Hebrew or Arabic and couldn't even tell them apart.

The boys were carrying a bucket and some dirty rags. That was easier to understand than their Arabic-accented Hebrew. Obviously, they wanted to wash my car. They spared me the embarrassment of asking how much. They cut through all that, holding up four fingers. For a moment, I just stood there. Four dollars was a lot of money for a dirty car wash. Then I remembered where I was. Four meant shekels, not dollars. Four shekels were equal to about one dollar in those days. For a buck, it didn't matter whether the car would be shining when I got back. At least I'd get rid of some of that sand and grime.

I patted the car and nodded my agreement. They nodded back. More big smiles.

"*Comma zman?*" the older boy asked. I hadn't yet learned that phrase for "how long," but since he was pointing to his watch, it was obvious he wanted to know when I would be back so he could get paid.

At last a chance to show off my Hebrew. I had already learned the word for hour. Or at least I thought I had. But instead of saying *sha'ah*, I got mixed up and told him *shanah*, the word for year. "In one year," I told him in Hebrew, filled with pride at my accomplishment. I started to walk away when I suddenly realized my mistake. I turned back to them, raised one finger, and said, "*Sha'ah.*" They nodded. They were polite enough not to say anything, at least not to me. I tried to not think about what they were saying to each other.

Learning a few words of Hebrew and then trying to put them together in a sentence was like trying to walk after both feet have fallen asleep. You know the ground is down there, but you're not sure where.

One summer day burned into the next as we continued our studies. The more we learned in class, the more we spoke Hebrew on the street, suffering the slings and arrows of outrageous mistakes such as telling a friend that because it was so hot that day, I wouldn't come by until the sun went down. The word for sun is *shemesh*. The word for oil is *shemen*. So, of course, I told him I couldn't come by until the oil went down. It did not enhance my self-image, learning Hebrew.

Historically, Hebrew had been used in prayer, but not as an everyday language. In Europe, Jews spoke the language of the country where they lived and Yiddish, a bastardized form of German folded into Hebrew. In Spanish-speaking countries, the Jews' second language was Ladino, an adaptation of Spanish into Hebrew. But except for occasional attempts to broaden its use, Hebrew was generally considered a holy tongue to be used only when speaking to God.

Theodor Herzl, the Vienna-born leader of the return to Zion, thought that perhaps German should be the official language in the new Jewish state he was trying to create. That's what he wrote in his diary back in 1895. He added that he had no objection to French or English, either.

But some of the early settlers, most notably Eliezer Ben Yehuda, seized upon Hebrew as the historic language of the Jewish people and literally breathed it into existence. He and his wife, when they arrived in Jaffa in 1881, spoke only Hebrew to each other. They spoke only Hebrew to their son who was teased by the other children for speaking such a strange language. The other children spoke the language of the country from which their parents had come. But Ben Yehuda did not give up and relentlessly dedicated his life to making Hebrew the spoken language of the Jewish homeland. He succeeded so well that by the time I came to Israel, I had no choice. Hebrew was the name of the game.

Compared to English, Hebrew has a small vocabulary. New words had to be created, especially to give voice to modern life. Fortunately for me, Palestine had been governed by the British since World War I, so many people in the Holy Land knew English. As a result, many new Hebrew words were not really Hebrew at all, but simply

Hebraized versions of English, a boon to my communication skills.

One of the first things I learned was that adding *tzia* to English words often produced Hebrew words. So in no time at all, I was navigating the Ministry of the Interior, harbor of all minutiae necessary for an immigrant's survival, to get *informatzia*. If they gave me the runaround, I'd tell them I had no time for so much *bureaucratzia* and demanded to talk to someone in the *administratzia*. Despite my rapidly growing vocabulary, my improved skill at pantomime, and my intense determination, I hardly got past the ubiquitous tea drinkers. That's when I learned something else about Israel, that no matter what language you spoke, government offices have a language of their own, the language of procrastination.

Undeterred, I kept expanding my English/Hebrew vocabulary. There were Hebrew words that were really English except that in the plural you added *eem* at the end, much as the letter "s" creates plural in English. I was off and running. At the auto-repair shop, I was bursting with confidence as I pointed to the underside of my car and ordered, "*Brakeseem!*" In the stationery store, I walked up to the saleswoman and knowingly asked for *clipseem*. And when it came to paying bills, the Israelis made it clear that instead of shekels, they would much prefer to take my American money, *dollareem*.

Hurray for English, I thought, as I learned that there were a lot of other words that were English. The only difference was that you had to change a "w" into a "v." I had come a long way since my days of "zeh, vah zeh, vah zeh" to point my way through the grocery store. Now I could walk up to the counter and confidently order a *sandvich*. In the department store, I could buy a *sveater*.

But the more I learned, the more I realized how much

I didn't know. My early euphoria disintegrated into verbal mood swings. There was a whole world beyond *zeh* and *sandvich*, a world that was flat and waiting for me to fall off. English had helped, but it could only take me so far. This was still the land of what Becca called "the Hebrews."

No matter how many tricks I learned, Hebrew was what people spoke. They did it with adjectives that were either masculine or feminine, not unisex like American adjectives where one description fits all. I hadn't known such anxiety since my days in high school trying to conjugate the verbs of Virgil in Latin.

It was just as bad with verbs. They changed as quickly as a chameleon to indicate future tense and past tense and other tension-producing tenses. But as I kept hearing in Israel, *ain brayrah*, there's no choice. It was either learning Hebrew or going hungry at the grocery store.

I did the best I could using the Hebrew words I knew to buy bread and rolls and whatever else I knew the words for. In times of dire need, I had the one advantage that belongs to all parents. I could send a child. The kids were learning Hebrew much faster and better than I. When it came to difficult words, such as toothpaste, watermelon, tomatoes, and 99% of the rest of the language, I would send out one of the children. Not very nice, perhaps, but the will to survive tends to overcome human kindness.

But even the children, a well as they did, were unable to express themselves as freely as they had in English. Laura came home from school one day looking particularly wistful. "I'm so charming," she said, "but no one here will ever know it."

Nor could they retreat into television as kids in America do. Everything was in Hebrew. Well, almost everything. One afternoon, Becca, who was once again trying to find something to watch, suddenly saw her old friend, Bugs

Bunny. She jumped up and came running across the apartment looking for David.

"David," she called out. "David! The rabbit speaks English!"

As my Hebrew slowly improved, my English got worse. Not speaking it as much as I did before we came to Israel, I became less fluent, often hesitating as I tried to call up the right word or complete a thought. And when I did use it, I tried to speak with small words so the Israelis could understand me. It wasn't like the cowboy movies I used to watch as a child when the hero would tell the Indian chief, "You gettum wampum. I give you horse." That's how movies were before Indians became Native Americans and folks became politically correct. I wasn't that bad, but I must have been perilously close to be reminded of those old films.

To make matters worse, my English began to be a direct translation from the Hebrew. Israelis speak with an abundance of infinitives, and it was not long before I was talking the same way, but in English. "Please to come in," I heard myself say one day as I opened the door. If someone thanked me for something, I would answer, "Not to thank."

The kids had the same problem, combining English with Hebrew. I was reading the paper one day, the English-language one, of course, with the chatter of the children in the background. Suddenly, I realized what I had just heard.

"What time is it?" Becca called out.

"Two and a half," David answered. He was thinking in Hebrew and talking in English. The Israelis don't say "two-thirty."

Another time, the phone rang, and from different rooms they both answered it. It was for David, one of his friends. Becca was obviously still on the other line when he called out, "Close the phone," again a direct translation. What ever happened to "hang up"?

Regardless of their problems, the kids did master the language while I continued to flail around helplessly. While the children had learned to think in Hebrew, I could think only in whatever words popped into my head at the moment, usually a combination of both languages. When a visitor from the States asked me what happened to our old coffee table, I told her, "The *shulchan* [table] is in the *machsan* [storeroom]." Another time I hesitated to ask the housekeeper to do something and asked Rosalind what she thought about it. "Is it okay if the *ozeret* [maid] scrubs down the *mirpesset* [terrace]?"

Things got worse rather than better. Worse is not remembering names. I was never too good at that in English, but at least in English, people are called Bill, or George, or Henry, something reasonable. In Israel, I met people called Yeshoshua, Amatzia, and Yehoram, names I could hardly pronounce let alone remember.

The ultimate frustration was the realization that even if I could ask a question in Hebrew, I was faced with the inevitable problem of not understanding the answer. I could ask the supermarket clerk where the tuna fish was, but when he answered me, I still didn't know where it was. What did he say? And why did he talk so fast?

I would walk down the street and ask someone for directions. But when he answered in copious detail and pointed to the right, then gestured to the left, and then looked back at me with a big smile, I still stood there helpless.

It was frustrating, but at least face to face a person was usually compassionate, would make an extra effort to point or gesticulate or do whatever else he thought would help me understand. Sometimes he would even try a few words in English. But on the telephone, things were terrible. On the telephone, there was only a disembodied voice. It's hard to be compassionate if you're disembodied. So the telephone, my longtime friend and companion, now loomed as my enemy, the source of anxiety, an inanimate object that charged the atmosphere with apprehension. As inevitable as death and taxes was its ring.

Ring. I wait. Another ring. I turn to Rosalind. "It must be for you," I tell her.

Ring. "You're standing right next to it," she says.

Ring. "Probably one of your friends," I tell her.

Ring. "Pick it up, already," she says.

Bravely: "*Shalom.*"

"*Shalom,*" the voice answers. So far so good. "*Yoel Roeh?*" the voice continued.

Recognizing my name in Hebrew, I answer yes. "*Cain,*" I say.

That's when it happens. An outpouring of words, all of them in Hebrew. And then more words. And then an inflection. You don't have to understand a language to understand an inflection. Clearly the voice had asked me a question. And then there was silence. The voice was waiting for an answer.

I put my memory on rewind, trying to hear the words again, recognizing one here and one there. Better yet, maybe I could get the voice to repeat the whole thing. I knew the Hebrew phrase for "one mo' time."

"*Ode ha-pa'am,*" I said.

The voice repeated itself. I made out a few more words in Hebrew and an important word that fortunately came from English, *televisia*. I made a leap of logic. He was talking about the television set. It may have been too loud. In that case, the inflection at the end was probably a request to make it softer.

"Okay," I said. Okay works in just about any language. Then I remembered the Hebrew for okay. "*B'seder,*" I said.

Gratefully, I heard the phone click at the other end. The ordeal was over.

"What was that all about?" Rosalind asked.

"Turn down the TV," I said.

"What about the call?" she said.

"He asked me to turn down the TV," I said. "I told him okay."

She turned down the TV. "So that's what someone was calling about?" she said.

"That's right," I said. I was hoping I was right. If I wasn't, I must have agreed to something else. Well, one day at a time. I got ready for bed and tried to forget the phone call.

Meanwhile, I was an embarrassment to the children. More than once they would stage-whisper to me when I was on the phone, "Speak in English." It was less embarrassing to them that I not even try to be a Hebrew speaker than it was to hear me torture the language.

"Daddy is really very smart," I heard Laura confide to Becca one day. "He just doesn't know Hebrew." Becca knitted her eyebrows and contemplated the idea. I saw her headful of curls nod up and down, signaling to Laura that she understood.

Another time, Devorah needed a note from me for the teacher, permission to take a class trip. "You're busy, Pops," she said, to make it easier for both of us. "I'll write it, and you can just sign it." It's not easy bringing up parents.

I was willing to admit that I was fallible. But not Rosalind. First of all, she was doing much better than I was. Furthermore, she was stubborn. One night, she insisted on writing her own note for the milkman. After the children were in bed, she sat down in the kitchen and methodically drew one letter after another, letters that ended up covering the entire page with the Hebrew words for "Please leave two bottles of milk." The next morning, she rushed to the door to see if she succeeded. She had. Two bottles of milk stood at attention. Underneath one of them was her note. With corrections. The milkman was kind enough not to grade it.

The summer days melted into weeks as I returned to classes day after day. July faded into August and then September as the sun burned hot into the dust and stones of Jerusalem. Through a shimmering transparency of light, its glare hovered over old buildings and dried-up gardens that stood still and pale like images in an old photograph, yellow with the stains of age. I stood in the dusty area outside the school building one day that September, sharing with the other immigrants, *hafsikah*, the fifteen-minute break between classes, when terrifying words began to spread among us in scattered phrases, in different languages. Instinctively, each of us gathered together with compatriots, English speakers with English speakers, Russians with Russians, a swift abandonment of Hebrew, a flight into our native languages to try to grasp the meaning of the fragments of news that passed among us. And then a middle-aged teacher came outside, short and stocky in her ill-fitting beige suit.

We all gathered around her as she started to speak in simple Hebrew. We listened, immobile like a moment caught in time by the click of a camera, a picture that would not turn yellow but would forever remain clear in our memory. The limpness of her body revealed this was not her first encounter with despair. The weariness in her eyes told us that her words were not about a moment of tragedy, but rather its continuity.

The event she spoke about was called the Olympics in a city called Munich, a terrorist attack, three decades before the destruction of New York's World Trade Center, long before an era of suicide bombings, a time when people rarely thought about such things. And if they did think about terrorism, they didn't think about it much because it was something that happened to people far away. This time it happened far away to eleven Israelis. The world was shocked not because the athletes were Jews, but because they were athletes killed at the Olympics. Avery Brundage, the president of the International Olympic Committee, stopped all the events, for twenty-four hours. Then life went on as usual.

We didn't understand every one of her words. We didn't have to. We understood enough to know what happened. And we understood more. That nothing changes. Even with our own homeland, we Jews are still expendable. That's another way that life—and death—go on as usual.

Weakly we tried to sing "*Hatikvah*," the Israeli national anthem. Few of us knew the words, except what *hatikvah* itself meant: the hope. In a sense, all Jewish history was summed up in that word.

I looked up beyond the teacher. No flags were fluttering on high to dignify the moment. Only laundry drying on a clothesline across the way. The scene was blurred. That shimmering of the intense sunlight, and the tears in my eyes, that first summer in Israel.

Chapter 13

Settling In

$\mathcal{I}$srael is like being in a crowded room with everyone standing next to each other. Not at all like Winnetka where people live within their bubbles of privacy. In Israel, everyone is a part of your life, just like that stranger who asked me how much we paid for our apartment. It's intrusive, but it does make you feel a part of the family.

Sometimes it's even helpful, like the time I planned to take Rosalind and the children on a short trip up north to Safed, an ancient town that had once been a Crusader fortress and for centuries has been a center of Jewish mysticism. Friends told me that we should stay at a small hotel called the Reemone Inn. I had already learned that *reemone* was the word for pomegranate. I hadn't yet learned that the word also means hand grenade. In Israel, words have to fit all sorts of situations.

Not knowing how to get to the Reemone Inn, I decided to call them for directions. But first I had to dial an operator for the phone number. Those were the days before the humiliation of having to talk to an inanimate recording that tells you to wait, even while assuring you "that your call is very important to us," though obviously not important enough to hire more people so you won't have to wait. In days gone by, people talked to people.

When I dialed, an operator answered, a nice Jewish lady. In my fragile Hebrew, I asked her for the number of the Reemone Inn. As many Israelis did as soon as they heard my American accent, she answered me in English. Not great English, but better than my not-so-great Hebrew.

"Can you give me the number of the Reemon Inn?" I asked.

"The Reemone Inn is in Safed," she said.

"Yes, I know," I said. "May I please have the phone number?"

"Why do you want to go that far north?" she said.

"Please," I said, "can you just give me the number?"

"The nights are cold in Safed this time of year," she said.

I wanted information, but not that much. "Please," I said, "the phone number."

A long pause. She was finding the phone number. She even gave it to me. As I jotted it down, I heard her parting words. "Be sure to take a sweater," she said.

In Israel everyone not only acts like he knows everyone else, he's often sure of it. Even at a traffic light.

When I first began to drive in Jerusalem I noticed that whenever I stopped at a light, the driver in the next car would twist his body around slightly and lean toward his window to peer at me. My first thought was that I must have done something wrong. Maybe I inadvertently cut him off. Maybe I was driving too fast. Maybe something was wrong with my car. Then the light would change, the driver next to me would speed off, and I would continue driving and let the incident fade from my mind.

Until the next day. Once again when I stopped for a traffic light, the driver in the next lane turned to stare at me. I was feeling annoyed and then paranoid until I finally realized what was going on. The other drivers were looking to see who was driving next to them. They figured they probably knew me. In such a small country, doesn't everyone know everyone else?

I felt that way myself that next spring when Israel celebrated its twenty-fifth Independence Day. From an office window looking out on Jaffa Road, I watched the country's young soldiers march by with a snap in their walk, young women strutting smartly in their miniskirted uniforms and slim Israeli boys standing straight, but not ramrod straight, because in Israel there is a limit to how seriously its people take the display of military power. The boys looked embarrassed at all the attention. The girls swayed their hips smartly, staying in step and holding their chins high, girls who in the United States might be going to a Spring Sing or a school dance at some college campus. I felt they could be my own children.

They marched briskly past the reviewing stand, past Jerusalem Mayor Teddy Kollek beaming at them, past Sephardic Jewish mothers ululating with the traditional high-pitched trilling they had learned in their native Arab lands, past old couples who had survived the Holocaust, past religious young boys wearing *kippahs* and nonreligious boys wearing blue jeans. Boys who were only eight or nine zigzagged through the crowd with their plastic hammers, harmlessly bopping passers-by on the head and then dashing on through the carefree crowd.

The celebration had the spirit though hardly the look of a Rose Bowl parade. No flower-covered floats or anything exotic. Just a few armored cars and a few massive tanks rumbling by and chewing up the streets that were not in such good condition to begin with. And as far as one could see down Jaffa Road, the soldiers, the young soldiers, trying to suppress their smiles and their glances at the crowds, trying not to turn their heads to search out a relative, trying to look serious.

I began to learn the rules about what it means to live in a country where everyone is part of one big family. If home is where they have to take you in, then a car is where you have to give a ride, especially to soldiers hitchhiking and eager to get home for a short leave. In those years before intifada suicide bombers laced the society with fear, just about every driver would give soldiers a lift, and I did the same, happily. Military service is compulsory, so you never think of the young men as strangers. They're somebody's son, maybe even your own.

One evening, I was in a late-night editing session in Tel Aviv. It was already two in the morning when driving back home, I made the final turn to Jerusalem and saw a group of soldiers at a bus stop trying to hail a ride. I pulled over and felt good watching them fling open the car doors and pile in, wrapping their heavy paratrooper boots around their bulging duffel bags and with long arms adjusting their M-16 rifles across their shoulders as they stuffed themselves into the seats.

The door slammed shut, and I raced on into the darkness. Only later as I sped on did I smile to myself thinking how quickly I had changed. In America, I would have been afraid to pick up a stranger in daytime, and there I was in Israel on a dark highway in the blackness of the night with four big soldiers armed to the teeth. For their part, the soldiers took it for granted that a stranger would stop for them because to them I wasn't a stranger. I was part of the family.

Other people were just as ready to help my children. Laura learned that when she was twelve. She was already fluent in Hebrew and had no qualms about jumping on a bus to wherever she was going. Her only problem was that like her father, she rarely knew where she was going. So even though the street signs were in English, Hebrew, and Arabic and she could read at least two of those languages, she would always take the precaution of telling the bus driver where she wanted to get off.

The trouble was that she spoke, as she still does, in that soft voice of her sheltered Winnetka childhood. She didn't yet know that in Israel everyone talks loudly and doesn't even hear soft. Taking the bus to visit a new friend one day, she blissfully rode along while passengers got on and passengers got off until finally she realized she was the only passenger left and the bus was coming to a stop at what was obviously the end of the line. She sat there silent, trying to hold back the tears.

As the driver turned off the ignition and glanced up at the rearview mirror, he was surprised to see someone still there. He turned his burly body around to get a good look at her.

"*Mah yashe?*" he said, something like "what's going on?" Putting her Hebrew words together carefully, something like threading beads one by one onto a string, she told him that she had missed her stop, that she thought he was going to call it out, and that she had no idea where she was.

The driver didn't answer. He didn't try to console her. He just started the motor, turned the bus around, and drove her, his solitary passenger, back to the street she was looking for.

We were beginning to get the idea. When we moved to Israel, David and Becca were only six and four, ages parents tell children not to talk to strangers. I told them just the opposite, that if they were ever lost, they should just stop anyone on the street and ask her to take them home.

Jerusalem was like a small town in those days and a safe

one at that. The saying in those days was that in the United States, the borders were safe, but not the streets, whereas in Israel, the streets were safe, but not the borders. It was strange. Life for Israelis was carefree, but never risk free. I learned that the first weeks we were in Israel.

I had already picked up a couple of small film assignments and was working on the projects in Tel Aviv with Danny Shik, a short, round-faced editor who, despite his need for aluminum crutches that helped him swing his polio-damaged legs forward when he walked, had a history of beautiful women in his life and was at the time married to a stunning, intelligent woman named Devorah. Danny, like many editors, worked in one of the small, low-rent apartments in a dilapidated part of Tel Aviv.

Just seventy-five years earlier, Tel Aviv was little more than sand dunes north of where many of the first assorted Jewish idealists arrived from countries like Poland and Austria and Russia. For many of those immigrants, the first sight of their new country was the squalor of Biblical Jaffa, the bug-infested Arab port where ships docked and passengers came ashore by wading through shallow water. Jaffa was the big city in those days when even big cities were not very big.

In time, a few hundred of those Jews built small houses on the sand that spread along the Mediterranean coast northward from Jaffa, and within five years more than a thousand people lived there. By the time I came to Israel, a whole city stood on those sand dunes. Nature is stubborn and the sand struggled to maintain its primacy, so that even today you see sand seeping out between the cracks of the stone sidewalks of that city, Tel Aviv.

One day, about a mile or so from where Danny and I were editing, eight members of Yasser Arafat's Fatah movement came ashore in Tel Aviv from a rubber dinghy, commandeered a seedy oceanfront hotel that pretentiously called itself the Savoy, and murdered eight hostages. Danny and I heard the news and kept working. So did everyone else in Tel Aviv that day. That's what Israelis do. That's how they cope. You hear the Hebrew expression again and again, *Ayn brayrah*, there's no choice.

I was learning that terrorism is always an imminent threat. There would be months of quiet and then suddenly another event. One day, terrorists commandeered an Egged bus on the highway between Haifa and Tel Aviv and killed several passengers. Another time, terrorists held hostage a group of schoolchildren in Ma'alot. At the end of Israel's attempted rescue, twenty-six people lay dead.

After these events, everyone is numb. For the next few days, everyone is depressed, watching on television the images of grieving parents burying their children. A few more days pass, and life goes on. That's how it is. *Ayn brayrah.*

In Israel, tragedy becomes the background music of everyday life. It played softly within the recesses of our psyches as we went about our lives.

We filled every free minute exploring our new surroundings and coming home to share our stories with one another. It seemed as if everyone was caught up in the mystery of Jerusalem, from tourists to natives. Christian pilgrims come to Jerusalem to retrace the footsteps of Jesus, but for Jews every day in Jerusalem is living in the footsteps of history, never far from the words of Isaiah preserved on those 2,000-year-old scrolls at the Israel Museum. Even Jews who are not religious can't escape that connection with the past.

Uzi Narkiss, the general who in the Six Day War led the Israeli troops in the recapture of the Temple Mount and the Western Wall and who was himself secular, stood with me one day looking out at the Old City and in a whisper confided, "I was born in this city, and yet I never take it for granted. Every day, I feel the excitement of just being here."

One way or another, Jerusalem reaches out from its dusty paths and takes hold of everyone, even Jews who are tired of hearing about centuries of persecution, Jews tired of hearing about the Holocaust, Jews tired of the burden of being expected to be a light unto the nations. Years ago at a lecture in San Francisco, I heard the Episcopalian bishop of California, James Pike, wryly observe that the Jews are the only people whom everyone expects to behave like Christians. A lot of Israelis just want to be left alone even as they know that to be Jewish is to forever feel the tight clasp of history's hand.

But to us, everything was new and exciting. Our favorite place was the *souk, Machanay Yehuda,* Jerusalem's outdoor market, which was filled every day with men and women pressing against one another along the narrow path that separated row after row of wooden cases overflowing with fruits and vegetables.

A frail woman from Ethiopia with beautiful dark skin cautiously squeezed past young soldiers with rifles casually slung over their shoulders. Men in cardigan sweaters and white shirts open at the neck went there on their lunch hour from the nearby Ministry of Foreign Affairs, picking out the oranges and grapefruits their wives told them to bring home that night.

Orthodox men in heavy black coats leaned back as far as they could against the lush watermelons overflowing from wooden racks lest any of the tall blonde girls from Switzerland with their stuffed backpacks accidentally touch them as they brushed by. Other shoppers flowed around and along the endless displays of green peppers and yellow peppers and melons and corn. Across from them, a vendor dipped into his huge canvas bags stuffed with walnuts and almonds to bring out the exact combination of the two that the old woman fumbling through her few coins was asking for.

People pressed forward like flowing lava, cutting paths through the masses of other shoppers who drifted right and left into their own rivulets that streamed past bright blotches of color of grapefruit and oranges and tomatoes and down other narrow aisles where the air crackled with the sounds of vendors shouting out the virtues of their avocados and onions as they tried to make themselves heard over the cacophony of other voices proclaiming that their fish was the freshest fish of all, while still other vendors called out with the speed of tobacco auctioneers the names of an endless array of cheeses, all at special prices.

Within that surge of people and voices, you breathe in the pungent aroma of lemons and spices mixed with the smells of cheeses and summer sweat, and yes, even with the sweat, you are swept up in the vitality and the energy and the excitement of life.

And yet as only in Israel, even within vast crowds, personal contact is always direct, even intimate. A huge, aproned man who sold herring out of a big barrel was always enthusiastic when Rosalind came by. One day, she encountered her first flirtation over a barrel of herring. As soon as the fish man saw her, he reached into the barrel, into the slippery mass of herring, and held up one that was implicitly his best, selected solely for her. "The day I see you in my shop," he said, "I eat my evening meal with renewed fervor." What woman in Winnetka ever received a compliment like that?

Another day, Rosalind stopped in front of a small cave of stone along one of Jerusalem's narrow streets, intrigued to see a fire in the middle of a stone platform and a man carefully leaning forward toward the flames of his makeshift furnace, steering over the fire a huge flat shovel overlaid with a pancake of raw dough. Within minutes, the fire transformed the dough into a crusty flatbread the Israelis call *aish tanoor*. The bread smelled so good that Rosalind immediately decided to buy it and bring it home.

"How much is it?" she asked him.

"Three shekels," he said.

"I'll take three," she told him and gave him a ten-shekel note. With swift, smooth strokes, he pushed fresh dough into the fire and quickly brought out more hot bread. From the day's opened newspaper lying nearby, he deftly slid off the top page, put the bread on it, and rolled the open page around it. With a broad smile, he handed her the package.

"My change," she said as she took them.

"It's all right," he told her. "You don't need change. I gave you extra bread instead."

What's a shekel or a bread between friends, even friends who never saw each other before?

That's how it was in those days, a simpler life for the simple reason that few people had enough money to make it complicated. Most people had enough to be comfortable, but that was about all. So one more bread or herring couldn't appreciably change anyone's life.

There was no pretense in those days because no one had anything to be pretentious about. Sephardic men in working-class neighborhoods wore baggy wash pants and open shirts. For *Shabbat*, they would wear their one pair of pants that was less baggy and a shirt that was white. German immigrants, many of whom were professionals in their old country, still wore suits through the streets of Rehavia though the suits were formless with age. At a time when the prime minister, Ben-Gurion, wore shirts that were open at the neck, the German Jews still wore ties even though they hung down from frayed collars.

It was not much better for women. No stylish mannequins with hips thrust forward tempted buyers with their stylish clothes. Instead, depressingly dark dresses stapled against cardboard peered out from dusty windows, a grim reminder of the storefronts of the Eastern Europe their owners had fled.

I hadn't seen any men's stores, but when I decided it was time to buy a new sports jacket, friends told me that the place to go was Hamashbir, that monolithic structure, that huge block of cement with windows, that passed as the city's department store, bigger at least than the storefronts down the street. Hamashbir at least offered a glimmer of hope at its entrance where there was a variety of products from cosmetics to jewelry to toys to clothing. That the numbers of choices within each variety was limited was something I hadn't yet learned.

With my Hebrew improving, I had no trouble finding the men's section and asking if they had sports jackets. The answer was yes, of course. Even in my size. One.

The last time I had bought a sports jacket was in Chicago where I browsed through at least twenty that were my size. It was quickly apparent that Hamashbir didn't have twenty of all the sizes put together.

I told the salesman I was a forty-two. He didn't actually have a forty-two, he said, but he did have one size forty, which he assured me would fit just as well. I wanted to tell him I didn't think it would fit just as well, but I didn't know the Hebrew word for "fit." I had no choice. Obediently, I held out my arms and slid them into the size forty that he held open for me. He looked approvingly at my reflection in the mirror as he pulled down the back of the jacket. He delivered a friendly punch into each of the shoulders and assured me that the jacket was, indeed, a perfect fit.

Before I could answer him, he had already called over several other customers and asked them if they didn't agree. Three of them did agree that the jacket looked good. Two were less enthusiastic. The salesman glowed. "You see," he said, "it's perfect for you. Makes you look trim, very trim." I looked at the strangers. They were looking at me, tilting their heads to see my mirrored reflection at a better angle, and then discussing it with one another. The vote stayed the same. The jacket was winning, three to two. I decided that since we were talking about my money, I was entitled to a vote, too—and even a veto. I voted no. I took off the jacket, thanked the salesman, thanked all the strangers, and left Hamashbir and the magic jacket that could fit any size.

The more I saw of Jerusalem, the less important clothing was to me. Walking down Jaffa Road, that worn-out main street littered with haphazard storefronts and broken sidewalks, I saw that the people there had neither the time nor the money to worry about fashion. The men I saw seemed as wrinkled as the pants they wore. Tired-looking Sephardic women with henna-streaked hair peeking out from their bright scarves passed by carrying baskets of vegetables from the *souk*. Orthodox women in long skirts pushed along babies in strollers, surrounded by an array of small sisters and brothers trying to keep up with the mother's pace.

Within that frantic struggle for existence, I would see some old lady or man hobbling along, their narrow shoulders a feeble hanger for their garments. Invariably, they clutched a worn shopping bag with little in it and yet stopped briefly at the sight of a tattered beggar leaning against a stone storefront at the edge of the sidewalk. They would drop a couple of agorot, a couple of pennies, into the hands of that person who in their eyes was not a beggar at all, but was just another Jew who happened to need a few coins. Over the years, I saw many beggars in Israel, but I never saw one person so poor that he didn't stop to help another, and I never saw a person left homeless on a street.

It's not even charity. Actually, there's no Hebrew word for charity. The word used is *tzedakah*, which comes from the word *tzedek*, meaning justice. Helping someone in need is not charity. It is simple justice.

One day I was on a bus whisking through the city streets when suddenly, in the middle of the block, the bus pulled over to the curb and came to a halt. I looked up to see what was happening just as the bus driver pushed a button that opened the front door. Opposite the door was a beggar sitting on the sidewalk. The driver aimed a coin at the shabby cap that lay upside down next to him. The coin dropped safely into its folds, the driver tossed a wave at the beggar, shut the door, and sped off.

Laura quickly absorbed the idea. When she came home from school one day, she told us she had passed a beggar and gave him a coin. She had gone a block further when she saw another beggar. Knowing it was the right thing to do, she didn't hesitate to give him a coin also. It seemed impossible, she told us, but a few minutes later, she saw a third beggar. Enough is enough, she thought, and fixed her eyes on a distant point straight ahead of her, determined to walk right by. She did pass him by. Almost. One step beyond him, she heard his voice quietly call out, "It's a *mitzvah*," a good deed. Her resolve vanished. She turned back and gave him a coin, too. "I had to do it," she told us. "It's a *mitzvah*."

It's not that there are so many beggars in Jerusalem, but rather that they are not invisible as they might be in New York. They are not part of the blur that disappears into the background as one races down the street.

Though all beggars may be needy, some, of course, are

more clever than others, like the one who always stood outside my bank. It was my bank, or at least the bank I banked at, for the simple reason that the bank gave their customers a refund for their parking fee. So whenever I made a deposit, I would walk away with a few coins. But not for long. I was barely out the revolving door when I would see the beggar standing a few yards away, the same beggar every time. My bank was his turf.

His eyes would search for mine. My fingers, ready to drop the coins into my pocket, were momentarily frozen in their grip. And then, at that critical moment, I released them, not into my pocket, but into the hand of the beggar. Free parking, I quickly learned, was not only good business for the bank. It was good business for beggars, as well.

The Western Wall is officially off limits to beggars, not to deny them their just due—there is a *pushkee* there for that, a metal box where people can drop in coins—but to discourage them from soliciting tourists.

A few weeks after we settled into our apartment, I took David to the Wall. I wanted to expose him to his Jewish heritage. I wanted it to be a special experience, just the two of us. When we got there, I pointed out the massive stones of the Wall, some weighing as much as two thousand pounds. I showed him how the Wall had been constructed, how each stone slab lay balanced layer upon layer, receding slightly from the one just beneath it. I pointed out the flowers that against all logic grew out from those cracks between the stones, a phenomenon some people see as a symbol of the Jewish people's insistent claim to life. I held his hand tightly and felt him press against me as we looked up at the Wall together. I felt that in the simple act of just being there, we had somehow become inextricably linked to centuries of Jewish history, my son and I.

My reverie was interrupted by my awareness of a large

man who seemed to have come from nowhere and was now standing next to me. He wore the traditional garments of one of the Orthodox sects, a black coat and a wide-brim black hat that framed a tumultuous array of red hair that ruffled into thick red curls beneath his ears and twisted downward into the circles of an unruly red beard. I felt his curls against my face as he leaned his lips close to my ear.

"Money for a poor family," he whispered, looking suspiciously healthy for a beggar in distress. With reflexes that were faster than my thoughts, I reached into my pocket, searching for change. There were no coins in the pocket, so I shoved my hand into the other pocket trying to find coins among a bunch of keys. There was none.

David was watching me closely. I felt the pressure of being a proper role model for him while, still searching for some coins, I felt annoyance that something about that man had crowded out my recent feelings of spirituality. Instead, I was feeling resentment. And to make matters worse, I felt guilty for those feelings of resentment, especially right there at the Western Wall. In desperation, I reached into my back pocket and pulled out my wallet, resigned to giving the man the smallest Israeli paper money there is, a five-shekel note, more than the coins I would have handed him.

I opened the wallet. Suddenly, a new problem emerged. The smallest note I had was ten shekels. I looked at the beggar. He was looking at me. I looked at my son. He was looking at me. I looked for the last time at the ten-shekel note and handed it over.

The beggar went on his way and I walked with David closer to the Western Wall, trying to recapture the spiritual mood I had already soiled. And yet in the sheer magic of that setting, I was quickly caught up in the atmosphere, watching with fascination the vagaries of the Jewish experience epitomized in the sight of Hasidim in long black cloaks swaying forward and back alongside American teenagers in tennis shoes who were wondering how you pray in Jerusalem. Dark-skinned Jews prayed nearby, Jews who looked like the Arabs from whose lands they had fled. Near them were dust-covered Israeli soldiers struggling to balance on their heads the stapled cardboard *kippahs* provided at the entrance for any Jewish man whose head was not covered.

Beyond the men were the women, on the far side of a latticed barrier. In the Orthodox tradition, men and women sit separate lest in a time of holiness men's minds wander off to thoughts that are not holy.

Elderly Jewish women were praying there, their small shoulders covered with sweaters, their hair covered by babushkas, their bodies swaying as they reached out to God. Off to the side, a Catholic nun mouthed her own private prayers in silence while two blonde girls, probably tourists from Sweden, watched in awkward reverence.

Just as I turned to go, I again heard those words, "Money for a poor family."

I turned to follow the voice and saw him there, that man in the black coat and wide-brimmed black hat and the ruddy face beaming out from that array of red curls. He came closer. "Money for a poor family," he called out to me.

I couldn't believe what I was seeing. Indeed, it was my beggar, the one with my ten-shekel note. His face was filled with poignancy. While I immediately recognized him, it was apparent that he didn't remember me. By that time, we were face to face, the beggar and I. But this time, his face looked even more downcast than before. "Money for a poor family," he said plaintively.

By now, my religious nature had succumbed to human nature. I was indignant. I pulled myself up straight, a full six feet, looked him right in the eye, and self-righteously announced, "I already gave money to your poor family." The beggar, perhaps finally recognizing me, didn't miss a beat. "So how about some money for *my* family?" he said. This time I kept the ten shekels.

The day, a Friday, ended as it had begun, with a beggar. Late in the afternoon, rushing to mail a letter, I saw a man standing on the stairs of the post office, holding out his cap. I knew it was wrong to turn my back to a beggar, especially just before *Shabbat*. On the other hand, I knew that the post office would close in just a couple of minutes. As I ran up the stairs, I made the calculation that instead of stopping by the beggar and risking not getting into the post office, I would quickly take care of the letter and then come right back to him. Which is what I did. Except that when I returned, the beggar was gone. The stairs were empty. I looked up and down the block. No sign of him. Certainly in those couples of minutes, he couldn't have gone far. Yet he was nowhere to be seen.

Years ago, I heard that Jewish mothers wring out guilt from their children like schmaltz from a chicken. My mother, even in Oak Park, had done her job well, just like generations of Jewish mothers before her. I was drenched with guilt. I had passed by the beggar, and he was gone. And before *Shabbat* yet. Like a madman, I jumped into my car and began driving up and down the streets near the post office. He must be somewhere.

I was just about to give up when I spotted him. I jumped out of the car and rushed to push a few coins into his hand. When I turned to walk off, I heard him calling me back. Turning around, I saw him holding out a bunch of wilted zinnias, their orange heads dangling over their wobbly stems. He was not a beggar, at all. He was a man who sold flowers. I thanked him and took the flowers, certain that whatever happiness my few coins brought him were nothing compared to the happiness I felt at that moment.

That night at our *Shabbat* table, with beautiful dishes laid out across a white tablecloth and the bright colors of fresh flowers bursting out from their glass vase, I set down my other flowers, the zinnias, their orange heads hanging limp over the small vase I had found for them. I told the children my story. They looked at the zinnias and agreed with me that somehow our *Shabbat* table had never looked more beautiful.

Chapter 14

The Hebrews Took All the Dolls

The problem with changing countries is that none of us really changes. We tried to be at one with the Israelis, but we weren't about to give up being Americans, and we couldn't have if we tried. The way we think, the way we act, even the way we move stays with us forever.

I remember more than once walking in the Old City, wearing jeans and an open shirt, certain that I looked no different from a dozen other men nearby with a similar build and similar features, and yet as soon as I stepped up to a vendor, before I even said anything, he would greet me in English. I was different. I hadn't said a word, and yet he knew I was different.

The children tried hard to be like the Israeli kids and did, in fact, integrate much better, but they ended up living in both worlds. My Yemenite friend, Ya'acov Yemini, pointed that out to us one day. "There are two Davids," he said, "the Israeli David on the streets and the American David in your home."

He was right. On Friday afternoons, I would proudly take our Roe Little League of three girls and one boy, together with a bat, a ball, and a catcher's mitt, over to the park for an improvised baseball game. Then a few hours later, they would be praying in Hebrew at the synagogue because it was the beginning of *Shabbat*.

After dinner, we would be Americans again. While a religious Israeli might read to his children about the revered Bal Shem Tov, I would be reading our little ones about Winnie the Pooh or telling the older ones about the Civil War. All that was natural and good within our home. But our home was not Israel.

The kids' first challenge, of course, was learning a new language. Our friends in Winnetka assured us that the younger children would have no problem, that they would pick up the language immediately. It might be harder for Laura and Devorah because they were older, our friends said, but not for the little kids. But how did they know? Had they ever moved to a foreign country? It didn't matter. They knew. And we were naïve enough to believe them. The fact is, they didn't know anything.

The kids who had the biggest problem adjusting were the little ones. They not only had to learn Hebrew, they still had a lot to learn about English. They could speak it, but hadn't learned to read it. Rosalind and I figured that Becca had enough to do just learning Hebrew, but that David was old enough to work on his English, too, so we found him a tutor. During the day, David learned how to read Hebrew from right to left. Then the tutor would come over and teach him to read English from left to right.

The tutor had all the proper credentials, and yet as time went by I sensed that somehow she and David weren't working well together. One day after a tutoring session, I asked David in my best offhand manner, "How did it go?"

"Not good," he said.

"Not well," I corrected him. After all, I thought, if he's supposed to learn proper English, I should do whatever I can to help.

"Not well," he repeated. "My teacher gave me a hard word to learn."

"What's the word?" I asked. My voice was upbeat, trying to inspire confidence.

"It's a hard word to say," he said. He was standing close to me and looking down. I looked down at him and could only see his wavy brown hair. He tilted his head up, and I could see his brown eyes. They were not happy eyes.

"Try it," I said.

He looked straight up at me. "It's what a rooster says," he said. "But I don't remember the word."

I thought a minute, wondering what on earth a rooster says. And then, a Eureka moment. "Cock-a-doodle-do?" I said.

His eyes turned happy. "That's the word," he said.

"Can you say that?" I said.

"I tried," he said. "But I can't say it. I really tried, but it's a hard word."

A long pause. "So what did you do?" I said.

Another long pause. He looked up at me again. "I told her I don't use that word very often."

There was a clutching feeling inside my stomach. I had been so anxious about my own problems that I hadn't thought much about the kids. I would teach him myself, I decided. I fired the teacher.

The problems were no less when David went from being an American in his home to not only being an Israeli outside, but a religiously observant Israeli as well. The school we found for him was Orthodox. Most of the kids there were from families who had come to Israel from Arab countries, kids who usually had dark curly hair and tanned skin. David's hair rolls backward in brown waves. His skin was light and his cheeks pink.

But the big difference was the way he wore his *kippah*. The boys had to wear it all the time. That was easy for his Sephardic classmates. They had worn a *kippah* since before they could walk. Clipped onto a boy's hair by an attentive mother using one of her bobby pins or a hair clip, it was as natural to them as a nose or ears. Not so with David. With him, it was as if the *kippah* knew it was a transplant that his body was always trying to reject. So instead of it resting comfortably within the waves of his hair, David's *kippah* always hung down the side of his face. So far down that it almost looked like an earmuff.

He tried desperately to look like everyone else, running around the school yard with his new friends in his short-sleeve shirt and short pants that barely covered his chunky thighs. I would sometimes see him from a distance racing down the soccer field as his classmates dashed back and forth in chaotic confusion and yet always able to spot their own teammates from all the other look-alike kids. Trying to emulate them, David succeeded in little more than running in circles in the midst of them.

He even tried to copy their mannerisms. He gamely imitated the macho look the boys would display to scare off any would-be assailant, eyes squinting, mouth pulled wide to the sides to show clenched teeth, looks that David called "mean faces." He also tried to show off his street smarts, hopelessly unaware that he didn't have any, that they didn't do street smarts in the streets of Winnetka.

It turned out that David was somewhat like the rest of us, warmly taken in and yet always an outsider.

Through it all, I carried the nagging apprehension of what the future would bring. When we moved to Israel just five years after Israel's overwhelming victory in the Six Day

War, it seemed that Israel was now safe forever. It made sense. It was what I wanted to believe. And it was easy to believe as long as I ignored Jewish history.

I tried to keep negative thoughts locked away deep inside me, but I didn't always succeed. Like the day I went to a class play at David's school. He was in second grade that year. When the play was over, the boys—they were six and seven years old—lined up to take their bows. I found myself looking closely at their soft faces. In my imagination, I saw their bodies become full grown and the smooth skin of their faces grow rough with the stubble of young manhood and I saw them as they would look in their army uniforms. My eyes went from one boy to the next and to the next and then I was looking at my own son. Quickly, my eyes moved on.

The day did come, some dozen years later, when I walked with David—just the two of us—to the induction center. A block before we arrived, he stopped to say goodbye. He would report to the army alone. We hugged, and I turned to walk back home, alone. It was the worst day of my life.

At the time, however, my anxiety about David at least had the comfort of lying well into the future. Our problems with Becca began shortly after we arrived. Unexpectedly.

We had enrolled her that fall in *gahn*, the Hebrew word for preschool. In Israel, *ghan* is a way of life. Most of the children there are between three and five. Some are as young as two.

It's an interesting word, *ghan*. It means garden. Maybe on some subliminal level, parents feel that's where they will plant the seeds that will grow into their dreams. That's not the job of seeds, but most young parents like us didn't know that. At that age, we thought that rearing children was simply a matter of nurturing our garden. We didn't know about the winds of chance. We didn't know about how many forces beyond our control shape the lives, and sometimes the deaths, of our children.

Gahn is a place of limitless love. Many of the women who take care of the children come from large families and, as older daughters, grew up taking care of little kids. They genuinely like children. You can see that in the way they talk to them and understand them.

At the end of the school day, you often see fathers as well as mothers coming into the classroom to help their children into their sweaters or jackets and take them home, not because they feel they are supposed to share the responsibility, but because they really want to. It's the complete opposite of New York. There is none of that American-style, time-and-motion efficiency of fathers getting their workout cascading down city sidewalks on rollerblades while steering the stroller in front of them. There are no scenes of mothers talking on cell phones instead of to their children as they walk with them down the street. Israeli children are not background music.

Maybe it's because life is precarious in Israel and therefore more precious. In America, young parents look at their children and talk about what university they might attend. In Israel, young parents look at their young children and know the years will fly by and soon they'll be in the army. Nothing is taken for granted.

I saw that anxiety in the lines of Hermona Lynn's face when I filmed the story of her family, one of the country's early kibbutz settlers who in those days of nation building thought they could build a homeland for the Jews and also be friends with the Arabs. Hermona is a beautiful, dark-haired woman with fine features, but after living through all of Israel's wars even her beauty cannot hide the apprehension that lives within her. Before the filming we talked, just the two of us, and she told me her story. As she spoke, her gaze wandered out toward the farmland nearby, but I could tell she was looking beyond the land and into her past, her life as a young woman.

"I remember when our third son was born," she said. Her lips revealed a nostalgic smile as she saw that new baby again. "And I remember him as a young boy playing with toy guns. My husband would say to him, '*You* won't be a soldier.'" She paused as if remembering that exact moment. "But he was a soldier," she said. "And now," she looked across the room, "you can see here our grandchild. We don't say to him . . ." She hesitated a moment. "We don't say to him 'you are not going to be a soldier.' We know, and we are afraid that he must be a soldier, too." Hermona looked directly at me. "This is our life," she said.

That's why in *ghan*, every child is special. That's why the teachers fussed over Becca and every other child there. But still Becca felt different. She hadn't grown up going to *ghan* since she was two like the other children. She was the new kid on the block, not knowing anyone and not knowing what to do.

Worst of all, she didn't speak Hebrew. A few phrases, yes, but not much more. The streams of sounds that swirled around her were beyond her comprehension, leaving her alone and isolated. And often embarrassed.

One day, she came home from school in tears telling us that the teacher had told the children to stand in a circle around a bunch of toys they could play with. Becca got the idea. The children formed a circle, and Becca moved into place with them. Then the teacher told them to cover their eyes. When Becca saw the teacher cover her eyes, she did the same, placing her small hands over her face. Then apparently, the teacher told the children to uncover their eyes and take a toy, but Becca didn't understand the words and kept standing there, her eyes covered.

Finally, hearing the other children moving around, she peeked out between her fingers and saw she was the only one still there. She looked down. The toys were all gone. She told us about it when she came home that day. "The Hebrews," she said—she didn't even know that her classmates were called Israelis—"the Hebrews took all the dolls!"

More tears.

Days later when Rosalind went to the *ghan* to walk Becca home, she was shocked to find Becca standing there, her head tilted to one side as if trying to see better. For days, Becca kept looking at everything strangely as if trying to bring the images into focus. We were terrified, immediately expected the worst, and brought her to a hospital fearing she had developed a brain tumor. The doctor examined her and found nothing.

But the problem continued and we didn't know what to do. She would come up to where we were sitting and tilt her head as if trying to find a position where she could see us better. Finally our family doctor, Moshe Rayman, a Chicagoan who had served in the American army during World War II, then worked in a displaced-persons camp with victims of the Holocaust, and finally fulfilled his lifelong dream of moving to Israel, told us not to worry, that it would go away. We worried anyway, but Moshe was right. After a couple of weeks of squinting and tilting her head, the problem did go away.

"Probably a reaction to tension," Moshe said. Our own tension subsided, replaced by a new awareness that as happy as the children seemed, we never really knew what fears they carried.

The year after *ghan*, Becca went to an Orthodox school and became close friends with a number of Sephardic girls.

They were generally poorer than the Ashkenazi Jews of Europe and also more religious, observing the Biblical injunction to "be fruitful and multiply." Growing up among many siblings, they showed the easy warmth and comfort of children who are close to one another and open in their affection. Their complexions were dark, their hair straight. In their midst, there was never a problem spotting Becca with her pink cheeks and brown curls.

She often brought her friends home with her. We loved having them, but it was soon apparent that they had never before seen such a large apartment. One day, one of the little girls walked over slowly from one living-room chair to another, cautiously touching each one, and then stepped into the dining room where eight more chairs stood around the table. For a while, she said nothing. Then finally she turned.

"Haval al ha kisot," she said to Becca. "A pity, what waste, there should be so many chairs." She was shocked at the excess, the breakfront, the buffet, the chairs in the dining room, the upholstered sofa and more chairs in the living room. Not to mention separate bedrooms for each of the children. Becca's friends lived in apartments less than half the size, took their meals together in the kitchen, and slept two or more to a room. Meanwhile, I had moved the lifestyle of Middle America to the middle of the Middle East.

As Becca got older, she showed a flair for language. From her awkward beginnings, she learned both Hebrew and English well and developed an elegance in both languages. By the time she was fifteen, she won an award for her poetry, presented to her by Yehuda Amichai, the earthy Israeli writer whose own poetry has been translated into different languages all over the world.

"Her writing is *nefla*, wondrous," Amichai told me years later. Becca's journey to self-expression revealed not only her talent, but also her sensitivity to the world around her and to the hurts and losses that she and other children endure and hide, particularly from their parents.

Even Laura screeched to a stop when she first came to Israel. It was a surprise to all of us and especially to her. For the first two years of her life, she was the first and only child, filled with the confidence that comes from being the center of the universe, a reasonable assumption on her part as the object of consuming parental attention. I certainly knew that her mother wasn't a virgin like Mary, and yet I looked at Laura with the kind of awe and wonderment that others must have felt when they saw the Christ child.

I still remember that rainy January midnight in San Francisco when she was born. Fathers were excluded from the delivery room in those days, consigned instead to a far-off waiting room with linoleum floors, orange plastic chairs, artificial flowers heavy with dust, and aging magazines. It was there that I first saw her, bundled within Rosalind's arms, already bearing a full head of dark hair, hair that as a teenager would become a bundle of long, curled tresses.

By age two, she was bursting with excitement, jumping up and down on the floorboard of the car at a time before grown-ups wore seat belts and strapped their children into car seats. Outside the car, she dashed here and there like a squirrel, her waves of energy almost convincing you that a bushy tail was flapping to and fro behind her. As a ten-year-old in Winnetka's Crow Island grammar school, she was one of the best students. And then she came to Israel, and I watched my ebullient daughter retreat into silence in the back of her classroom.

We enrolled her in gymnasia, a secular high school for bright youngsters. Classes, of course, were in Hebrew, which she quickly learned, and yet for weeks Laura sat there silently, her confidence lost somewhere between Winnetka and Jerusalem. And then finally the day arrived when she had a chance to shine. It was during history class. The teacher asked the students what event marked the year 1492. No American could resist that pitch lobbed across the plate. For the first time, Laura swung at the ball—and missed. Her hand shot up in the air to signal that she knew the answer. Gratefully the teacher looked past the other children's waving hands and pointed to Laura. At last she would hear from this new student.

"In 1492," she said, "Columbus discovered America." The teacher listened and said nothing. Neither did the other students, silenced in surprise at her answer. In Israel, everyone knows what happened in 1492, knows it as well as they know their names. Fourteen ninety-two! That was the year the Jews were driven out of Spain. Columbus? What did he have to do with anything?

It was a quick lesson for Laura and for the rest of us. America was not the center of the world, especially if you don't live in America. If anything, the center was Jerusalem, which is exactly how Jerusalem appeared in the maps of the Middle Ages.

Laura not only had to learn about events like the Inquisition, she had to learn the names of important historical and literary figures, as well. George Washington and Abraham Lincoln were not among them. Instead, she heard names out of history like Theodor Herzl, names of political figures like David Ben-Gurion, names out of literature like Bialik and Agnon, names out of philosophy like Maimonides and Rashi, names that no one ever heard of in Winnetka.

In time, she did learn those new names and much more and settled in comfortably with her classmates, many of whom knew English and who as children of professors and government officials had even lived in the United States. Before the year was out, Laura was one of the gang, a typical teenager, gossiping and giggling with the rest of them. In Hebrew, of course.

Devorah was our family WASP with her blonde pageboy and flashing blue eyes. When Crow Island school mounted its musical presentation about the cartoon character, Peanuts, there was Devorah in her crisp white shirt and red-and-black plaid skirt belting out the songs with the best of them, shoulder to shoulder with her classmates while swaying her hips to the beat of the music.

Despite her classroom performances, Devorah was basically shy, so much so that at our local synagogue where she and Laura wanted to join the children's choir, Laura had to do all the talking and explain to the teacher that she and her little sister wanted to be part of the group. The teacher nodded her agreement and told her they would be more than welcome. "But where is your little sister?" the teacher asked. Laura turned around, and the teacher followed her look. Crouched down hiding behind a desk was Devorah, waiting for the verdict.

Just as there were two Davids, there were two Devorahs. Perhaps all of us are two or more different people. There was the Devorah who on the ship to Israel eagerly shimmied down the water slide, her eyes shut tight and her nose squeezed between thumb and forefinger as she plunged into the ship's swimming pool, and there was the Devorah who was not only religious, but who was almost spiritual.

Even in Winnetka, when she was just six or seven, we used to call her the *rebbitzin*, the Yiddish word for a rabbi's wife, as she conscientiously observed in our home the religious ceremonies she was beginning to learn in Sunday school. By the time we came to Israel, it seemed only natural to enroll her in the prestigious Orthodox religious school named after its French benefactor, Evelyna de Rothschild. In reputation and in deed, the school merited the prestige and reputation of the Rothschild name. Sadly, all that prestige was housed in a rambling old building left over from the days of the British mandate, a building whose thick stone walls in winter insulated the classrooms within penetrating cold. It was so cold the January night I first went there for a meeting with Devorah's teacher that I not only kept on my coat, but my hat and gloves as well, in a desperate effort to stay warm. The kids who studied there, of course, couldn't do their schoolwork wearing gloves. They simply did the best they could writing their lessons with cold fingers.

Devorah loved the school. In spring, she joined the scouts who on *Shabbat* afternoon gathered together on the grass at French Square, kitty-corner from the prime minister's residence, and went on long marches together. The boys and girls were *Shabbat* clean, the boys with their *kippahs* clipped to their hair and the girls in white blouses and navy-blue skirts. One of my most exciting memories was of the day I saw Devorah with her blonde hair and blazing blue eyes marching proudly with her classmates. It was the day it was her turn to hold aloft the Israeli flag.

The biggest change in the lives of us all was learning more about our Judaism. Because of the influence of the religious political parties in Israel, all but a few synagogues follow the Orthodox tradition. As a result, Israelis who prefer the less-strict Reform or Conservative movement don't go to synagogue at all, or at most go only on Yom Kippur. From these alternatives, we decided to join an Orthodox congregation.

It wasn't easy, but as we learned more about the traditions we felt they were enriching our daily lives. *Shabbat* was the highlight of that deeper understanding as I learned about the traditional observances of the Friday-night Sabbath meal. My favorite moment was the blessing of the children, when all four would slide out of their chairs, the girls in fresh clothes for the *Shabbat* meal and David in long pants and a white shirt, and stand before me as I placed my hands on their heads, felt the softness of their hair, and whispered the centuries-old prayer asking God to bless them. We always had friends with us at our *Shabbat* dinners, and at the end of the meal we would sing traditional Hebrew songs and psalms. On the festive table, the silver wine cups flickered with the reflections of the candles' glow.

The next day, Saturday, was a time of quietude, shutting out the everyday pressures and anxieties, a time when instead of running past one another, we would stop long enough to see one another.

I began to see the world differently. I stopped taking everything for granted. I began to understand that a miracle is not the parting of a Red Sea. A miracle is every day

Even David's little *kippah* opened new worlds to me. I knew that an Orthodox Jew must have his head covered whenever he says a prayer, but I wondered why he would wear a *kippah* or a hat all the time. Then it occurred to me that maybe it was so he would always be ready to pray. I had learned that there are special prayers for just about everything—from hearing good news to seeing trees blossoming for the first time in spring to seeing a rainbow. I imagine that often these prayers are recited in a rote manner and yet the observance revealed to me a remarkable sensitivity to life that I had been oblivious to in my days as a suburban achiever.

From the recesses of memory, I found myself recalling lines I had memorized in high school. At the time, I had little interest in an English poet named William Wordsworth. He was just another homework assignment. Now, so many years later, I found myself remembering some of his words.

The world is too much with us, he wrote,
Late and soon,
Getting and spending, we lay waste our powers:
Little we see in Nature that is ours;
We have given our hearts away, a sordid boon.

I think Wordsworth would have understood those Orthodox Jews.

For me, it was easy to feel religious. It was comfortable sharing a moment of meditation with God and hoping that somehow my thoughts would penetrate the mysterious unknown. But it was difficult, really difficult, to learn to be part of an Orthodox prayer service.

In our Conservative congregation, the prayers were in Hebrew on the right page of the open book, but on the left was the comforting reassurance of the English translation. So all we had to do was pray in English. But in our Orthodox synagogue in Jerusalem, the Hebrew was on both sides. What do I do now?

I not only couldn't read the prayers, I had never seen so many of them before. The siddur, the Hebrew name for prayer book, is filled not only with prayers you say, but even prayers you don't say.

There are prayers you say only in the morning and different prayers you say only at night. There are prayers you say every day, and others you say only on *Shabbat*. There are prayers for men and others that are just for women. There are prayers used only for some special holiday or event. And there is prayer you say on the first day of every month. I didn't even know the Hebrew names for the months and never knew which month it was, let alone when the month began.

It isn't easy to be a Jew, especially when you're trying to pray.

Still learning my way through Hebrew, I would read like a child, making the sounds the letters make, struggling through the first line while out of the corner of my eye, I would see everyone else already turning the page. Quickly, I would turn my page and try to figure out what to pray next.

I didn't really mind the effort, and I could handle the frustration. What was difficult was the endless embarrassment. Everyone knew what he was doing except me.

After a while, men sitting near me would see me fumbling through the pages and politely point out where I was supposed to be, usually about four pages ahead of wherever I was.

I also had to learn when to stand and when to sit. Jews do a lot of standing and sitting when they pray. And because Jews for some genetic or cultural reason find it difficult to stay in one place for any length of time, a man who was standing up and sitting down and standing up again could also easily drift a few rows one way or the other with no perceptible impact on the waves of movement that undulated through the synagogue.

Haim Donin was my guardian angel, or guardian rabbi to be exact, for he had been a rabbi with his own congregation before moving to Israel from Detroit. I used to play tennis with Haim on Friday afternoons before *Shabbat*. Before he died at a young age, he wrote a wonderful book, *To Be a Jew*, which people are still buying thirty years later to learn many of the things Haim taught me just in passing.

Often during the service, Haim would pray his way over in my direction so he could reach over and turn the page of my prayer book to where I was supposed to be. Other times, some stranger behind me would reach over my shoulder to point out the right passage. Little by little, I learned what to do, and sometimes I could even feel what it means to tremble before God. Even all the standing up and sitting down felt good because it made me feel in my very body that I was connected to all those Jews who had been praying like that for thousands of years. Down deep I felt at peace with myself.

Peace is a rare commodity in Israel.

The phone rang one day, and I picked up the receiver.

"Pops, I'm okay." Devorah's voice.

Devorah always runs her words together. Even in English, it is not easy to understand her. I had no idea what she was talking about.

The words tumbled out. "A bomb. In the open market. I'm okay."

It's strange how the mind works. I heard the words. I even understood them. But I couldn't comprehend them. Bombs don't go off in markets. Bombs are something you read about in newspapers. And even though you know that sometimes things like that happen in Israel, it doesn't really happen to you.

"Are you all right?" still struggling to accept what I had heard.

"I'm okay," she told me again.

"Devorah, slow down. What happened?"

"A bomb, in *Machanay Yehuda*," Devorah repeated. "Something happened. They say it's a bomb. I'm coming home."

She hung up the phone. I didn't hang up. I sat there for several long moments. I was getting the idea. I was living in what used to be "somewhere else."

For us, it was the first time we were so close to terrorism. For Israelis, it is a part of life. It soon became a part of our lives, beginning in small ways. Laura coming home from school one day to tell us about her silly classmates who pushed her aside when she playfully tried to kick away a package of fresh gum someone had dropped on the sidewalk. "They said I shouldn't touch it," she told us, mocking the girls' frantic voices. We laughed along with her, but within weeks our attitudes changed. Laura and the rest of us learned to see everything and touch nothing. We learned what every Israeli knows, that anything could be an explosive.

One day, I called the police when I saw near a doorway a small crunched-up brown bag, obviously with something in it. The police came, circled it, studied it, carefully opened it, and then showed me its contents, three pitas. I was not embarrassed, and the police were not upset. We all knew that the first rule is to be careful.

Terrorism was nothing new to the Israelis. Long before al-Qaeda, there were Germany's Baader-Meinhof gang, Japan's Red Army Faction, America's Weather Underground, and Italy's Red Brigades that committed terrorist acts in several countries, including Israel. One of those attacks occurred a few weeks before we moved to Israel, and to my chagrin, Rabbi Dresner spoke about it that farewell evening when we were honored at the synagogue. I looked over at my children and hoped they were already bored with the ceremonies and weren't paying attention.

I don't know why but the Rabbi insisted on talking about the three members of the Japanese Red Army who gunned down twenty-four tourists who had just arrived in Israel. The terrorists had flown in with the other passengers, went through passport control with them, and then to the baggage area where with the other passengers they waited for their luggage. When their bags arrived, they ripped them open, pulled out Kalashnikov rifles and grenades, and started gunning down everyone in sight. The assault went on for a full five minutes until their ammunition ran out. By that time, the arrival hall was stained with blood and littered with bodies of the dead and wounded. Two of the terrorists blew themselves up, and a third was captured.

It was not the kind of story I wanted our children to hear, especially just before moving to Israel.

It is insidious, terrorism. It is different from other threats. It is not distant like a war. It is not something gone awry like an airplane crash. It is not a force majeure like an earthquake. It is a threat that lurks unseen, something that happens in places that are part of your everyday life, the open market, the mall, buses. You don't overtly dwell on the threat but in a way that is deeply sublimated, you consider for a moment whether you should perhaps walk instead of taking a bus, whether you should buy those vegetables you want at the grocery store rather than in the open market, the *souk*.

A typical Israeli response is what I call the *dafka* reaction. *Dafka* is a hard word to explain. It means doing the opposite of what is expected, just to be stubborn or ornery. If you prefer white, *dafka!*, I prefer black.

So when there was a big explosion at the supermarket at Agron and King George streets in Jerusalem and many people were seriously injured, *dafka!*, the next day hundreds of Israelis went to shop at that supermarket. Whether the Israelis do that to send a message to the enemy that they're not going to be pushed around or whether they do it to reassure themselves, I don't know. But that's the reaction. *Dafka!*

When those things happen and newsmen report it on television, that five people were killed and twenty-four injured, it's just numbers, like a football score. It's reported, and then it's over. At most, people may be shocked that so many were killed. But "injured," there's something amorphous about that word that evokes little reaction. Injured sounds like something that happens and then gets better and goes away. The fact is that injuries from terrorism often mean the loss of a limb, shrapnel embedded in your head, a fragment that enters your eye and blinds you, nails exploding out of the bomb and ripping your stomach open.

Five dead and twenty-four injured. It's more than a score.

For the loved ones of those killed, there is the loss itself and the raw suddenness of the event. A child goes to school and never comes home again. A mother goes shopping and never comes home again. The agony is compounded by the rules of burial, again determined by Orthodox Jewish law. The person killed must be buried the same day. So you can wave good-bye to a child in the morning and stand helpless that afternoon or evening watching her, draped in a white sheet, being lowered into a grave.

Reason enough, I have often thought, why Israelis smoke relentlessly and drive so recklessly. There's a lot of tension living in Israel.

I saw terrorism up close once, in the heart of the Jerusalem shopping area on Jaffa Road. My cameraman and good friend, Yehoram Pirotsky, was filming with me near Zion Square, the center of the city where people gather to shop and meet friends for coffee. Suddenly, we heard a shattering sound, five kilograms of explosives ripping through pedestrians and storefronts and cars. In seconds, the busy intersection was littered with hundreds of pieces of broken glass that reminded me of the jagged pieces of ice I used to crunch across on a winter day in Chicago.

A Palestinian had driven a small truck to the center of

the downtown area. In front of a toy store, his partner got out to unload a heavy refrigerator. A passerby, an Israeli named Shabtai Levi, saw him struggling with the heavy refrigerator and stopped to help him pull it onto the sidewalk. Minutes later, a timing device set off a huge blast that exploded out of the refrigerator killing thirteen people and, as they say in the newspapers, injuring seventy-five.

People were shouting and rushing in every direction as Yehoram ran toward them with his 16mm camera capturing the horror. I ran with him accomplishing nothing, but running because we were always together when we filmed, and so there we were together again in the middle of all the confusion. A soldier ran past us with a young woman in his arms. Others were running in other directions. Some were slumped against storefronts or lying in the streets. Ambulances arrived. It was amazing. Though we were just a block away when it happened, it seemed as if they got there as quickly as we did.

Out of nowhere, the ubiquitous mayor of Jerusalem appeared, Teddy Kollek, who had been mayor for almost a decade and whose name was already inextricably linked to the city that he loved. Teddy, recognizable to everyone with his full wavy hair, large belly, and thick build was moving steadily through the madness, his very presence reassuring to whoever saw him.

Yehoram, tough and wiry, kept pushing through all the tumult, his camera going nonstop, filming, filming. I looked around and saw there was no other camera crew there. It was our story, ours only, and it was on the ABC network the next morning. I have often asked myself why should we record such terrible events. I have often wondered whether our films helped people understand the difficulties Israel faced or whether they just fed viewers' voyeurism as they watch in newscast after newscast the same shots of horror repeated again and again. There were times when I felt that what I was doing was pointless. But that's what I did.

Even more upsetting than what we saw were the raw feelings conveyed in the stories of people we filmed, feelings like those shared with us by a sensitive musician from Pine Bluff, Arkansas, who three years after Israel's War of Independence decided he would return to his historic roots and move to Israel. That's exactly what he did, in 1951.

His name was Hanoch. He married an Israeli woman and changed his family name to Tel Oren. That's how you say Pine Bluff in Hebrew. Obviously you could take the boy out of Arkansas, but you couldn't take Arkansas out of the boy. Hanoch and his wife had seven children. Until 1976. That's when terrorists commandeered that Israeli bus traveling to Tel Aviv on the Haifa Road. Both Hanoch and his fourteen-year-old son were shot in the attack. Thirty-one Israelis were killed. Hanoch's son was one of them.

"I never dreamed such a thing could happen to me," he said. Hanoch is a delicate man, a flutist. His right arm was shattered by bullets and was still bandaged when I spoke to him. He tilted his head as if trying to see something discernible only to him. "I'm trying to digest the horrible fact," he said, "that one of the seven is missing." He tried to make me understand his feelings, but he was still sorting them out himself. I listened in a pall of sadness. There is a point beyond which one cannot feel the pain of another.

Hanoch struggled with his own feelings. "I don't want anybody else to experience it so he would understand it," he said. "No one. If you have the ideal, you go on, regardless." He said it quietly, with resignation. "You go on."

In Israel, there is still another dimension to terrorism. It is the reminder of a brooding past from which no Jew is ever free, a past stained with blood through centuries and a past that is still within recent memory, the Holocaust. Perhaps more than any other country, Israel is memory. It is the memory of the killing of one out of every three Jews in the world, a memory so recent that many of us have lived through that period.

Every year, on a spring day, the mournful sound of a siren reverberates throughout the country at exactly ten o'clock in the morning. The day is Yom HaShoah, the day that commemorates the loss of six million Jews. When that siren sounds, every Israeli walking down the street stops and stands still. Children at play stop and stand still. Every driver stops his car, gets out, and stands silent. Those old enough to remember stand there, each alone with the memory of days they survived or days they heard about, all of them with the memory of an event that every Israeli feels and that no Israeli can ever come to terms with. Then the siren wails again. Drivers climb back into their cars and drive on. Pedestrians resume their walking and children their playing. As if nothing had happened.

Nor are the memories only once a year. They invade your life. They become a part of you, and you never know when they will recur. I was shocked into that memory one day during the most mundane activity. I was at Geva Studios in Givataym doing a sound mix for one of my films. My engineer was Haim Avish, a man in his forties, about my age at the time. He even looked a little like me, about the same size, similar features, dark hair always a bit askew.

Many days Haim and I sat together, watching the 16mm images of my films projected onto a large screen, those edited rushes with faded colors and scratch marks that were the guide for the technicians who, wearing white cotton gloves, would later carefully cut and splice the negative to match our edited rushes and produce a clean, crisp copy of the film. As Haim and I worked, we were accustomed to the imperfect images and concentrated only on the sound, fading in the music at the proper times, making sure that spoken words matched the movements of lips, balancing the music with the narration track and with the live sounds on the film itself until all the sounds were smoothly integrated.

Because of the heat and humidity so near the Mediterranean, we usually wore light clothes, chinos and short-sleeve shirts. As I sat next to Haim and we leaned forward at the audio console, carefully scrutinizing the rushes of the film, my eyes strayed from the image on the screen to the image on Haim's forearm, a row of numbers. That was his memory of another time. And I thought how strange fate is, that we were born in almost the same year and were both teenagers during World War II, but that I was lucky enough to be born in a town in Illinois. Haim was born in Czechoslovakia. I tried to look away from the numbers.

In Israel, the past is always present. Sometimes it even augers the future. When I first came to Israel, I met a rabbi who had lost a son in the Six Day War. Neither of us ever imagined, as we talked together, that within a year, he would lose another son in still another war.

Micha Lynn, Hermona's husband at Kibbutz Mishmar HaEmek in the Galilee, told me one day, "We live for Israel, we die for Israel." He gave a slight shrug. "That's our life."

I was beginning to understand. *Ain brayrah.* There was no other way.

Chapter 15

Making a Living

eople usually condemn ignorance, but I think it has its virtues. It was my faithful companion in Israel, never more so than in trying to make a living. Ignorance kept me from knowing that what I was doing couldn't be done.

Sure, Burt Harris had warned me that business backers often drop away after their first burst of enthusiasm but I didn't worry about that. I had in my desk signed legal agreements from my partners. So there was nothing to worry about even though when Joe Perlman signed the contract, he did mention in passing that any contract can be broken. I didn't pay any attention to the remark and only thought about it months later.

When I finally got to Israel, I heard that old, not-so-funny joke—how can you get a small fortune in Israel. The answer: Come there with a big one. I didn't worry about that either because by sheer luck my little business got off to a fast start. Within just a few weeks, I made my first sale to none less than the mighty CBS television network. I couldn't believe my good fortune.

It was embarrassingly easy. I had read a new book, *The Israelis*, by Israeli journalist Amos Alon. It was a strong story and as I read it I could see it as a great television special. The world was still awed by Israel's spectacular success just five years earlier when in six days its military forces destroyed the Egyptian air force, pushed the Syrian army off the Golan Heights, and drove the Jordanian army out of East Jerusalem and what is today called the West Bank. That military campaign is still studied today in military academies.

What was even more shocking to the world was that all this happened less than three decades after the world had seen one-third of the Jewish people shot, gassed, and cremated by the Nazis. Overnight the exaggerated image of the Jew as hapless victim was transformed into the equally exaggerated image of the Jew as a superhero capable of surmounting all military odds. Even years later after Jimmy Carter's humiliating military failure trying to rescue the American hostages in Iran, I overheard people on the streets of New York saying, half in jest and half seriously, "Why didn't he send in the Israelis?"

So I was simply riding the crest of public sentiment when from Israel I dialed CBS in New York and asked to speak to Bill Leonard who was running CBS news. Bill got on the phone, liked the idea, and told me, "We'll do it." Television was like that in those days, a lot of fast seat-of-the-pants decisions. "Our top producer is in London right now," Bill said. "I'll have him fly over to Israel."

I was thrilled. My first project since moving to Israel and I succeeded immediately. What I failed to notice in our phone call was Bill's use of that little pronoun, "we," when he said, "We'll do it." I thought that we meant CBS and me. What I found out was that he meant CBS, as in the sentence, "We at CBS will do it."

My dreams of producing a network special were quickly shattered. CBS sent me a thousand-dollar check for my trouble, not bad for a twenty-minute phone call, but like so many other Jews what I really wanted was to be in show business. And yet I was encouraged that my idea was so quickly accepted. So were my investors. It seemed to prove that even from Israel, I could make things happen.

Other business followed. Somehow or other, the BBC found me and asked me to handle the arrangements for an interview with an Israeli general down in the Negev. I had only been in Israel a couple of months and didn't know anything about Israeli generals, but I got the name of the one they wanted to film and, together with the BBC producer, met him at the general's ranch.

That anybody had a ranch in Israel was my first surprise. Israel is a small country with a lot of desert, not exactly the kind of place where people have ranches. Highly polished boots were my next surprise. Here I was in a country where just about every man walked around in ill-fitting pants and a short-sleeve shirt, and suddenly my eyes were focused on a pair of expensive, highly polished boots, above which was a very English jodhpur into which was tucked a full white shirt covering a hefty belly and a massive chest. The man sat down, the BBC journalist sat opposite him, the cameraman started to roll his 16mm 7247 color film, the soundman signaled "speed," and we began the interview with General Ariel Sharon.

That's how it is making films. It takes you to all sorts of places where you would normally never go and to all sorts of people you would otherwise never meet. In time to come, I would sit across the desk from Yitzhak Rabin while my crew filmed his brilliant explanation of Israel's security arrangements. Other times we filmed Ingrid Bergman on location for her motion picture role as Golda Meir, Zubin

Mehta preparing to conduct the Israel Philharmonic Orchestra, Danny Kaye in performance at the Jerusalem Theater, and even Elizabeth Taylor and Richard Burton who were sneaking toward their honeymoon suite at the King David Hotel after successfully eluding the entire press corps at Ben-Gurion Airport.

On a tip from the chambermaid I found out in which room they would be staying. My crew and I raced up the stairs, got there ahead of them and were waiting at the door of Richard and Elizabeth's suite as they came down the hall. They granted a short, but rather nice interview so they could get past me into their room, while my cameraman conscientiously filmed the cart of Scotch and hors d'oeuvres that would begin their repast. The material was on ABC-TV the next morning.

Ordinary people were even more intriguing because they would invariably share private thoughts they would never express in their everyday lives. To this day, I don't quite understand how this happens, but I have found that as soon as the camera starts running, some magic takes over that evokes the most-intimate revelations.

I also learned that there is something intimidating about the camera that makes people strangely obedient. One day, I almost lost an Israeli cabinet minister when I was filming him on a hilltop overlooking the Dead Sea. Peering into the viewfinder, I kept telling him to back up a little, and then a little more, and then still more as I tried to get just the right composition. When I finally stood up straight to survey the scene, I was horrified to realize the man had backed up to the very edge of the cliff. One more directive and he would have toppled over. But as they say, that's show business.

One of my assignments was to make a documentary about a young American family that lived in Metulla, a rustic, small town in northern Israel that looks very much like northern California. There was more than a slight difference, however. Metulla is the northernmost point of a narrow strip of land that on the map looks like a finger pointing upward. As you look closer, you see that on one side of that narrow point of land is Lebanon. On the other side is Syria. Israel was technically at war with both countries. Metulla is a town where the land is beautiful, life is tenuous, and that young American family was very brave. I called the film "The Last House in Israel."

If my company had been big like America's corporations, it would have had one of those mission statements that were so popular in the 1970s, laying out in pretentious phrases the company's resolute commitment to the public good. Within a decade, mission statements faded from favor, but the phrases lived on in advertising like Archer-Daniel Midland's commitment to feed a hungry world. Their real objective, of course, is to make money to feed themselves. That's what my company was all about. Never mind saving the world. I was too busy trying to save myself.

So I let my imagination roam and soon came up with an idea for a series of half-minute children's commercials that I managed to sell to General Mills. The idea, called "The How Come Show," was simplicity itself and, I hoped, charming. First an animated graphic backed by an attention-getting musical sting announces "General Mills presents, 'The How Come Show.'" Then a blonde Tom Sawyer-type boy of eight, whom I found in a family of Christian neighbors, spins around on a stool to face the camera and says something like "How Come Birds Don't Fall Down?" Then there's a twenty-second visual explanation—aerodynamics made easy—and the kid comes up full screen again saying with amazement, "I didn't know that."

Music up over a closing graphic with a "brought to you by General Mills" credit and that's that, all in half a minute.

Another commercial showed a half-dozen kids of different ethnic backgrounds tumbling down a slide, one after another. A different kid is the questioner this time asking, "How Come People Come in Different Colors?" Then there's an answer to that and a good-bye from General Mills. We made twenty-five of those commercials and got an order for another twenty-five.

The business was growing, money was coming in, and certainly within three years I would be at break-even. At least, that's what I thought until Burt Harris's words of caution started to come true. Partners started dropping out.

The first to go was Bob's friend who simply changed his mind. He would lose his initial investment, and he knew that, but he wanted out. My problem was that the company would lose the remaining five installments that I expected from him. It was not good news. But after all, I consoled myself, we still had the remaining seven investors.

Six months passed. The stock market had broken upward through the 1,000 figure, which in those days was heady territory. But soon it broke through the 1,000 figure a second time, going down. It not only went down—it kept going down, the worst market retreat since World War II.

I was in the States on business when Zig Porter found me in my hotel room in Chicago.

"The market is terrible," Zig said on the phone. "I think I have to pull out."

"Don't do anything hasty," I said. "Let's get together. We'll talk about it."

We got together that night at a cocktail lounge. Zig's forefinger drew small circles through the condensation of his Coke on the rocks. My forefinger was stirring the ice cubes through my vodka just the way my old television boss, John Mitchell, used to do it.

"Markets always turn around," I told Zig. "The important thing is to not panic."

Zig stared at me.

"And besides," I said, "we're already getting business."

Zig continued to stare.

"Quit staring at my teeth!" I blurted out.

"They look nice," Zig said. "Very nice."

At last, Zig looked me in the eye. "Okay, Yale, okay. I was thinking about it some more on the way down here." A pause. I waited. "I'll stick."

"Great, Zig," I said, reaching for his hand.

Zig shook my hand. With his other hand, he reached over and lifted my upper lip so he could see my gums.

"Get your hand out of my mouth," I snapped at him.

He let go of my lip and looked at me instead. "The gums look good," Zig said. "Very good."

A few days later, I flew back to Israel. Meanwhile, the market kept going south. Six more months passed, and one day, I got a letter from Zig. He wrote that he just couldn't stay in the game any longer. I didn't argue with him. I just felt sorry he had lost his money. At least I still had my gums.

Don was the next one to throw in the towel, or more literally, his stock. Once again a letter, another explanation of the burdens of a declining stock market, and another partner was gone. Now we were five. The investment capital had been reduced by more than a third. I had a problem, and it was serious.

I thought back to a lunch I had with Ralph Baruch before I left for Israel. Ralph had been a CBS executive who had the good fortune to be around when the government forced CBS to divest itself of ownership in programs such as "I Love Lucy." CBS did a deal with Ralph, who got those valuable properties to syndicate to TV stations under the aegis of a new company called Viacom.

During that lunch, Ralph told me that CBS had produced an audiotape tour of the Civil War battlefield of Gettysburg narrated by Walter Cronkite. Thinking once again about that conversation I didn't have to make a great leap of imagination to transpose that idea to Israel.

Emotionally Masada is to Israel what Gettysburg is to Americans, the site of an extraordinary national event. Masada is a stone fortress that hovers 1,300 feet above the Dead Sea in the Judean desert where almost two thousand years ago, after the Roman general Titus captured Jerusalem and burned the Holy Temple, 960 Jews fought on for more than two years against the Roman governor, Flavius Silva, and his soldiers of the Tenth Legion who set up eight camps that surrounded the Jewish stronghold.

In time, the Romans methodically constructed a siege ramp. When they finally attacked and reached the top of the mountain, they found only two women and five children alive. In the face of imminent defeat, the other Jews had committed suicide rather than surrender. Two thousand years later, that event, described by the Roman historian, Josephus, is as stirring a tale as any told by Shakespeare and has entered into Israeli lore. Today in Israel, when the tank corps is sworn in after completing its training, they repeat the line that is burned into the psyche of every Israeli, "Masada shall not fall again."

If a tape about Gettysburg works for American tourists, I thought, a tape about Masada will be perfect for visitors to Israel. And it could be the beginning of a business of producing videotape tours at other tourist sites, creating another source of revenue for my company.

I even had my answer to Cronkite. The man who would

be perfect as the narrator would be General Yigael Yadin, the tall, thin, debonair, mustachioed, English-mannered archeologist who at age thirty had been the acting commander of the Jewish defense forces in the 1948 War of Independence.

It was Yadin who in the 1960s had led the excavations of Masada. It was Yadin, the gifted storyteller, whose charm and intellect for years had entranced the heads of state and virtually every other VIP visitor to Israel as he personally escorted them across that rocky mountain fortress, pointing out the remnants of the synagogue, the ritual baths, the storerooms, and other reminders of lives and events that reached back twenty centuries.

Yadin's voice was clipped and very British. His explanations were crisp and understated as he guided his guests around the restored archaeological sites and told the story of the Jewish rebellion in such a mesmerizing fashion that the visitor looking out at the Judean desert through the shimmering waves of the heat could easily imagine seeing hundreds of Roman troops below, building the massive ramp for their final assault. They would feel the desperation of the Jews who, watching the Romans' inexorable progress, knew that disaster awaited them while seeing in the eyes of their children the look of trust that everything would somehow be all right. The Jews knew that everything would not be all right. As they looked at their children, they tried to hide their own feelings of hopelessness.

Yadin would relate the story matter-of-factly, its impact intensified by the visitors' knowledge of the inevitable outcome. At the same time, like the children themselves, the visitors would listen hoping that somehow against all logic the Jews would be saved.

Yadin would be perfect, but I didn't know Yadin. Masada

would be perfect, a national treasure like Yosemite or the Grand Canyon, but I didn't know who was in charge of Masada. So I started making phone calls and quickly learned that Masada was part of the National Parks Authority and that the man in charge was Ya'acov Yannai, another war hero. I was learning something else too, that in Israel with its small population and citizen army that had fought three wars in only twenty-four years, just about every man had been in at least one war and that many of those ordinary-looking veterans were reserve commanders and generals.

It wasn't difficult reaching Yannai. In the United States, a prominent person is usually too important to talk to just anybody. In Israel, no Jew is ever intimidated by another Jew. If one Jew is successful, another might still say, "So he has money. Big deal. He's still a schmuck." I had no trouble making an appointment to see Yannai.

I arrived on a humidity-drenched August afternoon in Tel Aviv, hopelessly lost within warrens of look-alike wooden barracks that housed important military and governmental bureaus. After I had wandered around for an hour, hardly able to ask directions in my feeble Hebrew and hopelessly unable to read any of the signs on the different barracks, the tenth stranger I stopped had compassion for me and took me by the arm almost as far as the door to make sure I would stop being lost.

There I found him, Yannai at last, a thin, taciturn man, his face as lined as the fir trees planted by the Jewish National Fund. His hair was combed from right to left, the way men who are balding comb their hair. He wasn't balding, but that's how he combed it. He stared at me impassively. To ingratiate myself, I told him I had just moved my family seven thousand miles to become a fellow Israeli. He didn't look impressed. And the fact is there was no reason for him to be impressed. My comfortable cross-ing of the Atlantic couldn't begin to be compared to what he and just about everyone else in Israel had gone through.

Besides that, Israelis are no-nonsense people who aren't interested in social amenities. I went right to the point.

"I want to produce an audiotape tour of Masada," I told him.

"So does everybody," Yannai said.

"It'll be great for tourists," I said. "Right now they don't know the story. We'll bring it to life, the two-thousand-year-old synagogue, the storehouses, the rooms where they lived, the resistance, the whole story that Josephus writes about."

Not a flicker of response. I told him I would pay for everything myself. It wouldn't cost the Parks Authority a penny. It would even make money for them. It would cre-ate goodwill with tourists.

He still wasn't impressed.

Enough, Yale, I thought to myself, ask for the order.

"I need your approval," I said.

He finally said something. "It's Yigael Yadin's park," he said. "If it's all right with Yadin, it's all right with me."

I finally understood. Yannai wasn't interested in tourists. He wasn't interested in audiotape tours. He wasn't interest-ed in developing parks. Yannai was in charge of parks.

The conversation was over. Yannai stared at me and said nothing.

"Then it's all right with you?" I said.

"Why not?" he answered.

I reached out to shake hands, that silly American way of saying good-bye.

Yannai had already turned away and was busy talking to a secretary. So I left the room. Never mind the handshake. He said it was okay. I was on my way. Now all I had to do was find Yadin.

He was at his desk at the Israel Museum in Jerusalem when I arrived, puffing on his pipe. I soon learned that Yadin was always puffing on his pipe. It jutted out from just below his small crisp mustache.

He was taking off his softly crushed plaid fedora that revealed a bald head. Really bald, not even warranting an effort to comb from right to left. When the fedora was on, as I saw a couple of days later, Yadin looked as if he had just come off the set of *My Fair Lady*. He looked like Rex Harrison's Henry Higgins.

Sitting tall and erect, he puffed away and listened thoughtfully as I explained my idea about Masada. I tried to suppress my anxiety. After all, when Yadin was commanding the Israel Defense Forces in the War of Independence, I was a self-absorbed fraternity boy at Northwestern. Years later when Yadin patiently explained to visiting world leaders the two-thousand-year-old secrets revealed within Masada's archaeology, I was at ABC-TV explaining to advertising agency time-buyers why they should run commercials in our new program, "To Tell the Truth," starring a young comedian named Johnny Carson. And now in 1972, there I was sitting across the desk of that important man.

I didn't feel uneasy or presumptuous because I really thought the idea of creating an audiotape tour of Masada made sense. It would make history come alive for tourists, and it would explain to visitors the centuries-old Jewish connection to the land. In the vernacular of our people, it was good for the Jews.

Best of all, I liked Yadin. I could see that he was carefully considering everything I said. Best of all, I saw that he felt comfortable with me. Before the meeting was over, he agreed to make the audiotape and to take me personally through Masada to record his commentary.

Two days later, in the same dark blue Volvo station wagon that I drove from our house in Winnetka, there I was pulling up in front of Yadin's home on Ramban Street in the Rehavia section of Jerusalem. He was on time, as I knew he would be, already outside and already puffing on his pipe, his crunched-up tattersall hat at a jaunty angle on his head. He was ready to go.

He jumped into the car and we were on our way. I couldn't believe it was happening. Only two months after my arriving in Israel, there was Yigael Yadin, hero of the 1948 war, host to heads of states from all over the world, traveling to Masada with me, just the two of us.

Jerusalem is a small city. It was even smaller in those days. In less than five minutes I drove through its narrow streets and onto the open road leading out to the desert. Yadin and I chatted amicably. I listened with fascination as he shared with me stories of his life in Israel. And yet as I drove on along roads that had pushed aside the hills and the desert, I sensed that something was wrong. I raced on, but could feel a restiveness in that man sitting next to me. On a hunch, I turned and asked him if he'd like to drive. He accepted in a second. Yadin may have been British in his bearing, but deep down he was as tightly wound as all Israelis. My idea of speeding along the highway was not speedy enough for him.

I stopped the car, we changed places, and Yadin pressed down on the accelerator. In an instant we were roaring ahead. Within an hour, we were near the Dead Sea, the lowest point on earth, and then up into the rocky fortress of Masada where Yadin took me still further, two thousand years into the past. I recorded every word he said.

He pointed down, and I felt that I could peer through the dust of centuries and see the Roman forces camping below. He walked me past rocks and stones laid out in careful formations that outlined where the Jews lived and where they worked. Through the brightness of the noon sunlight that splattered across the stony surface, I felt I could actually see those Jews awaiting their fate.

Yadin showed me the piles of rocks that marked the synagogue where Jews prayed facing east toward Jerusalem just as Jews do today. And he showed me where, twenty centuries after the battle of Masada, young Jewish tank lieutenants at a torch-lit midnight ceremony under an eternal sky are sworn into Israel's tank corps.

It was more than I had ever imagined. What I didn't know at the time was how many things happen in Israel that are beyond imagination.

The day after our trip, while Yadin's recording still lay on my desk, the phone rang. It was Yadin.

"Yannai wants to see you," he said.

"Anything important?" I said.

"You'd better go see," Yadin said.

It was obvious there was trouble ahead. I was back in the warren den of Tel Aviv the next day, this time finding my way easily to Yannai's barracks office.

Yannai got right to the point.

"We have problems," Yannai said.

"But Yadin said it's okay," I said. "You said it was Yadin's park."

"It's Yadin's park," Yannai said. "But where you do the business is our business," he said.

"That's not a problem," I said. "We'll put the audiotape display at the entrance where people walk in."

"Not enough room there," Yannai said. "We already have a girl there selling tickets."

"All right," I said. "We'll set up right next to her. How much more room can that take?"

"Too much room," Yannai said. Clearly he was not a conversationalist.

"Okay," I said. "We'll set up where people enter the cable car."

"That's worse," he said.

"Where they get *off* the cable car," I implored. "On the top. On the top of the mountain. There's plenty of room on top of the mountain."

"Not *there*," he said. "We can't sell things on Masada. It doesn't look nice." Yannai looked at me with disdain. I could hear him thinking, "What kind of a person are you?"

Yannai didn't mind if Yadin wanted to record an audio-tape. Yadin didn't mind if I wanted to produce it. He just didn't have a place for me to rent it. Close to a thousand Jews had once lived on top of Masada and two thousand Romans managed to hang out at the bottom for a couple of years, but for my little rental stand there wasn't enough room.

I gave it one last try. "We'll set up a stand in the parking lot," I said, "where people are driving in. There's plenty of room in the parking lot."

"In the parking lot," Yannai said, "you might get run over."

Never mind being run over, I thought to myself, I'm being run out. For sure, my patience had run out. I began yelling at him. I don't usually yell at people, but for him I made an exception. "I thought we had a deal," I yelled, "that if it was alright with Yadin, it was alright with you."

"We don't have a deal," he said, confirming what was already obvious. "We'll have to hold a public tender," he said.

"Why suddenly a tender?" I snapped. "Until I walked in here nobody ever produced a tour. Nobody ever worked with Yadin. And now that I gave you the idea, you're going to have a public tender?"

Yannai just went on. ". . . and we'll let everyone make a bid. Then we'll decide who we want."

It was obvious it wouldn't be me. I turned to go, feeling like a balloon when the air goes out.

"*L'hitraot*," he called out behind me, the Hebrew equivalent of "so long."

I answered him in Anglo-Saxon.

For a second time in history, Masada was lost.

I was furious as I drove back to Jerusalem. Masada was one of the country's biggest tourist attractions. General Yadin was one of the most impressive people in Israel. And I let the whole thing get away from me. I was burning with anger, but at the same time I knew I was on to something. I knew I had an idea that was waiting to happen. Where else could I do this? I thought to myself as I drove home.

Within a couple of days I came up with the answer, the place that had captured my imagination the first time I saw it—the Shrine of the Book at the Israel Museum. The building itself suggests the sense of mystery within. It is not a shrine at all in the literal sense. It is not a place of worship. And yet it evokes a feeling of wonder because it houses the Dead Sea Scrolls, documents that bear the words of Isaiah and other Jewish prophets copied onto papyrus and parchment scrolls more than two thousand years ago by a Jewish sect that lived near the Dead Sea.

A Bedouin shepherd found those scrolls, hidden in clay jars, within a cave in 1947. That was the same year that the United Nations voted to create a Jewish state. The words of redemption that Isaiah wrote two thousand years earlier were discovered at virtually that same moment in history when the Jews fulfilled his vision and returned to their ancient homeland. It was eerie to contemplate. Things like that seem to happen in Israel.

News of the discovery soon came to the attention of a famous Israeli archaeologist who immediately understood the importance of those scrolls and took steps to acquire them for the museum. The archaeologist was my new friend, Yigael Yadin.

The Shrine of the Book fascinated me. The structure is part of the Israel Museum, which in itself is a remarkable story. The museum was new, only seven years old at the time. Jerusalem Mayor Teddy Kollek had started it in 1965, a time when the city needed housing, better streets, community centers, and jobs for the Jews it had rescued from Arab countries and Europe. But Teddy thought that was no excuse for not having a museum. He had grown up in Vienna where culture was a part of life. What is a great city without a museum?

"There was a lot of opposition," Teddy's secretary, Shula Eisner, told me as she reminisced about those early days of the state. "The country was facing so many other problems. But Teddy was determined."

"If we hadn't started soon," Teddy confided years later, "it would have been impossible. If we had waited until all the problems were solved, we still wouldn't have a museum, but we would still have problems."

Meyer Meir, who worked with Teddy during the early days of the museum, had his own insights into Teddy's feelings. He illustrated it with the tale of a Chinese man, terribly hungry, who had earned two sous. With one, he bought himself some bread. With the other, he bought a flower. When friends asked him why he didn't spend it all on food, he told them that he used one sou to feed his body and the other to feed his soul. There wasn't much food or anything else in Israel in those days, but Teddy felt it was important to nourish the soul.

So only seventeen years after Israeli independence, Teddy Kollek began to build the Israel Museum. Its modern architecture blends seamlessly into the ancient Judean hills. As you enter the grounds of the museum, you immediately see the Shrine of the Book, a large white dome that suggests the lids that covered the clay urns in which the parchments were found. Opposite stands a black basalt wall. The contrasting colors and shapes, the purity of the white dome so near the boldness of the black wall, recall the spirit of the ancient Jews who saw themselves as the forces of light struggling against the forces of darkness.

To enter it I walked down a stone staircase that brought me into a long, dark corridor that evoked the feeling of entering the cave where the scrolls were discovered. I followed its narrow path that led me past dimly lit displays of relics found in those ancient caves. The corridor then opened into a large, circular room that recalls the shape of the urns in which the scrolls were preserved. In the center is a circular display case illuminating the words of the Isaiah scroll. Nearby is a smaller case displaying part of the original scroll itself. In front of the displays stood Israeli children effortlessly reading and understanding this ancient script that was their heritage and yet twenty centuries later was still relevant to their lives.

I felt I was touching eternity to see the words of Isaiah and other prophets that artisans had meticulously copied into those scrolls so long ago, writings that are studied today in the same land by the descendants of those prophets.

It was ironic. Secular pioneers had been the driving force in the rebirth of Israel to shape a Zionist future for the Jewish people, where Jews would live the way all other people live in a normal country with its scholars, its scientists, its madmen and even its prostitutes. In doing so, they had released a mystical force within the ancient country of the Jews, the spiritual past of Jewish history. I was beginning to intuit that there may be wisdom more visible to the soul than to the mind.

Exploring these feelings, I realized how ignorant I was of the history revealed in those ancient documents. And I knew thousands of visitors would be as ignorant as I was. Even after looking at the scrolls.

One scroll in a display case was labeled Manual of Discipline. What on earth was that? Another scroll was identified as the Habakkuk Commentary, but how many people had ever heard of Habakkuk, a minor prophet who six centuries before the Common Era railed against the same iniquities that still plague people today. In another display case, an opened parchment was identified as the Thanksgiving Day scroll. I had no idea what that was either, but I knew that like me every visiting American would read that and start thinking about turkeys.

Once again, I turned to Yadin. Once again, I found him in his office at the museum. He greeted me warmly. Yadin had lived among Israelis too long to be surprised by my problems at Masada. He had also seen too much of life, and death, to get upset over my audiotape tour.

I didn't need commiseration. I was already excited about my latest idea.

I told him immediately that I thought the exhibit of the Dead Sea Scrolls was remarkable and profoundly moving. But what a pity, I told him, that hardly anyone seeing them understood their significance or their place in Jewish ethics and Jewish history. As I heard my own words coming out like an assault, I was shocked at what I heard. I already sounded like an Israeli, blunt and direct.

"We have to produce an audiotape tour to explain all this," I told Yadin. I didn't have to pound the desk. My voice was doing enough pounding. For a moment, I feared I was beginning to sound like Professor Harold Hill in the Broadway production, *The Music Man*, as he told the ladies that "what this town needs is a band, a brass band!"

The smoke puffed up into small clouds from Yadin's pipe. As usual, he was listening closely. And as usual he made up his mind quickly. "Okay, Yale," he said. "I'll do it."

"Great," I said, jumping up and slamming my hand down on his desk. That time I really did hit his desk. I had planned to be more reserved, but the excitement of the new project, following so soon after my defeat at Masada, was too much to contain.

Yadin tried to contain it. "But remember," he said, "we need the permission of the museum director." I don't know how I looked at that moment, but however I looked, Yadin immediately saw my apprehension. He stood up and put his arm on my shoulder. "Don't worry," he said. "Go see Danny Gelmond. It'll be okay."

Danny had been a fighter in Israel's pre-state ragtag army, the *Haganah*. He was a huge hulk of a man who overflowed the austere Israeli chair behind his desk. Being an Israeli, he was not upset that I had simply walked into his office unannounced except for a mild knocking at the door. Danny liked people in general, and he particularly liked new immigrants, impressed by anyone who would link his fate with his fellow Israelis. I told Danny what I wanted to do. My heart sank as I listened to his reaction.

"You're making a mistake," Danny said.

I started arguing with him. I couldn't believe this was happening to me again.

"But it will help people understand what they're seeing," I said.

"I know that," he said. "I'm not worried about that."

I braced myself for what was coming. Danny hunched toward me, his thick arms stretching out from his short-sleeve white shirt. Danny laid out his concern.

"The idea makes sense," he said, covering my hand with his thick hand that was about twice as large as mine.

"So there's no problem," I said, trying to make the hesitation that was in the air go away.

Danny squeezed my hand. He meant to squeeze my hand, but he was almost crushing it. "I'm worried about you," Danny said.

"Now what's going on?" I thought. Some polite letdown?

"I'm not sure it's a business," Danny said. "What if the idea doesn't work? What if you lose your money?"

"I'll take my chances," I said, trying to figure out where he was coming from. I was annoyed he was throwing up barriers to my idea. At the same time, I was wondering if this complete stranger was really worrying about this new immigrant. Was that possible? I studied him closely.

His massive head atop broad shoulders generated a feeling of relentless power, and yet his broad smile made him look like a big uncle.

"Look," he said. "You're new here. It's not so easy in Israel. You have to be careful."

"I also have to make a living," I said.

Danny laughed. "You call that a living?"

That's how people talk in Israel.

"You're a nice guy, Yale," Danny said, "but you're out of your mind."

"So?" I said.

Danny held out a huge hand. "So good luck," he said and shook what was left of my hand. Then he stood up and looked at me straight in the eyes. "Be careful," he said.

In those days, audiotape tours were still a new idea. Most museums didn't use them. The Metropolitan Museum of Art in New York was first trying them out. Even the equipment was not sophisticated. In Jerusalem, I began with unwieldy audiotape players that the tourist carried in one hand while trying with the other hand to keep the listening device in his ear from falling out.

We set up a display case at the entrance to the Shrine of the Book and gave students working their way through university a percentage of income to encourage them to make money. The first week, we made money. The second week, we made a little more. Tourists not only rented our tours, but often asked if they could buy them to take home, so we began selling them as well. We kept making money, the students were making money, and the museum received a percentage. It was good for everybody.

I was on my way. Now it was time for some promotion. I had seen in the tourist offices racks of brochures describing hotels, historical sites, tours of the Old City, restaurants, and everything else a tourist would look for. I thought we should have a promotion piece about the Shrine of the Book audiotape tour. I went ahead and produced five thousand glossy cards designed with handsome graphics and printed in attractive colors describing the audiotape tour of the Dead Sea Scrolls at the Shrine of the Book, narrated by the famous Yigael Yadin. As a special inducement, I even offered a 25-percent discount to anyone presenting one of the cards.

My plan was to distribute the cards through the hotels and best of all through the tourist offices. One day, clutching a handful of them, I strode over to the tourist office where I even knew the man in charge, Uzi Michaeli, whom I had met when he worked for the Israel Consulate in Chicago.

In his office I proudly slid one of the cards across his desk. "Here's another perk you can offer tourists," I told him. "Everyone has heard of the Dead Sea Scrolls and now they can hear Yadin himself explain what they're all about." I paused. "At a discount yet." Another pause. "And it won't cost you a penny."

No reaction. I went on, undeterred. "We even made them the exact dimensions to fit the racks in your tourist offices. All you have to do is put them in along with the other brochures."

"Okay," Uzi said.

"You mean it's all right?" I said.

"I mean okay, it won't cost us a penny."

"That's good," I assured him.

"That's a problem," Uzi said. He paused and looked at me wearily, as if this was not the first time he had tried to explain the ways of the Middle East. "You see, the job of the tourist office is to promote tourism. Now if you had come to us with your idea to produce audiotapes for tourists and had asked us for a loan of ten thousand shekels so you could make them, I probably could have helped you. We have money to help people build tourism." He paused again and looked at me closely to be sure I was following him. No point continuing unless I was getting it.

"But, Yale," he said, "you're not asking for money. That's a problem."

Suddenly my thoughts flashed back to Yannai. Was this déjà vu all over again? And how do you say déjà vu in Hebrew?

All my newfound Israeli bravado seeped out of me. I was puzzled. I was meek. "But Uzi," I said, "I just want you to put the cards in your racks."

I could see the compassion in his face.

"I'll ask the committee," he said.

Franz Kafka meets *Catch-22*.

"Isn't there just one human being we can talk to?" I said.

"There are no human beings," Uzi said. "Only commit-tees."

I felt an impenetrable wall rise up between Uzi and me. I gave up.

"All right," I said. "Turn it over to the committee."

I walked out feeling completely depressed. What was I

doing in this crazy country? What was so terrible about America? And as for Uzi, I could already see the future. After all, what is the purpose of a committee except to say no anonymously?

I walked down the street remembering that old line that a camel is a horse created by a committee. I began to wonder if that's why there are so many camels in Israel.

Within two months, I had my answer. The committee had voted no. By then I had overcome my sense of defeatism and was ready to do battle again. I returned to Uzi's office.

"There must be someone I can talk to," I insisted.

"How can you talk to a committee?" he said.

"But there must be a head of a committee," I said.

He smiled at me sympathetically like a father being patient with the simple son. "It's a committee," he said. "Everybody's equal."

"But someone must at least conduct the meeting," I said.

"All right," Uzi said, worn down by my persistence. "You can call Mordechai."

"Who's Mordechai?" I said.

"He's the guy who does what he wants after the committee tells him what to do."

I was too worn out to try to understand how that happens, and I was getting to the point where I didn't care. Uzi scratched out the phone number anyway.

I was resigned. "I'll call Mordechai," I said. And the next day I did.

Even that became a major undertaking. First I had to wait until his phone stopped being busy. Phone lines were scarce in those days and people often waited months until they got one. So people like Mordechai only had one line, the same line his secretary used to order tea and talk to her mother.

I kept trying. At last an answer, and I quickly asked for Mordechai. The secretary said he was out and hung up. Obviously taking messages was not part of her job description. I called right back before the line could get busy again and barked out a message before she could hang up.

It didn't matter. Several days went by before I figured out that Mordechai didn't return calls, which is probably why his secretary hung up without asking for a message. So one day, I just walked in to Mordechai's office. I had already learned that is what people do in Israel. Even though the telephone had been invented, people don't use it to set up meetings. People just walk in if they want to have a meeting. I was lucky that day. Mordechai was there.

He was very nice. Most Israelis are nice. A little difficult, but nice. He knew all about my discount cards. He assured me there was nothing he could do. The committee said no. "Not only that," he continued. "But they were right."

"Mordechai," I said. "I know I'm in a different country, a guest in someone else's house so to speak."

"We're all in the same house," Mordechai assured me.

"I know I have to learn to do things the Israeli way," I said.

"Not to learn," he said with a sweep of his hand.

"I don't mean to sound patronizing," I said as I heard myself sound patronizing, "but in the United States, if we have a problem, we don't just say 'no.' We don't just say 'nothing can be done.' We start all over again and say, 'We have a problem. Now how do we solve the problem?'"

"So what's your problem, Yale?"

"You know what my problem is," I said. "I can't put my cards in your tourist offices."

"That's right," he said.

"But you have everyone else's brochures there," I said. "What's wrong with my cards?" I started to lose my patience. "I'm helping tourism! I'm helping Israel! What's the problem?"

He didn't take his eyes off me as he reached for my discount card at the side of his desk. He didn't take his eyes off me as he placed the card in front of me and pointed to the bottom of it. "It says here, 'The Shrine of the Book.'"

"That's right," I said.

"But it doesn't say, 'Available at.'"

"But if I list the location, it implies that it's available at." I was almost shouting at that point.

"Not to imply, Yale," he said.

"You mean, Mordechai, that if I add the words 'available at,' you'll put the cards in your tourist offices?"

Mordechai pushed himself back in his chair and threw out his hands expansively. "Why not?"

And that's what happened. The tourist office put up our discount cards with the added words, "available at," our business was doing well, and everything was humming along. I was making a small contribution to my new country, I was helping kids work their way through college, and I was adding a new revenue stream to the film business. What's so difficult about moving to a new country? I thought. Momentarily.

But nothing exceeds like success. Instead of just letting things be, I was already thinking about a new idea, an idea so obvious that I wondered why I hadn't thought of it before. The Western Wall, the most holy spot in Jewish history.

It marks the place where once stood the Holy Temple of the Jews. Religious Jews from all over the world follow the Biblical injunction to gather there three times a year— for Passover, Shavuot, and Sukkoth. Joseph and Mary brought Jesus to the Temple when it stood there.

No doubt about it. With all that history and all those

tourists, the Western Wall was the perfect place for an audiotape tour. Its rows of stone, assembled without mortar, rise to a height of fifty-eight feet, evoke history and inspire awe among the worshipers below. The largest blocks of stone weigh more than a hundred tons. The lower stones are about three-and-a-half feet high and ten feet long. Some stretch out as much as thirty-nine feet.

When the temple stood, that wall loomed up almost twice as high as it does today. Nineteen rows of stone still lie buried, still unexcavated, beneath the feet of today's worshipers. I thought about how intimidating that wall must have been to people living twenty centuries earlier and gazing up at the Western Wall that reached up more than one hundred feet above them. And higher still, above that wall, worshipers saw the majestic Holy Temple.

It was a time before people were inured to majesty, before flying 35,000 feet above mountaintops reduced those mountaintops to insignificance, a time before 100-story buildings conditioned people to look down at others instead of up at the heavens. I tried to imagine the sense of awe a person must have felt standing at that site centuries ago.

There was so much that an audiotape tour could tell. What an opportunity, I thought, to explain the source of those feelings, the history of that past.

On Yom Kippur in the days of the Temple, the *cohanim*, the priests, entered the inner chamber, the Holy of Holies, to invoke forgiveness for the Jewish people. Tradition holds that the *Schechinah*, the divine spirit, dwelled there. Many friends who visited me in Israel, Christians as well as Jews, have told me about feeling God's presence, that sense of the *Schechinah*, at the Western Wall.

And yet, as with the scrolls at the Israel Museum, I sensed that few visitors seemed to know much about the Wall. They felt the emotion, but knew little about its significance.

I decided to see if my hunch was right by stopping people at the Western Wall and conducting my own personal survey. The question-and-answer session went something like this:

Q: How do you like being here?

A: Fantastic. It's just fantastic.

Q: (Pointing to the Wall) What would you say that is?

A: (Look of incredulity at being asked such an obvious question) The Wall. The Wailing Wall. I mean, the Western Wall.

Q: What do you think that wall was?

A: Are you being funny? Part of the Temple. Something like that.

Q: Which temple are you talking about?

A: What do you mean which temple? The temple. The Jews had a temple there.

I would thank the tourists and make a careful retreat. They were just like me and most other tourists who want to see all the sights when they travel. I remembered my own visits to Rome.

"The Church of St. Peter," the sign said. I would look up at the Church of St. Peter, glance at my tour book, and skim over a few facts. "Very impressive," I would think. "The Church of St. Peter." I didn't absorb much more, but it was one of the things I was supposed to see in Italy.

Now I had a chance to make things better for tourists at the Western Wall. An audiotape tour would tell them everything.

It didn't take me long to find the rabbi in charge. He sat in the Ministry of Religious Affairs in one of the many small depressing rooms called offices. A clutter of religious texts were scattered across his desk, their Hebrew titles embossed in gold against bindings of blue and black and maroon.

The rabbi himself seemed to reflect the disarray, the

metal frames of his glasses slightly bent, his shoulders slightly bent, his stained tie hanging down from a worn, oversize collar. His face was weary, but welcoming.

"*Lekennes,* come in," he said when he saw me at the doorway.

I sat down cautiously on a rickety wooden chair, carefully pulled it toward him and explained my idea, that an audiotape tour would enrich tourists' visits, educate them about Jewish history, and even make a little money for the Ministry of Religious Affairs. To my surprise, he seemed interested in the idea. At least that was my impression.

That's all I had, an impression, because he began speaking in Yiddish, which I didn't understand at all, then switched to Hebrew, which I understood sporadically. I answered in my tortured Hebrew, which seemed to torture him as he strained to understand me. Then I switched to English, which he understood about as well as I understood his Hebrew. Freely translated, what I think he said was:

"Of course, you mustn't set up your display case near the Wall. It would be disrespectful."

"I agree," I said. "I want to be respectful."

He got up and walked over to a large drawing of the Temple compound where the Wall stood. He pointed to a location far off to the side. "Over there would be all right," he said.

"But people don't pass by over there," I said.

He tipped his head slightly to one side, studied the drawing carefully, and idly pulled on his earlobe that was bushy with black hair. He looked to where he had pointed and nodded. "You're right," he said.

"Maybe on top of the staircase," I said. "The one by the *souk.* There were two staircases going down toward the Western Wall and a third entrance by the Dung Gate. At least a third of the people had to pass by the staircase I had in mind. And it was a respectful distance from the Wall.

"That's an idea," he said.

I was trying to figure out if his response was an agreement or an evasion. I remembered what my old girlfriend, Meta Mittleman, told me years ago about how she would respond to baby pictures of babies who were not so attractive, but that proud parents insisted on showing her. "Did you ever see such a beautiful baby?" they would ask. Meta would nod her head. "*That's* a baby!" she would exclaim. The parents would beam with delight. "*That's* a baby" made them happy, and it spared Meta from telling a white lie.

I wondered whether the rabbi's "That's an idea!" was similar obfuscation.

"Go see the rabbi at the end of the hall," my rabbi told me.

"What does he do?" I asked.

"He's in charge of things like that," my rabbi said.

"But I thought you were . . ."

He smiled at me, an understanding smile. A patient smile. "I'm in charge, too."

"Thank you," I said, feeling like Alice in Wonderland.

"And send me a letter," he called out after me.

"I'll send you a letter," I called back as I wandered down the hall, moving slowly from one office to another, my lips forming the sounds of the letters written on the signs outside the doors as I tried to find letters that spelled out the name of my next rabbi.

I found him. During the next nine months, I found several other rabbis as well, three lawyers, two accountants and a treasurer. I felt like an archaeologist unearthing the hidden mysteries of a society. It seemed that no meeting was ever the last meeting. It seemed that no matter how much authority a man had, he would invariably refer the matter to another official. And at each encounter, there would be endless forms and questionnaires.

The Bible had promised the Jews that they would be as numerous as the stars in the heavens and the sands of the earth. In Israel, the only thing that seems to have approximated that promise is not the number of Jews, but rather the number of papers they have to fill out.

Each aliyah, each period of immigration to Israel, had brought to the country the influence of new immigrants. The ones from Eastern Europe filled Israel with bureaucracy and minutiae. The German immigrants were more organized. They took the minutiae and gave it structure. They codified the chaos and encased it within impenetrable procedures. If the committee had not already been invented, Israel would have invented it. Israel was a bureaucracy pretending to be a country.

Everyone liked discussing decisions but no one wanted to make one. And even when I got what seemed to be a decision, even if I got an agreement, I had already learned to question whether it was real. In studying Israeli history, I had come across the story about Levi Eshkol, Israel's second prime minister, who is reputed to have once said, "Of course, I promised him. But I didn't promise to keep my promise." It wasn't that people were trying to be deceitful. Instead it was something of a world outlook, that in the great sweep of things, life is change, and that while a person should make an agreement and, of course, honor the agreement, on the other hand—and then the changes begin.

Maybe it was simply a matter of history. Many of the founding fathers—Ben-Gurion, Levi Eshkol, Haim Bar-Lev, and others—had come to Israel from the *shtetls*, the small villages of Poland and Russia. While their struggle to create an Israeli nation was an act of vision and intellect, their internalized past was the *shtetl*. Maybe they could only think of Israel, smaller than the state of Maryland, as a country, yes, but, a *shtetl* just the same.

That was the heritage that confronted me as I tried to get approval for my audiotape tour of the Western Wall. No matter. I finally got it. By then the search for a decision had traveled full circle. The original rabbi was satisfied because the higher rabbi had approved it after he, in turn, had been assured by the controller that he had no objection because the lawyer had told him it was all right with him because he had heard it had the approval of the original rabbi. Whatever. The decision was made, and it was in my favor. Cautious after my handshake deal on Masada, I made sure I had a contract this time that was approved and signed by everyone concerned. This time nothing could go wrong.

By the time the contract was ready, so was I. I had searched out Israel's leading expert on the Wall and from him learned everything there was to learn, its history, archaeology, and religious significance. I wrote the text and rewrote the text, walking from one end of the Wall to the other and into its underground excavations, pacing the distance carefully, timing each segment, and laying out clear instructions for the user so the recorded explanation would play out at just the right time as he traveled the prescribed route. Satisfied at last that the instructions were clear, that the information was accurate, and that the timings were realistic, I had the script translated from English into Hebrew, French, and German and recorded announcers reading those scripts in all four languages. I had a special display case designed and constructed to show off the tape recorders through clear plastic doors. I had plastic signs printed in four languages and hired a young college student to make the sales. Not a moment was lost. The same day that I finally received the contract, I was ready.

My salesman and I pushed the heavy display case up the

incline from the parking lot to the Wall and then carried it up fifty stairs to the place where we had permission to work and where at least a third of the tourists had to walk by. Everything was in place. We could begin the next day.

Early the next morning, my salesman and I hurried to our location, eager to start our new business. Impatiently we drove to the wall, parked the car, ran across the open plaza, and dashed up the stairs to our display case. To our horror, we found it flung over on its side and all its windows smashed.

I was shocked. I turned to the soldier standing guard at the stairs. I assumed that as long as he was guarding the Western Wall, he would also guard my display case that was just twenty feet from him.

"What happened?" I called out in Hebrew. I was already fluent in sentences of two words or less.

He turned out his palms and hunched his shoulders upward, Israeli for "who knows?"

I was furious. I snapped out the words. "I'll call the police," I said.

He looked at me, surprised. "They're the ones who did it," he said.

"But I have permission," I said. "I have permission to be here."

"Do you have *their* permission?" the soldier asked. "You have to have *their* permission."

"Not again," I thought. "Is there no end to permissions in this country?"

I had spent nine months getting written permission from the Ministry of Religious Affairs, the governmental body in charge of the Western Wall. You can't get more permissioned than that. At least that's what I thought. "Why didn't they at least call me?" I said.

Again the soldier hunched up his shoulders and turned

his palms upwards.

"Never mind," I called back as I raced down the stairs and over to police headquarters. I shoved the door open and kept moving forward as I called out, "Who's in charge here?"

Someone pointed toward a staircase. I bolted up, found a man in a uniform sitting behind a desk and immediately turned on him.

"Are you in charge?" I asked.

"Maybe," he said. I grabbed a chair and pulled it up close to his desk, leaning forward as close as I could get.

"I have permission to rent audiotape tours at the top of the stairs and somebody . . ."

His palms turned out, just like the soldier. Then he leaned forward toward me. I could see this was no bureaucrat. I could see that this guy was serious.

"Listen," he said, "a terrorist could break into your case at night and put an explosive in one of those recorders."

"Then we'll take the recorders out of the case at night," I said.

"A terrorist could rent one of your recorders and return it with an explosive inside," he said.

"If a terrorist wants to plant a small explosive somewhere," I shot back, "he doesn't need my recorder. He can leave it in a prayer shawl right where everyone is praying. He can put it in one of the charity boxes. He can hide it inside a hollowed-out prayer book. He doesn't need my recorders!"

"We can't be too careful," the man said.

I stood up impatiently.

"On the other hand . . ." the man said.

I looked back at him, still naïve enough to think I could work my way out of this disaster.

"You could put your display case at the far end of the

plaza," he said.

"But tourists don't walk past the far end of the plaza," I said.

Once again, the shoulders hunched up, the palms turned outward.

I walked away defeated. I tried to understand what happened. I thought to myself that if one man doesn't promise to keep a promise, why should a second man promise to keep the promise of the first man? A question for a Talmudic scholar, I thought, and I was no Talmudic scholar. I wasn't even a purveyor of audiotape tours. I wasn't even in business. Stonewalled at the Wall, my epitaph.

I walked away despairing. I had lost nine months and a bunch of money at the Western Wall. I had lost four months and less money at Masada. I had succeeded at the Shrine of the Book, and that was making money. I was finding clients for my film business, and that was okay. On balance, not great, but I was making a living.

The longer I lived in Israel, the better I understood the country's gallows humor.

First man: How's business?

Second man: You call that a business?

Chapter 16

My Not So Military Career

*W*here you sit has a lot to do with where you stand.

I never dreamed I'd be standing, figuratively at least, next to Charlton Heston. Just because we went to the same university didn't mean we'd have identical ideas about everything. I certainly never shared his passion for guns.

But one day things changed, and there I was, just like Charlton Heston, waving a rifle around. I even fired it once.

It all began when Israel asked its citizens to sign up for Mishmar Ezrachi, civilian guard duty. I remembered things like that from World War II. I was too young to be in the army, and my dad was too old, but he did join the civilian guard. Sometimes I'd go along to keep him company. His job was to walk around our neighborhood carrying a big flashlight.

Looking back, I'm not quite sure what they expected him to do. People didn't worry about terrorists back then. The only thing they worried about was an air raid, which in our case was unlikely since Oak Park was about a thousand miles from the Atlantic and two thousand miles from the Pacific.

On the other hand, you never know.

So he was out there doing his duty. Just in case there was an air raid and Oak Park would be blacked out, my dad was at the ready with his flashlight.

It seemed the right thing to do, to help guard your neighborhood. Like my dad before me, I, too, volunteered.

That's where the rifle came in. In Israel, you don't walk around carrying a flashlight. You walk around carrying a rifle.

I had never even seen a rifle except in the movies or on television. I came from a home where we wouldn't kill a fly. Whenever we heard his maniacal buzzing and saw him banging himself against a windowpane, we would carefully reach over to the window and push it open for his convenience. So for me, actually handling a weapon was a big step forward, or backward, depending on how you look at it.

But one day, the civilian guard called me in to not only show me a rifle, but to teach me how to use it. The day I was to appear, I went to a big open field. A lot of people were standing there, patiently waiting in a line. I took my place at the end of the line and waited for someone to call my name. Far out in the field were colorful displays of circles. That was easy to figure out. We were supposed to hit the inner-most circle, the bull's-eye. A lot of people were already there, standing in a long row like people practicing their golf shots. They were firing away at those circles, or at least in that general direction.

I was surprised at how quickly the line kept moving. It wasn't long before I heard someone call out my name. I looked in the direction of the voice and in the distance saw a serious young soldier looking toward me.

I walked over to him with brisk steps, trying to appear at least a little bit militaristic. I told him my name, to reassure him he had the right man. He didn't seem to care. He thrust a rifle into my hands. This was the first time I ever touched one. It was long and smooth and a little heavy. I had never thought about whether a rifle is light or heavy. It was just a rifle.

Next he handed me a metal case small enough to fit into my palm, a little smaller than a pack of cigarettes. The soldier told me that was a magazine. Inside were smooth-beveled cylinders. I had never seen a bullet before, but it didn't take a great leap of imagination to figure out that's what those pointy things inside the magazine were.

Then the soldier showed me how to put the magazine into the rifle. And finally he showed me how to hold the rifle.

I would never admit it to Charlton Heston, but the touch of that rifle was sensuous, as smooth as a woman's thigh. And the metal where your finger pulls the trigger, that was smooth, too, and cold. Just holding the rifle made me feel virile.

The soldier pointed in the direction of a distant target, and I immediately stopped thinking about women. The target he pointed to wasn't one of those big colorful circles. My target was shaped like a man. It was mesmerizing standing there holding that rifle. I felt a surge of power. On the other hand, the sight of a target shaped like a person took some of the fun out of the fantasy. No matter. It was too late to back down. I did the best I could.

I placed my left foot forward to plant myself firmly against the ground and raised the rifle, pushing it up tight against my right shoulder. The soldier stood there waiting. I had the feeling he was expecting more. I pointed my rifle straight ahead, tightened my forefinger around that cold metal trigger, and tried to line up that cardboard man in my gun sight.

I suppose that's easy to do, but not for me. Somehow I

wasn't quite sure whether or not I was aiming directly at the target. I was more like a golfer than a rifleman. I knew it was out there, something like a distant green on a golf course, and I was focused on that faraway spot, not exactly at the tee, but at least in the direction of the green.

I had the feeling that my soldier expected me to be a little more precise.

I couldn't stand there forever thinking about it. So I aimed my rifle somewhere in the vicinity of my cardboard enemy and pulled the trigger. I don't know if I hit my intended victim, but at least I hadn't killed any real people. I looked at the soldier, and he looked at me. He looked relieved. He took the rifle from me and tossed me a slight wave of the hand. "*B'seder*," he said, Hebrew for okay. That was it. One shot and I was part of the civilian guard.

That's how I came to spend a couple of evenings a week feeling my way through the darkness and up and down the 142 stairs of Yemin Moshe, the area right across from the Old City walls.

Yemin Moshe had been a no man's land after the 1948 War of Independence. It was a small valley where squatters lived in makeshift houses between the Jordanians who had driven the Jews out of the Old City and the King David Hotel area controlled by the Israelis. After the war, there was a cease-fire of sorts, which meant that firing went on only occasionally, usually above the heads of the squatters.

Yemin Moshe fell into Jewish hands after the Six Day War and the shelling from the Old City stopped. So Teddy Kollek, who during his twenty-eight years as mayor of Jerusalem was obsessed with beautifying the city, decided to make Yemin Moshe an artist colony.

Poor artists were given subsidized housing to encourage them to move into the area. Jewish squatters who lived there, most of them poor Jews who had fled Arab countries, were paid money to leave. I still remember an old Iraqi woman rocking back and forth on the stone entrance of her house under a trellis of bright green grape leaves, trying to rock away her despair at being forced to move.

For the next twenty years, Yemin Moshe was filled with workers tearing down old hovels, jackhammers chomping into the stone, Arabs building new Jewish houses, and donkeys swaying under bags of heavy gravel as they picked their way down the steep steps, marking their pathway with a trail of dung.

Slowly, house by house, that no man's land with its unobstructed view of the Old City walls became home to painters, silversmiths, artisans, and writers, all subsidized by the municipality. Then with the passage of time, like a variation on Gresham's law, just as the poor artists had driven out the poor squatters, wealthy immigrants from Britain, South Africa, and the United States began to buy homes and drive out most of the poor artists who at least were not poor any more because of the rapid increase in the value of their homes. The neighborhood was just beginning to change in the year that I was assigned to patrol it. On a moonless night, you could hardly see your first step down, let alone the 141 that followed it.

Citizen guards patrolled in pairs. My partner was often Gloria Kramer, a tall, blonde from Chicago who with her husband, Mike, had settled in the area about the same time I did. As Gloria and I trudged forth into the darkness, I was never quite sure if I was supposed to be protecting her or whether she was protecting me. Neither of us had the slightest idea of what we do if we suddenly spotted an armed Arab crouching in the bushes.

Our instructions were to carry the magazine of bullets outside the rifle. I don't know what I could have accomplished if I actually had to use the rifle. By the time I would remember how to insert the magazine, aim the rifle, and fire it, any Arab intruder could have run all the way home and still have time to smoke an entire nargileh of hashish.

Fortunately, no one ever hid in the bushes. Just as well. Gloria and I were such liberal Americans that if we had found an Arab lurking there, we would have probably invited him in for tea.

One night, my civil guard partner was the son of a prominent rabbi, a fervent right-wing nationalist who would repeatedly remind me that even though the Arabs and the Jews are all children of Abraham, the Bible says God gave Israel to the Jews. Period. End of discussion. If it had been up to him, he would have cast out all the Arabs the same way Abraham cast out Hagar.

We talked about things like that as we patrolled deep inside a dark alleyway in the Old City. It was late and silent. Not even the sound of a radio. Shadows disappeared into the stone walls on either side of us, shadows that became apparitions of our imaginations and our fears. Alone in that darkness, you can do a lot of imagining.

As we trod on, one of the shadows evolved into the visage of a tall Arab coming toward us, alone. The rabbi's son, a short, benign-looking young man, stopped the Arab and asked for identification papers. The Arab took them out and handed them over, slowly. His silence was his hostile statement. The rabbi's son examined them slowly. That was his statement. It was like a game of chess, each move deliberate and filled with implications.

After studying the papers, the young man looked up at the Arab and then down again at the papers. I was a step removed from them, watching the chess game. I could sense that the papers were okay and that the Arab was okay, but the game between them stretched on. I wanted to be somewhere else, anywhere else. I wasn't afraid. I was embarrassed. The time it took, the way the young man looked the Arab up and down, the way he made him wait before he would let him pass had nothing to do with guarding Jerusalem. It had everything to do with sending a message. We are the rulers of this land and don't forget it.

My partner shoved the papers back into the Arab's hand, looking only at his hand not at his face, and walked past him. I followed. I don't know who felt more humiliated, the Arab or I. The only difference is that he was probably used to it.

I had never seen an Arab until I moved to Israel. I knew nothing of their history or their culture. But you can't live here without learning all that.

I learned that it's almost impossible to be more gracious and inviting than the shop owners in the Arab *souk* of the Old City. If you enter one of their small stores to examine olive-wood camels, or silver crosses, T-shirts emblazoned with a big Shalom across the front, rings or trinkets, or backgammon sets, or whatever at that moment you are sure you can't live without, they will almost always call over a young boy to bring out a brass tray of small cups filled with sweet coffee or steaming tea flavored with nanna, fresh mint leaves.

Hospitality is a way of life among the Arabs. Perhaps it comes from the culture of the desert, to offer food and drink to the stranger. You even read about that tradition in the Bible when Abraham welcomes the angels to his tent. Abraham may have been a Jew, but he was also a nomad and lived within the culture of a nomadic society, the same culture as the Arabs who back in the seventh century emerged as a people from the sands that are now Saudi Arabia. That tradition remains deeply ingrained in today's Arab culture.

One day I picked up two Israeli soldiers who were

Druse, an Arab sect with its own secret religious traditions. Their homes were not far off the main highway. I thought nothing of turning off the road and taking them right to their door. As they got out, I waved goodbye, but they refused to let me leave until they had brought me into their home and introduced me to their father.

When they entered their home, the first thing they did was to greet him and kiss his hands and then tell them about their new friend. The father motioned me to sit down. To do otherwise would have been an insult. I sat down and immediately saw a young Arab girl peeking at me from behind a curtain in their living room while other girls brought out fresh pitas and platters of desserts shining with honey.

The Arabs are not only hospitable, they are charming. They have a flair for captivating virtually every prospective buyer, smiling at a pretty girl, putting their hand around the shoulder of a young man, or whispering into the ear of a housewife that they have a special price just for her, all the while mesmerizing the tourists and selling the merchandise. How can anyone not succumb to such charm?

Other Arabs I met were the workmen, the ones who move in your furniture, who fix your walls, and who at six o'clock in the morning collect your garbage. We were happy, and they seemed happy or at least reconciled to the world around them. For centuries, the Arabs have seen conquerors come and go. The Arabs of today, in my own lifetime, have been ruled by the British and then the Jews. They are experienced at adjusting to new rulers, quietly confident that each will disappear just as each disappeared during the centuries gone by.

But even when I first arrived in Israel, I could see the beginnings of change. Arab acquiescence to Israeli rule was slowly evolving into resentment and then to anger and finally to hate. But back then, even though there were occasional acts of terrorism, the tenor of daily contact was benign.

Rosalind and I often took friends into the Arab part of the Old City at night to have dinner at an Arab restaurant. My film crew and I would eat lunches of hummus and tehinah with Arabs in Ramallah. A number of my friends socialized with Arabs and entertained them in their homes. One night, I even found myself at a dinner sitting next to Elias Freij, the Arab mayor of Bethlehem.

At the same time, there were incidents that revealed the deeper feelings of many Arabs, feelings that at first I was too naïve to acknowledge. Like the time I took the family into the West Bank for a picnic and, finding an empty area under some beautiful olive trees, decided to stop and put out our things. We got out of the car, opened the rear of the station wagon, and began to take out our baskets of food. Suddenly from nowhere, little Arab children appeared and started throwing stones at us.

It never occurred to me that that isolated empty space was someone's land, but there they were throwing stones. I didn't know where the children came from, and I had no idea what to do with them when an Arab man appeared and motioned for the children to stop. At the same time, with a nod of his head, he motioned for me to leave. I herded everyone back into our car and drove away.

These were not the friendly Arabs of the *souk*, and this was sixteen years before the first intifada. Only in retrospect did I begin to understand the sensibilities. This is our land, not your land, all of it, they were saying. This was the message beneath the surface, beneath the politeness, beneath the hospitality. It was not much different with Elias Freij. At the dinner table, he was charming. Freij was a Bethlehem merchant who almost by accident ended up becoming mayor. He had many friends among the Israelis as well as among the Arabs, and that night at my friends' house I certainly felt he was my friend. But months later, when I interviewed him with my film crew and started asking him some pointed questions about the PLO, he jumped up, pulled the microphone off his lapel and abruptly left the room, calling back over his shoulder that the interview was over.

The tensions were more obvious in the Gaza Strip. The first time I filmed there, I had to stop for gas. Gaza then was like Gaza today, a hellhole of poverty, people living in shacks of aluminum sidings, inadequate sewers, insufficient water, and every other misery you could think of. Egypt had grabbed Gaza away from the Palestinians in the aftermath of the Israel War of Independence in 1948. And then they lost it to the Israelis in 1967.

In 1979 when Sadat made peace with Israel, he demanded and got back every bit of his "holy land," but he was clever enough to not insist on taking back Gaza.

Gaza, you couldn't give away.

I didn't know much about Gaza the first time I filmed there. As my gas gauge flirted with empty, I didn't know how difficult it would be to find a gas station there. And when I finally found one, Yehoram tapped me on the shoulder and told me it would be a good idea to first drive to a nearby army base and pick up an Israeli soldier to accompany us.

It seemed a waste of time to me and, more importantly, a waste of our declining supply of gasoline. But since Yehoram had fought in the 1967 war and I hadn't, I thought it would be prudent to listen to him. I followed his advice, drove over to the army base, asked them to loan us a soldier, and then finally went to fill up the tank. I had hardly turned off the motor when the soldier took a position next to the car, his legs spread wide, holding a rifle across those legs, and standing next to the Arab pumping gas. Even I could figure out this must be dangerous territory. And that was thirty years ago.

But day to day, in Jerusalem or Tel Aviv, the tension lay hidden. Sure you passed the Daheisha refugee camp near Bethlehem enclosed in its wire cage that reached up higher than anybody could climb and where, behind that cage, dirty children and mothers scrambled around like animals in a zoo. It was terrible but in a way not much different from the cages called tenements that I used to see from the elevated train I rode from Oak Park to the Loop when I was a kid. I'd look out through the grime of the train windows and see staring out from the grime of the tenement windows a disheveled mother holding a wriggling infant against rusted iron bars, trying to find some air to breathe on a stifling August day.

Another day I'd see an unshaven young man in an undershirt sitting in the window of his one-room apartment, sitting there motionless, looking out at our train from empty eyes. Every trip to the Loop would be like that with all those people staring out from their hopelessness. Then the train would race on, and all that misery would slip away, and I wouldn't have to think about it very much. Chicago, Jerusalem, it's pretty much the same. We shut out the Blacks or the Arabs or anyone else whose plight makes us uncomfortable.

On Saturday afternoons when we gathered with friends at the *Shabbat* table, everyone had strong ideas about what to do. Some people resented the Arabs. Some people thought we should do more to help them. But the one thing everyone seemed to agree on was how ungrateful they were. After all, they certainly had better lives in Israel than their Arab brothers had in Jordan or Saudi Arabia or wherever. What were they so upset about?

Meanwhile, the problems of the Middle East continued as they had for centuries past. My footnote to that history was my small role helping patrol the streets. Sometimes I even took turns guarding the synagogue. Nothing ever happened, but I was prepared, or at least tried to look prepared. After a while, I no more thought about carrying a rifle than carrying a loaf of bread.

That's how I arrived home one Friday night after finishing my guard duty at the synagogue, running up the stairs and clutching my rifle. I opened the door, kissed Becca and David who were standing there to greet me, and then taking a couple steps forward saw a short, friendly looking middle-aged woman wearing a beige and white plaid suit. For some reason, she reminded me of the photos in *Hadassah Magazine*. In any case, it was obvious she was there for dinner that night.

Our guests for *Shabbat* included friends from Jerusalem and tourists visiting Israel and friends of friends who had given our names to their friends. There were times I suspected we were listed in the tourist directory. We had become something of a curiosity, this family that had actually moved to Israel. So by the time I met Mrs. Klein, I wasn't surprised to see someone I had never met before.

Rosalind came forward to introduce me. Mrs. Klein greeted me pleasantly, and I stepped toward her to greet her pleasantly. As I reached out to shake hands, I forgot that my right hand was still clasped around the rifle. Mrs. Klein leaped back at the sight of it.

Realizing my faux pas, I quickly set the rifle down on a table and tossed the magazine of bullets alongside it. Mrs. Klein turned white. I stepped forward, put a reassuring arm around her, and guided her into the living room. It wasn't something to be proud of, especially on *Shabbat*, but I did find some small satisfaction in the thought that at least this is one guest who will not be recommending us to her friends.

I was hardly the only one with a rifle. Since Israel's army is a citizens' army with every boy going into service at age eighteen, the streets are filled with young soldiers with rifles slung over their shoulders. Soldiers walking around town are as much a part of the scene as children running to school, old men shopping for bread, or men and women on their way to work.

I thought I had already adapted well to Israel and was used to seeing all those soldiers until one January morning when the cold rain was tumbling out of the sky in such big drops that they bounced back off the sidewalk. To find refuge, I leaned my shoulder against the door of Bank Leumi, pushed my way in, and stood there for a moment, shaking myself off like a wet dog. Straightening up, I saw a tall, young soldier in front of me, slowly dislodging the wet gear on his back.

His dubon, the quilted jacket issued by the army, was drenched. To take it off, he reached back with his arm and swung the rifle off his shoulder. That's when I burst out laughing. A man with a rifle in a bank and everyone went about his work completely unperturbed. If the same thing had happened in the United States, everyone would have been screaming.

Just as no one pays particular attention to the sight of a soldier, the soldiers themselves pay no attention to the role they are in by virtue of their uniforms. In Israel, there is no prestige in being a soldier. It's simply a duty, something you have to do. You go in the army after high school, you serve three years, and you're subject to being called up for a month of training, sometimes fighting, every year until well into middle age, an intrusion in your studies, your work, and your life. As to the uniforms, the soldiers take them off as soon as they get home and spend free weekends in jeans and a T-shirt.

There were exceptions, of course. Dr. David Weiss, a respected middle-aged research scientist with a German accent loved the idea of being called up by the army and the prospect of lying in the mud, gripping a rifle, and preparing for an enemy attack. Although born in Germany, David was brought to the United States as a child and perhaps had fantasies about John Wayne. But for most Israelis, there is nothing glamorous about the military.

I had my own encounter with the army shortly after I arrived. As a full-fledged Israeli—any Jew who moves to Israel is immediately anointed with citizenship—I was subject to the draft.

Even in the early days of the country, Ben-Gurion said that more than even money or arms, the country needed Jews. On that score, I qualified. In the United States, immigrants have to be in the country a certain length of time and learn American history and pass a test before they become citizens. In Israel, if you're a Jew, all you have to do is show up. Zap, you're a citizen.

I felt good about that. I figured that if I moved to Israel, the least I could do was be a citizen. Best of all, that didn't affect my American citizenship. According to American law, I could have dual nationality, citizenship in both countries. To put it another way, I had the opportunity to serve in the war of my choice. At that time, the United States was still fighting in Vietnam. And at most any time, every five or six years, the Israelis were fighting the Arabs. That's why, even though I was more than twice as old as the average recruit, the Israeli army was looking for me.

My children didn't want me to go. It's not that they were worried about me. They were worried about being embarrassed.

"At your age, you'll be checking ladies' purses in front of the department store," Laura said.

"I can't handle it," Devorah said.

But of course, I went.

I had expected to see rows of young soldiers in their underwear lined up to get their shots, the way it is in all those World War II movies. Instead I found myself called into the office of a solitary doctor sitting behind a small wooden desk with nothing on it except a nameplate that said Dr. Friedman. He was a man of slight build, and he was balding. His wire-rimmed glasses were slightly askew.

Dr. Friedman looked down at the papers I had filled out and asked me how long ago I had my hernia operation and what I was allergic to. Then he ran through a list of just about every ailment known to man. Did I have any of them? No, no, no, and more noes. I didn't have any of them.

"Take off your shirt, pants, shoes and socks," he told me without looking up. At last it was getting to feel like the movies, I thought, as I stripped down to my briefs. With a metal hammer that had a black rubber cover at the end, the doctor tapped here and tapped there. With another instrument that looked like a pliers, he peeked into my ears. With something cold attached to tubes going into his ears, he listened to whatever he could hear inside my chest. Then he told me to stand up. I stood there, slightly ill at ease. Clothes may not make the man, but they usually make him look better than he looks without them. I was wishing I had my clothes on.

The doctor slid himself onto the top of his desk, rested his chin on the fingers of one hand, and stared at me thoughtfully. I followed the direction of his stare. He was staring at my feet. His face, which until now had been immobile, had melted into a look of compassion. He said nothing. I shifted my weight from one foot to another.

"Your feet," he said. I was right. That's what was fascinating him.

"Your feet. They're as flat as—do they say that in America?—as flat as pancakes."

"That is an expression," I mumbled.

He kept staring at them. "Worse," he said. "They spread out like batter before it becomes a pancake."

"That's possible," I said.

At last, he raised his gaze and looked at his chart. "And you seem to have high blood pressure," he said.

"I didn't know that, sir," I said. "Can I put my clothes on now?"

"You can put your clothes on."

I put my clothes on. In the World War II movies, soldiers are just rushed along and inoculated. But this wasn't World War II. It wasn't even America. It was Israel, and once again I could feel the difference. Dr. Friedman's face was filled with more than compassion, maybe even concern. I was hoping it wasn't concern.

"I think you should see a doctor," he said.

"But you're a doctor," I said.

"Your private doctor," he said. "It can't hurt."

I thanked him and turned to go. I started to walk out on my flat feet.

"And come back again in a year," he called after me.

I walked out feeling uneasy, as if he hadn't completed the sentence. Did he really mean, "Come back in a year—if you're still alive?"

That was the extent of my military service in Israel. A year later, I got a notice telling me I was permanently excused. I guess they figured that at that point, only six years away from turning fifty, I just wasn't worth the effort.

Chapter 17

War

*Y*ou know that sound when you hear it, even if you never heard it before. In an instant, you know. An air-raid siren.

That scream pierced the silence that was Yom Kippur. It was two in the afternoon. I was leaning against the guardrail of our terrace, savoring the early October sun, looking out toward the Old City walls that century after century stand indifferent to the cares of those who walk by.

The synagogue services had recessed for an hour. We lived only two blocks away, close enough to walk home for a brief rest.

That's when I heard it.

Yom Kippur had begun the night before. All Jewish holidays begin at sundown and continue until the next sundown. That year, Yom Kippur, the holiest day of the year, fell on *Shabbat*, the holiest day of the week. A day of fasting and contemplation and asking forgiveness for one's sins. A day when even nonobservant Jews feel compelled to enter a synagogue, to pray the prayers of centuries or their own improvised prayers or simply stand among other Jews and share a moment of dread as they glimpse into a future unknown. A day when, in Jerusalem, even sound is suspended.

At the synagogue the night before I waited for the service to begin, waited to hear the familiar and disturbing chanting of Kol Nidre that begins the twenty-four-hour period of introspection and prayer.

We pray on that day that God forgive us for our sins. But even that is not enough. It is the tradition to ask each family member and everyone close to us to forgive us for the hurt or harm we may have caused any of them in the past year. Even God cannot forgive on behalf of someone else.

In the synagogue, Rosalind and the girls are together in a balcony upstairs, the women separate from the men. David and I sit together downstairs on wooden folding chairs. His short legs barely touch the floor

There is silence. Then several men stand up and walk to the front of the congregation. One of them opens the doors of a large wooden cabinet. Each man reaches in and takes out a large Torah scroll that is standing there. Then each man turns to face the worshipers.

That is when from out of the silence, we hear the first notes of the cantor's sobbing cry of Kol Nidre. The melody penetrates beyond memory and mystically connects us to Jews who long before we were born trembled at that same haunting incantation. We can feel the pleading in the voice of the cantor. We can feel the fragility of life. We feel apprehension if not dread of the year to come.

Kol Nidre is a moment when life seems suspended, when feelings beyond life permeate the silence.

The service is not long, maybe only ninety minutes, but in that brief span of time everyone's mood is transformed. When the service ends, parents with their children go out quietly into the night, clusters of families dabbed against the darkness.

The next day, the early morning silence nestled against the warmth of autumn as David and I returned to the synagogue, holding each other's hand. Rosalind and the girls would join us soon.

As I walked along, distant images blurred into my vision, appearing and disappearing as if in a black-and-white movie, images of people rushing to prayer. A young boy holding the hand of his older brother runs alongside him to keep up with his pace. Two young girls in white blouses and long skirts look as solemn as the day itself. A shadow emerges from the sun's early morning glare and becomes a Hassid in black moving forward in long strides, leaning forward as if in a windstorm. His prayer shawl flutters back from the shoulders of his coat. On his head rides a wide-brimmed, fur-trimmed hat, the same kind his grandfather wore a century earlier inside the chilly synagogues of Eastern Europe.

From another direction comes a man with a white robe drawn around him. It covers him all the way down to his ankles. It is a *kittle*, a garment that in its whiteness represents purity, a robe he wears on Yom Kippur and the next Yom Kippur and for every Yom Kippur until the end of his days when he is returned to the dust, wearing his white *kittle* for the last time

David and I walked into the small synagogue, nodded at some friends, and sat down together near the windows.

To pray on Yom Kippur is to be immersed within centuries of Jewish history. Time, for the Jewish people, is not a yesterday, today and tomorrow. It is a continuum. It is like the unrolling of a scroll on which is laid out the story of a people and their God, the story of a people that began with Abraham, persevered through struggles, stood at Sinai, and ultimately entered the Promised Land. Within that story every Jew who ever lived is contemporaneous with one another.

At Passover, Jews are reminded that each one reading the story of the Exodus at the family table should think of himself as standing at Sinai, that the Ten Commandments were given not only to those who were there, but just as much to those not yet born.

In the Talmud, a Jew studies intricate arguments between scholars arguing with commentators who may have lived three centuries earlier. They voice their own differing interpretations of the laws. It is all written there, views that may be challenged by still other scholars who live centuries after them, and yet the arguments are studied as if everyone lived at the same time. And in a Jewish sense of time, they do.

David and I stood there that day praying with our friends in that small synagogue, in a sense praying with all the Jews who have ever lived.

The service itself is uplifting and exhausting, an intense dialogue between man and God. It takes effort to pray with *kavanah*, that complete dedication of spirit to the Almighty.

In Jerusalem, the prayer service is different from the American experience where frequently the congregant arrives at the synagogue as if going to the theater and sits back waiting for the words of the rabbi or the chanting of the cantor to stir his feelings. Prayer in Jerusalem is a passionate reaching out to God, imploring, arguing, and pleading that the gates of life and health remain open for another year.

It is tiring to pray, especially from one evening into all the next day. Fasting is tiring, too. The idea of fasting, of course, is to afflict the body as well as the soul and to remove distractions at a time of spiritual intensity. Unfortunately, fasting is often its own distraction.

It shouldn't be that way. When you think about it, fast-

ing from one evening meal until the next is simply going
without breakfast and lunch one day. That's not so much to
give up, and yet it's enough to occupy everyone's thoughts.
Even the traditional holiday greeting, "Have an easy fast,"
is a reminder that despite our best intentions, we often
focus on the wrong part of the ritual.

I fasted, and I prayed with as much dedication as I
could muster. Still it was a relief to return to our apartment
when the one-hour recess was announced shortly before
two o'clock. Rosalind went into the bedroom to remove her
hat. David and Becca went into the room they shared to
play with their toys. Laura slumped into the large foam-
rubber chair in the living room and closed her eyes.
Devorah went to her room with a book of psalms.

I stretched out on the sofa, a simple retreat into nothingness. I had tried to concentrate on each prayer, to feel
God's presence on that special day so I could make up for
so many other days when I was too busy for God. But six
hours is a long time to be holy.

I tried to rest, but I was really more restless than tired
and finally got up. I went up to the roof garden to get some
air and to stretch and to perhaps find God in the heavens
as well as in the prayer book. I squinted my eyes against the
brightness of the sun and felt it comfort me as I peered out
into the quiet. Then I heard footsteps on the stairs.

It was Phil Masler, a tall, good-looking, blond boy from
our synagogue back in Illinois. Alone, Phil had moved to
Israel. When he met us, he adopted us and made our home
his hangout whenever he needed a place in Jerusalem. Like
most young men on Yom Kippur, Phil wore a white short-
sleeve shirt and cotton slacks for the holiday.

Phil came over alongside me. We nodded to each other
and stood there. It felt good, the warmth of autumn and
the comfort of the peacefulness that embraced Jerusalem.

That's when it happened, when the silence of Yom Kippur was ripped open by the piercing shriek of the air-raid siren.

I had my insides slashed open like that once before. I was six years old. My grandfather had died and lay in an open coffin, his head resting against a small white pillow. It was more comfortable, I am sure, than any pillow he had ever rested on in life. I stood next to the coffin, holding onto the hand of my thirteen-year-old sister, Charlotte, unafraid as I felt her by my side. And then a cry pierced the silence and my heart. My mother had just entered the funeral home and from the back of the room I heard her cry out, "Pa!" and then she rushed down the aisle toward the coffin. I had rarely heard my mother raise her voice at all. I had grown up in a home where people didn't raise their voices. But then—that shriek!

That's how the air-raid siren felt.

I knew nothing and in a second knew everything. Something terrible had happened.

I looked down at the *kikar* and saw a white car suddenly race out from the emptiness, slam to a stop near the curb as two soldiers dashed in, and then lurch forward down the empty street. I learned later that wireless contact was being made with soldiers throughout the country even before the siren sounded. All soldiers were ordered back to their bases immediately.

Phil and I glanced at each other and said nothing. We paused for just a second. Then he turned and ran down the stairs to our living room, grabbed his rifle and backpack, and spun down the four flights of stairs to the street. Another car appeared out of nowhere. Phil waved at the driver. The car hardly stopped as a back door swung open and Phil leaped in and was gone.

Again the street was empty, for a minute and for still

another minute, and then again a lone car swept by, stopped briefly a block away, picked up two more soldiers, and sped off. It was like watching a silent ballet, forms appearing on stage and then dashing off stage, the choreography of the surreal.

We were at war. It was different from what happened in 1967. Then everyone was waiting for war. Tension had gripped the country for days and weeks. For months, Egypt's leader, Gamal Nasser, had been calling for the destruction of the Zionist Entity. Arab threats resounded from every neighboring country. And then the threats changed into action. Egypt blockaded the Strait of Tiran, an act of war. Everyone knew that actual fighting was imminent. Everyone knew it was coming.

This was different. In 1973, war came like an electric shock. Just six years earlier, Israel had decimated the Arab armies and emerged from the war arrogantly confident of its power. Hostile rhetoric poured out from the capitals and mosques of the Middle East, but everyone was so accustomed to Arabic bombast that it faded into dissonance. No one expected war.

Even Golda Meir's kitchen cabinet, actually meeting that day in the prime minister's kitchen, didn't think the Egyptians would attack. They were aware of Egypt's ominous troop movements, but could the Egyptians really be crazy enough to try such a thing?

David Elazar, Israel's head of the Southern Command, was an exception. He took the bombast seriously and wanted to launch a preemptive strike. But Israel had done just that six years earlier. World leaders would have excoriated Israel if it did it again. The year was 1973, thirty years before President George W. Bush made preemptive strikes American policy. In 1973, the idea of attacking first was out of the question.

Israel's legendary general, Moshe Dayan, vacillated. So did Golda Meir. Israel did not mobilize for war.

The one person who didn't vacillate was the Egyptian ruler, Anwar Sadat, the man who would go on to make peace with Israel. But first he was determined to make war.

On Yom Kippur, 1973, Egyptian troops crossed the Suez Canal and overran Israeli positions in the south. Syrian tanks swept through the Golan that Israel had captured in 1967. Then they pressed on into Israel itself. From the north and from the south, Israel was under attack.

It was a while before any of us knew what was going on. The country's one television station and its radio stations are owned by the government, and on Israel's most sacred day the stations do not broadcast.

Secular Jews started tuning in the BBC and heard fragments of reports. Orthodox Jews don't turn on the radio or TV at all on Yom Kippur. But as soldiers received orders to report back to their units, the word quickly spread that Israel was at war. Beyond that, everyone knew nothing

I ran down the stairs to see Rosalind by the front door kneeling down with her arms around David and Becca. Laura and Devorah were pushing in close against her. Whatever was going on, the best place to be was next to Eema.

Suddenly we heard a knock on the door. I opened it, and Naomi Cohen from across the hall almost fell in. She was dressed in a dark, severe dress. Her body was hunched forward. In the best of times, Naomi looked serious. That afternoon, she looked more serious than usual after a morning of praying for forgiveness from sin, though I am sure that no sin has been invented that could possibly corrupt Naomi.

No matter. At that moment, prayers about sinning had been forgotten. Living is all everyone was thinking about.

Jews see no glory in dying. They even tell God that dying is a bad idea. "In the grave who can praise you?" says the psalmist. Even when raising a glass of wine to make a toast, Jews don't waste the occasion with something as meaningless as "cheers!" The toast is always, *L'chaim*, to life!

Naomi had lived through wars before. She knew what to do and was there to tell us what to do.

"The bathtubs!" Naomi called out. "Fill the bathtubs with water. You may need it for drinking."

Now we knew this was real. Knew it for sure.

Habits of a lifetime, like cleanliness, fled from my thoughts. Drinking from the bathtub, no problem. Naomi disappeared. I had hardly reached the closest bathroom when the front door flew open again.

"Take the children down to the basement," Naomi called in to us. "Your storeroom. And take water and cookies." Naomi stepped back into the hall, swinging the door behind her.

It's amazing how fast the body reacts, faster than the mind. The scenes, the events were so much beyond our experience that we couldn't even process them. But the body, like a hand jerking away from a flame, moves at once. Rosalind was in the kitchen, grabbing thermos jars and empty bottles to fill with water. I ran into our bathroom, put in the stopper, and quickly opened the cold and hot faucets all the way. Without waiting for the tub to fill, I ran into the children's bathrooms and did the same thing and then ran back into ours to stop the water before the tubs overflowed, and then I ran back to the children's tubs.

The kids grabbed whatever was precious to them as Rosalind and I herded them to the door. They moved obediently, trusting us to take care of them, not wanting to think about what they viscerally knew, that there was little we could do. We swung the door open and heard another neighbor's voice from down the stairwell, "Bring a flash-light!"

"Keep going," I told Rosalind and the kids. I dashed back into the kitchen, grabbed a flashlight, and joined them in seconds as we raced down the stairs.

There was no time to question, no time to contemplate, not even time for fear. Our bodies had switched onto auto-matic and were leading us.

Reaching the basement, we turned down the corridor to our storeroom, passing sackcloth bags that slumped against the metal bars of the windows. They were stretched out of shape by the sand and the pebbles and small stones stuffed into them long ago and whose weight over time had opened holes here and there. Small streams of sand had spilled out of those holes and onto the window ledge.. They were left-overs from the last war. Or maybe the war before that.

The first time I saw those sandbags, I was fascinated by them. I had never seen a sandbag before. I had seen them in newsreel photos of London being bombed night after night during World War II, but until I came to Israel I had never seen a real one, nor touched one. The novelty passed, of course, and before long I hardly glanced at them when I walked by, never thought much about why they were still there. Laziness, no doubt. But this time as I ran toward the storeroom, a different thought flashed through my mind. Maybe they were left there for a reason, maybe by someone who knew much more than I did, someone who under-stood there is no such thing as security and that life is always tenuous, especially in the Middle East. You never know when you'll need a sandbag.

Entering the storeroom, I bent low so I wouldn't hit my head. I pushed aside bicycles and boxes to make room for Rosalind and the children. At the last minute, she had grabbed one of the kids' blankets and brought it down with us. Once inside the storeroom, she sat down on a box, pulled the blanket across her lap, and drew Becca and David close to her.

We sat huddled together in that small space and waited, pressed against old pieces of luggage and the bicycles and cartons of books. David and Becca munched on the cookies and drank some water. Little children don't have to fast on Yom Kippur. No matter. If it had been otherwise, we would have broken the rules.

David looked up at Rosalind. "I'm not going to have good dreams tonight," he said. None of us answered him. Sometimes there are no answers.

We sat there silently, not knowing what more to do, each of us receding into their own thoughts. I started thinking of stories I had heard about the Six Day War. We, at least, were together. Back then no one knew if their loved ones were safe—children were at school, fathers at work, mothers at home or at their jobs, many sons and daughters in the army. In those first few hours, greater than the fear of war was the fear for their loved ones. Would they hear from them? Would they get home safely?

Another thought went through my mind, that we were not the first Jews trapped in Jerusalem worrying about whether there would be water to drink. A few months earlier Devorah had talked me into walking with her through a tunnel of frigid water that came up to my waist and almost to her chin as we eased our feet along slippery stones.

That tunnel went back to another war in another time, twenty-five-hundred years ago. The Assyrians had laid siege to Jerusalem, but King Hezekiah was determined to build a tunnel to bring water to the city from the nearby pools of Siloam.

That was the tunnel that Devorah and I were trying to walk through. Although modern Israelis had installed some lighting in that ancient tunnel, it was still dark inside. We edged forward timorously, holding each other's hand, Devorah always a couple of steps ahead of me trying to rush into history while I moved more cautiously trying not to fall into history. Inside that tunnel, we had entered a past that went back to the time of the prophets. The furthest thing from my mind at the time was that within months, like Jews of centuries long past, I would sit huddled together with my own family, worrying about whether there would be water to drink.

A crackling sound interrupted my thoughts. Each of us looked up. What was that?

Static from a radio. Then we heard words, sporadic words and then more static and then more words again, disjointed words. "Syria . . . tanks . . . surprise attack." The sounds came from the far end of the basement. We were not the only family down there taking refuge in their storeroom. There was another, and they had a radio, and they had picked up the BBC. It had to be someone not religiously observant, probably the Erlangers, someone not worried about playing a radio on Yom Kippur, worried only about war.

Next we heard a whining sound. They must be turning the dial searching for word from anyone, from any voice that would speak to them out of the ether. Then there was English again, words and phrases, "caught off guard . . . in retreat . . ." Then the static again.

I wanted to run over to them and find out what they had heard, but I was afraid to leave the family in case something happened. We sat there, and we waited.

Then after a few minutes, another sound, this time a siren. An air raid? Was it another air-raid warning? Could it be an all clear?

We didn't move. Soon we heard voices coming nearer.

The Erlangers had left their storeroom. They were walking toward the stairs, and as they walked the sound of their radio grew louder. I called out to them. They seemed surprised to see us, but too absorbed in the news to slacken their pace or come toward us. Instead they waved for us to come out.

"All clear," one of them called out in English. For a moment, they must have sensed our bewilderment. "It's okay," they said. They kept walking toward the stairs. We crawled out of our small space and followed them.

We were still numb from shock as we went back to our apartment. I was surprised to see the disarray, the signs of our grabbing a blanket here and a toy there. A box of raisins lay spilled on the floor. Rosalind must have knocked it out of the cabinet when she reached for the cookies. Out of habit I started picking things up, wondering what you're supposed to do when there's a war on. Especially on Yom Kippur when you're supposed to do nothing but pray.

I looked at my watch. It was a couple of minutes before three. I looked back at the children. Each of them had found some chair to slump into and sat there caught up in their own confusion, waiting to be told what to do as if by virtue of being parents we would know.

I felt angry at my helplessness. I was angry at whomever was threatening us on our most holy day. I was frustrated at not being able to do anything. And then I thought of the one thing I could do. *Dafka*, I thought, already comfortable with that Hebrew word for being contrary. I would go back to the synagogue. I would like to think I was being religious, but I was really just being defiant. Whoever they are who started all this, I thought, they're not going to tell me what to do.

I picked up my prayer book. "I'm going back," I said. It didn't occur to me to take anyone along. I just assumed the kids would be safer at home than anywhere else. I was closing the door behind me when I heard a soft voice. It was Devorah. "I'm going with you," she said. She ran over and took my hand.

The afternoon sun was beginning to slide behind the orange roofs of distant buildings. Other people were returning, too, their stark forms silhouetted against the sun's rays. An occasional car raced by as we walked, more soldiers returning to their bases. For the rest of us, there was nothing to do but wait . . . and pray.

It was surreal. No bombs were falling around us. There were no sounds of an attack. It was almost as it was before, the silence of Yom Kippur in Jerusalem, and yet we already knew from the radio that just a few hours away, something terrible was happening, that Egypt had attacked us and Syria had attacked us.

Most of the people returned to the synagogue, but there were a few empty seats. The seat next to Moshe Stein was empty. That's where his son always sat. That afternoon, Moshe prayed alone.

A couple of rows behind him was Aaron Goldwater with his sons, but only two of them. The third, the oldest, was not there.

Everyone who was there was praying, and yet the tension was palpable. You could see it in the faces of parents whose sons had quickly returned to the army. As their lips moved with the prayers of the congregation, you knew they were adding their own prayers. You knew they were pleading with God. There was not a person there who did not have someone in the army, a relative or a friend or the child of a friend. There was not a person there who did not feel the stirrings of memory, the memory of other wars, for some the memory of the Holocaust. Each of us struggled alone with his own fears as the ritual bound each of us to one another. The service proceeded as it had for centuries, the same prayers of contrition, the same fears of what a new year might bring.

As I sat bent over, reading from the prayer book, I felt someone push in next to me. It was David. I looked up at the balcony and saw Rosalind there. Devorah and Laura were taking their places next to her. I put my hand on David's knee, to reassure him and to reassure myself. I was glad they had come. We were together. At a time like this, I thought, it is good to be together.

The prayers we had prayed for years seemed to take on a new meaning that afternoon

"On Rosh Hashanah will be inscribed and on Yom Kippur will be sealed how many will pass from the earth and how many will be created . . ."

Nothing had changed, of course, except our perception, a sudden reminder of how precarious life is.

Through every day of the year, each of us lives his life as if he will live forever. And then on Yom Kippur, in a brief period of introspection, we hear words that remind us of the fragility of our lives.

"Who will live and who will die..."

On that Yom Kippur day, death was as real as life.

"Who by water and who by fire..."

For most Israeli soldiers it was their first war, for still others their second. For some, their third.

"Who will be harried and who will enjoy tranquility..."

When I worshipped in America, my prayers were little more than the chanting of disembodied words that weaved in and out of my thoughts. That Yom Kippur in Israel, with the sound of the air-raid siren still reverberating in my mind, I heard every word for the very first time.

The Yom Kippur service draws near its conclusion with the N'eila prayers and the imagery of the gates of repentance closing as the sun sets and the day of Yom Kippur ends. It is late afternoon. There are few lights in the old synagogue and as the sunlight fades, the sense of the gates closing becomes so real that we feel we can discern them in the distance. We feel the chill of apprehension as to what the year may bring.

This war was not America in Vietnam with soldiers few people knew fighting 10,000 miles away in a country hardly anyone had ever heard of. This was Israel where we knew our soldiers, knew the land, and knew that within our small country, there was no place to retreat. In Israel, the alternatives are stark, winning or dying. We prayed hard for forgiveness that afternoon . . . and for life.

At last sundown, usually a relief after the long hours of fasting and prayer. Traditionally a time for festivities when young men and women come together in a celebration of music, dancing, food, and wine. In 1973, no one felt like celebrating. Outside the synagogue, we nodded to one another and again wished friends the traditional *G'mar Hatimah Tovah*—your future should be sealed for life and health.

The gates of repentance are now closed, an awesome thought. On the other hand, Judaism being Judaism there is always a second chance. During the following eleven days, through the last day of Sukkoth, a Jew can still repent and slip through those closed gates. That's what it's like to be Jewish. There is always a fragment of hope. How can a Jew live without hope?

Everyone clung to that hope as they hurried home to turn on radios and televisions. Even as we ran up the stairs to our apartment, we could hear the sounds of news reports from other people's radios. Across the street, we could see television screens flickering blue and gray through neighbors' windows. Everyone was desperate to hear the news.

The first reports were fragmentary. The Egyptians were

crossing the Suez Canal. Syrian tanks were racing across the Golan. No details yet, just the shock, the surprise, and the sense that the scattered reports reflected something more serious, that the Israeli armed forces were in disarray.

It seems that as quickly as everyone turned on the news, they were on the telephone, calling sons in the army or relatives and friends whose sons were in the army and wives whose husbands had fought a war just six years earlier and may have been called back to fight again.

And then for thousands of families throughout Israel, the waiting began, hoping that the doorbell will ring and that it will be their son on a twenty-four-hour leave, the good fortune of Israel being so small that a soldier can be home within hours. There was another kind of waiting, hoping that the doorbell would not ring lest you open it to find three people in military uniform. In Israel, everyone knows what that means. Three strangers and you don't want to hear what they have to say.

Ruth Rayman, the wife of Moshe, our American pediatrician, didn't wait. Somehow she sensed what had happened.

We went over to see Ruth and Moshe right after dinner to find out if they had heard from Jacob. I had seen him just a week earlier, home on a weekend leave from the army, gobbling down pieces of fried chicken before rushing back to his base near the Syrian border. That's where, we learned later, the Syrians launched their attack as eight hundred tanks and three infantry divisions swept past the cease-fire line and through Israel's Golan settlements.

Ruth was looking at their family picture albums when we came in, pictures of Jacob as a baby, other photos of him growing up in the United States, then at school in Israel with his buddies and with different girlfriends, and then with the Israeli girl he planned to marry. Pictures, too, of Jacob in his army uniform, tall, good looking. Slowly

Ruth turned the pages of the past. She was already in mourning.

There was no news, we reassured her. None of us knew what was happening, we said. There was no reason to jump to conclusions. Ruth kept turning the pages, studying each picture.

"He's dead," she said without looking up.

"You shouldn't say that," we told her.

The following day, October 7, I went back to Ruth's apartment. I ran up the stairs and opened the door without even knocking. Chaim Potok, the writer, was there. He was visiting Israel that year. Somehow Moshe knew him.

"Jacob is dead," Chaim said. Three soldiers had come to the door. It was official.

Chapter 18

War, the First Days

*E*ach night we cover the windows with blankets, bedspreads, tablecloths, anything we can find. Even an old bathrobe. There is a blackout in Jerusalem. There have been no more air-raid sirens, but you never know.

The parking lights of an occasional car, like fireflies darting through the dark, pierce the blackness. The streets are silent.

It is a strange feeling. You know terrible fighting is raging in the south and in the north, and yet in cities like Jerusalem people continue their routine, at least as best they can. Kids go to school, people go to work, and mothers cook meals. Delivery men deliver bread, and shoemakers repair shoes. Life goes on. With a dull ache.

Wherever you go, you hear the radio. You hear it from apartment buildings you pass and from cars passing you. Even in the bus, the radio is on. There is news on the hour, and if you hear an announcer's voice from a car passing by, you glance at your watch and you see that another hour has gone by, and you realize that despite the news broadcasts you've heard no news. The government stations aren't reporting it.

Maybe it's part of the confusion after the surprise attack. Maybe it's because the news is bad and the government doesn't want people to know. But people do know.

Fragments of news are passed by word of mouth, reports from a soldier who phoned home, news from another who hitched a ride, rumors from someone who knows someone in the government. The only thing everyone knows for sure is that things are going badly.

Meanwhile, like the public at large, the army clings to routine. It has to. A lot of soldiers have to make meals for a lot of other soldiers. Soldiers have to man the communications systems, move trucks, repair armored cars. It takes a lot of people just to make an army function, even before the fighting. But of course, much has been added to the routine. Extra jobs, like hauling tanks up north to the front. The roads are filled with tanks being brought up to the front.

Other soldiers sit around and clean their rifles and do what soldiers always do, wait. Then some of them stop waiting and, like the tanks, they too are moved to the front.

At Hadassah Hospital in Jerusalem, doctors still deliver babies and care for cancer patients and kidney patients. But anything that isn't urgent is postponed. Helicopters are landing on their pads at Hadassah in Jerusalem and especially at Rambam Hospital up north in Haifa. Ambulances pull up at the entrances. Nurses and soldiers rush in the new patients.

Wherever you go, people want to help. But every hospital has already posted signs that say "No Volunteers Needed." They have all the volunteers they can handle.

Some people find places to help in the schools. There are vacancies there. A lot of teachers are now soldiers. It's a citizen army, and a lot of men have been called up.

I want to do something, but nobody needs me.

I walk through the Hadassah Hospital by myself. From my regular film work, I already know a lot of people there, and I have no trouble going wherever I want. I feel a compulsion to see with my own eyes what is going on.

I pass a burn unit and see the nurse and doctor carefully treating a young man. His entire side is a raw, searing red. I go over to the operating rooms. Surgeons are amputating limbs.

Deep inside, I'm hurt at what I see, but I don't know how to show the hurt or share the hurt, so it comes out as anger. I am very angry. I want the whole world to know what we're going through.

During those first couple of days of the war, David developed trouble breathing and became seriously ill. Watching him try to pull air through his chest brought back suppressed fears from my own childhood when I too struggled for breath, was rushed to the hospital and placed in a huge steam room while doctors talked about performing a tracheotomy. When I saw David breathing so hard, I was scared and called Moshe Rayman.

Moshe came right over, the way old-fashioned doctors did when I was a kid. It was comforting to see him. He sat down on David's bed, listened to his breathing, stroked his head and assured him, "You'll be just fine. Just be a good boy and take the medicine I'm going to give your daddy." I could feel tears burning in my eyes as I watched Moshe worrying about my son, no longer able to worry about his own.

We kept the radio on all day long. Everyone did. Certainly there would be a bulletin, a new report, something. And there were reports, but we could feel that more was going on than we knew.

Only after the war did we learn the whole story, that the war had begun with a barrage of thousands of bombs and shells fired by the Egyptians, followed by a crossing of the

Suez Canal by 8,000 soldiers in fiberglass boats. By nightfall, more than 30,000 Egyptians had crossed the canal. On the Israeli side were 436 Israeli soldiers, three tanks, and seven artillery batteries. One of those soldiers was my friend, Avi Yaffe, a recording engineer doing reserve duty at the canal that Yom Kippur day. As the Egyptians literally rolled over and past the line of bunkers where he was stationed and then pushed on even deeper into the Sinai Desert, Avi reflexively did what he had always done. He flipped on his recording equipment, memorializing shouts and cries no one wants to hear.

Further on in the Sinai, small groups of Israeli reserve soldiers were haphazardly thrown together into makeshift units. Ill equipped, not yet assembled into integrated forces, the soldiers got caught up in chaotic battles and suffered terrifying losses. The skies that the Israeli air force had dominated in the Six Day War were Egyptians skies in 1973. Egyptian planes and surface-to-air missiles penetrated deep behind Israeli lines, firing relentlessly at the disorganized Israeli soldiers and tanks on the ground.

Avi and his buddies miraculously stayed alive for several days in the middle of all that death and destruction. Finally they took a desperate chance and began walking through the chaos, behind the Egyptians who had overrun their bunkers, walking and walking until their luck finally turned, and they spotted an Israeli tank unit that brought them to safety.

The attack from Syria was just as furious, but Moshe's son, Jacob, wasn't as lucky as Avi. Thousands of tanks bore down from the north, an arsenal not seen in action since World War II. Helicopters swept in with Syrian commandos who quickly overran Israeli positions. Syrian planes attacked Israeli radar surveillance facilities atop 6,000-foot-high Mount Hermon.

I couldn't stop thinking about Moshe's son, the shock that a young man of such vitality whom I had just seen is—as they say in Hebrew—*is no more.* It was too much to absorb. Even the idea of the war itself. It seemed impossible that young men were being killed only a hundred miles away from where I was. In Jerusalem, warm in the October sun, the air seemed too hushed for war.

I felt the frustration that there was nothing I could do. With the country at war, I was just a hanger-on.

I felt frustration, too, about the dreams I had about a life in Israel. Maybe Dick Gottlieb was right. Maybe a person doesn't just pick up a family and move thousands of miles away. Not to a country where there are wars.

I wanted to get out of the house, go somewhere, anywhere. I wanted to escape the confinement of my helplessness. It was a beautiful day. It seemed strange that such a beautiful day could be so terrible.

I walked down Balfour Street and then left at Ben Maimon toward the home of Shula and Shmuelik Toledano. They had three sons. One was a high-school classmate of Laura's. The other two were in the army.

The army is where Shula and Shmuelik met during the War of Independence in 1948. He was her commanding officer.

Growing up in Jerusalem at a time when Jews and Arabs lived among one another, Shmuelik spoke perfect Arabic and had many Arab friends. As years went by, he became Arab affairs advisor to Golda Meir when she was prime minister. He later became a member of the Knesset, the parliament, where he was outspoken about the need for peace between Arabs and Israelis. On the day I walked over to their house, his sons were fighting Arabs, just as he had done.

I climbed up the stairs along his carefully tended trellis

of bright red geraniums. I opened the door and walked in. Shula was sitting there, blonde, tall, erect, against a stuffed red sofa that was more typical of Arab furniture than Israeli.

Life was comfortable for Shula, but it hadn't always been that way. As I greeted her, I remembered the story she told me about peeling an apple for her son when he was only five. It was during the War of Independence and Jerusalem was under siege. Food and water were in short supply. Shula peeled the apple and cut up little pieces. Slowly, the boy ate the small chunks and then looked up at her. "What are you going to eat?" he asked. There was only the apple.

Except for the wars that had happened in the meantime, the Suez War in 1956, what the Israelis call the War of Attrition during the 1960s, the Six Day War in 1967, life was better twenty-five years later. From the kitchen, you could smell the aroma of fresh pastry. Shula's family owned a famous bakery in Israel, and I had quickly learned that the best desserts in the country were in Shula's kitchen. She smiled at me slightly as I walked in, but just sat there. She was staring straight ahead, listening to the radio news. Shmuelik was pacing back and forth behind her. I nodded to them both and sat down next to her. That's another part of life in Israel. You don't always have to say something. Especially during a war.

Suddenly a tall, young paratrooper burst into the house. The greetings and rapid questions drowned out the newscast. "I've seen Udi," the boy said. "He's all right!"

The paratrooper sat down and put his big arm around her. "He's all right," he repeated. Shula listened to him, her face expressionless, frozen between the relief at the news and the fear of what might have happened since then. She just looked at him, waiting to hear more.

"He shot down four Egyptian planes," the boy went on.

Shula clutched herself. Her body trembled involuntarily. She didn't say anything, yet I knew what she was thinking. Jews don't like being killers. After the Six Day War, the world looked on Israeli soldiers with awe, but Israelis didn't feel that way. Maybe it's because every Israeli family knows what war is all about, firsthand.

Then the questions began. Where is he, Shula wanted to know. How does he look? How does he feel?

I got up quietly to leave. So many feelings to sort out, they should be alone. Down the stairs and out onto the street again. I walked aimlessly through their neighborhood.

That night I lay in bed dozing and then waking again, tired but unable to sleep, fearful of admitting my fears. Was it just little more than a year ago when we boarded that ship, when I felt such excitement, when I was so sure of what I was doing? I didn't feel that way anymore. I wasn't certain of anything. It seemed that I couldn't understand anything.

I started thinking about Moshe's son. How old could Jacob have been? He was tall, more than six feet. Nicely built, strong, but not bulky. Mature looking. Is it possible he was only nineteen?

I looked at the numbers on the clock shining red through the darkness. Three-thirty in the morning. It would be eight-thirty at night in New York. I had an idea. I tried to slip out of bed without Rosalind noticing me. She was either asleep or pretending to be asleep. I closed the door behind me and dropped into a chair next to the telephone.

I still remembered the phone number of ABC-TV where I had worked for fifteen years. It was an easy number. Almost all sevens. Even at eight-thirty at night, people would still be working in offices, control rooms and studios. The operator answered, and I asked for the newsroom. She rang the number, and I heard an impatient hello.

"This is Yale Roe," I said, hoping that I'd be lucky

enough that whomever I was talking to might have heard my name during all those years. But he hadn't heard of me, and it was obvious he couldn't care less what my name was. But I wanted him to care and started to tell him that I was a former ABC guy.

Strange stories seem to come to mind in all sorts of inappropriate moments, and I found myself recalling the day when the program manager at ABC had been fired. And I remembered that a few weeks later he phoned one of his buddies at the network to ask for a favor. He wanted a couple of tickets for a big sports event. "Sure," his friend said, relieved at the chance to ease his guilt at still being alive and well at the network after his friend had been fired. "I'll take care of it," he said. "Just go to the box office and tell them . . . tell them . . ." and he searched for the right words. "Tell them who you—*were!*"

That's where I was in my life, telling them who I had been. So I told him. I told him about those fifteen years at ABC and that I was calling from Jerusalem and . . .

Impatiently, he interrupted me. The word Jerusalem got his attention. "Okay," he said, "what's going on?" I made up the answer as I went along. I told him I knew ABC had its regular crew in Israel and I knew there were more foreign reporters in Jerusalem than just about any other city in the world, but that only twenty-four hours after war broke out, there probably wasn't a crew from New York and that I could send him stories every day that he could play in New York, which was the network's biggest station. "Don't worry," I said, "I know what you need."

"Okay, Yale, it's a deal." He gave me his name. "Send them to me, and I'll take care of the rest."

It was typical network. I had never been a producer for ABC, and he had no authority to make a commitment to me, but television in those days was still 50 percent seat-of-the-pants, maybe 90 percent. I knew he would make it happen. I hung up the phone feeling better. While I wasn't going to help win the war, at least I could give people a sense of what was going on. Nothing of profound importance in the great scheme of things, but at least it made me feel better. I would be doing something. By the next morning I had located a cameraman and a soundman and was making my way through the Jerusalem hospitals, getting my first stories.

Thirty years doesn't seem like such a long time ago, but in terms of technology, it was like living in the Stone Age. There was no videotape then with its instant pictures, no sending images thousands of miles by satellite. Instead, we shot with 16mm news film that was called fast film, inferior in quality to the regular 16mm film, but requiring less time to develop. Then we either edited our material into a story or packaged it as raw footage together with a script. We would rush it to the airport, and it would be on its way to New York on the next plane.

That's what I did every day, sending out stories about ordinary people in wartime and what they went through. Back in New York, those stories connected with people. Within days people we had filmed told me they were getting phone calls from people they hadn't seen in years, even from people they hardly knew. I hadn't bothered to talk to ABC since that first night of the war so that was the first confirmation I had that the material was actually getting on the air.

Producing those news stories helped, but I still felt pretty useless. It was hard to come to terms with the fact that I was nothing more than an average immigrant with flat feet who didn't speak Hebrew well, someone of little use to a country at war.

Even our seventy-year-old neighbor, Charlotte Bergman, a large, impeccably dressed European with a priceless art collection, was doing something, driving her massive Cadillac convertible—a head-turner wherever she went—up and down the highways to pick up hitchhiking soldiers going home or back to their bases.

By Friday, I decided I'd drive to every place I could think of where I could possibly do something even though the "no volunteers needed" signs were everywhere. Laura and Devorah, home from school because of the Sukkoth holiday that begins four days after Yom Kippur, said they wanted to come with me. "Let's go," I answered, already feeling better at the thought of their company. A friend had told me years ago that to have a daughter is like falling in love again. That's how I felt about daughters, especially in those blissful years before teenage rebellion. The girls were used to my habit of moving quickly. As I soon as I told them it was okay, they slung their knapsacks over their shoulders and raced down the stairs with me.

We jumped into the car and were on our way. The only thing that seemed to have changed is that there were more "No Volunteers Needed" signs than before. Pulling away from Hadassah Hospital, I saw a soldier hitchhiking. The Israelis don't hitchhike the way Americans do with the thumb pointing back over the shoulder. The Israeli way is to point the forefinger down toward the road. It made sense. At any rate, as soon as I saw him, I stopped the car. He jumped in, slammed the door shut behind him and said nothing. I continued on down the hill.

"Where are you going?" he asked me in Hebrew.

"Wherever you want to go," I tossed back in Hebrew, grateful that Laura and Devorah whose Hebrew was much better than mine were with me in case the conversation got more complicated than that.

He looked me over carefully and said, "The Jericho Road."

"No one just goes to the Jericho Road," I said, trying to lighten up the mood. "Where are you going?"

"The Jericho Road," he repeated.

"No problem," I said even as I realized something was strange. Israelis are gregarious and start chatting as soon as they bounce into a car. This soldier said nothing. He sat staring straight ahead. As the road opened, I increased my speed, driving east, then turned north through the five-thousand-year-old town of Jericho. Suddenly the monotony of the flat desert gave way to splashes of color sputtering from the deep green leaves of orange and lemon trees. You could see them in the distance among large Arab villas and along the storefronts of beige plaster that lined the streets where robed Arab men huddled together or played *sheshbesh* as they puffed on their narghiles. And then as quickly as it had appeared, the ancient city slid behind us and we sped on.

There was a barbed-wire fence along the right side of the road. I had passed by that fence many times. Jordan stretched out beyond it. Before the Six Day War, the road I drove on had been part of Jordan. So had Jericho. And the rest of the West Bank.

The brief history of Jordan was a strange one. After the First World War, League of Nations diplomats met and, perhaps after too much brandy and cognac, marked up a map with little regard for natural borders and decreed among other things that the part of the old Ottoman Empire called Palestine would by administered by the British.

Then in 1921, the British colonial minister, the same Winston Churchill who in less than two decades would be the British prime minister during World War II, continued the British foreign policy of buying Arab loyalty. For King Abdullah's Bedouins, he carved out from that mandated territory an area that spanned both sides of the Jordan River. It was named—what else?—Transjordan.

When the United Nations divided the remainder of the Palestinian Mandate into two states, one for the Israelis and one for the Arabs, and war broke out in the area, Abdullah used the occasion to take the West Bank and East Jerusalem that had been assigned to the Palestinians and make it part of Transjordan.

In 1950, King Abdullah shortened the name to Jordan and granted citizenship to all Arabs living in the West Bank and East Jerusalem. A year later, Abdullah was assassinated on the steps of Jerusalem's Mosque of Omar.

Abdullah's seventeen-year-old grandson who was with him that day, Hussein, took over the throne. It was King Hussein, by then thirty-three, who was the ruler of Jordan in 1967 when the Six Day War broke out. During that war, Hussein gave in to pressure from his fellow Arabs and sent his well-trained troops against Israel from the east while the Israelis battled the Egyptians in the south and the Syrians up north on the Golan. The Jordanians fought well in that war and were respected by the Israelis, but in the end they, together with Egypt and Syria, lost the war and lost land. Jordan itself lost the West Bank.

In the 1973 war, Hussein sent troops north to Syria in a gesture of support for his fellow Arabs, but never pursued the war aggressively.

After the Yom Kippur war, the Israelis joked that King Hussein made two mistakes: attacking Israel in 1967 when he lost the West Bank and not aggressively attacking Israel in 1973 when the Israelis were reeling back from the Egyptians and Syrians, and Hussein had a real chance to recapture the West Bank.

Timing is everything, and maybe that was Hussein's bad luck. On the other hand, in light of the rising tide of

Palestinian nationalism that had begun a decade earlier, it may have been his good luck that he was spared owning the West Bank.

In the autumn of 1970, the fedayeen of the Popular Front for the Liberation of Palestine hijacked four international airliners and tried to assassinate Hussein. In what is today remembered by Palestinians as Black September, the Jordanian army in ten days killed more than two thousand Palestinian fighters and thousands of refugees. In the long run, Hussein may have been more clever than people thought in not trying to seize the West Bank in 1973. Two million more Palestinians inside Jordan might have been the end of his Hashemite Kingdom.

At any rate, I had other things on my mind as I kept driving without the vaguest idea of where I was headed. Occasionally, the soldier would interrupt the silence with a few questions. Where was I born? How long had I been in the country? Then more silence. It was obvious that he was taking my measure although I figured I couldn't look too threatening with two young daughters in the back seat. I kept on driving.

On the left, from the midst of abandoned mud and sand huts, an Arab boy with jet-black curly hair and a smile of stained teeth waved at us as he rode bareback on his donkey. Occasionally we passed an Israeli kibbutz, little more than an array of long containers used on ships that the Israelis moved onto hilltops and along borders and lived in. A few bunks beds and some old chairs converted them into instant homes. For some strange reason, the Israelis call those containers "caravans," a curious name since the settlers had absolutely no intention of ever moving their "caravans." Their sole purpose was to provide a quick and affordable way to "create facts," as the Israeli expression goes, and establish an Israeli presence on the land.

There were a few modest cottages there, as well, and a dining hall of sorts. Past rusting farm equipment that lay in disarray, toddlers held hands and waddled dutifully behind a young woman wearing a long full skirt and a sweater whose sleeves stretched beyond her hands. The settlers who lived there were mostly young people in their early twenties whose commitment to the land exceeded their knowledge of it. But they were learning fast, and you could already see the early efforts at fences, crops, and some sheep. We sped on. Then again the land was empty except for the sea of sand split open by the stretch of black asphalt that we pretended was a road.

The shining sunlight reflected from billions of grains of sand cast a hypnotic spell as I drove on. The soldier's words snapped me out of my reverie.

"Turn right here," he said.

I glanced over to the right. There was nothing there but sand. And then, a narrow road. I swerved the car sharply toward it, wondering what would happen next. What happened was a large army base beyond a huge sand dune. Soldiers, tents, and armored cars. "Stop here," the soldier said.

He flung the car door open and came over to my side as I got out. The girls got out of the backseat and looked around, fascinated by their first view of hundreds of soldiers.

"Now do you want to do something else?" the soldier said. He was big and stood so close to me that I found myself backing up against the car. "The first thing I want you to do is to forget where this base is."

I knew he was serious, and the situation was serious, but I had been in Israel long enough to know that somehow everyone in Israel seems to know everything. It was totally inappropriate, but I found myself thinking about the old story of Ginsberg, the spy. Ginsberg was living in a big city, posing as a schoolteacher. A man is assigned to make contact with him.

When the man arrives at Ginsberg's apartment building, he finds to his dismay that among the more than a dozen names listed, two are identical, Ginsberg. Which bell should he push? What if the wrong Ginsberg answers, and he blows the cover of the other Ginsberg? He has no choice. He has to take a chance. He pushes the first bell. The latch on the apartment building door snaps open and the man enters the hall. Quietly, he goes up one flight of stairs where he sees the name Ginsberg. He knocks on the door, and a man answers.

"Ginsberg?" he asks.

"I'm Ginsberg," the man in the apartment answers.

"I'm Schwarzbach," he says. He studies Ginsberg carefully, looking for a glimpse of recognition. There is none. Carefully, Schwarzbach pulls back his jacket, slightly revealing a silver medallion clipped to the inner lining. There is no response until slowly a smile spreads over the other man's face.

"Ah," he says, pointing up the staircase. "You want Ginsberg the spy."

I had the feeling that the army base, hidden as it was, was about as unknown inside that small, busybody country called Israel as Ginsberg the spy. No matter. I told my soldier I wouldn't say a word.

As I walked into the camp with my soldier, other soldiers came toward us in groups of twos and threes. They were youngsters, eighteen or nineteen years old, obviously new recruits, many of them without a trace of facial hair. Their uniforms hung on them in that usual disarray of Israeli soldiers. Dust and sand covered their shoes. The army is not glamorous. It's just there, the something that comes after high school, something you have to do. Just as their fathers did. And if you are scared, you don't say so.

Laura was fascinated at the sight of so many nice-looking young men coming over to see us. She was fourteen that year, going on twenty, and was sure all the soldiers were coming our way just to meet her.

My soldier put his hand around my arm and pulled me close. "Look," he said, "these guys haven't been off the base since the war broke out. Haven't been able to call home. For all their families know, they could be in the Sinai right now. Or dead."

I got the idea.

"You want to help? Get word to their families that they're okay. But nothing else. Not where you saw them. Nothing." He was still clutching my arm, waiting to make sure I got the message. "*Mayveen?*" he said in Hebrew. "You got it?"

"*Havanti,*" I said. "I've got it."

By now twenty soldiers were pressing around us. My soldier nodded to them, and suddenly everybody talked at once and started shoving scraps of paper into our hands. Notes with a name, usually just the first name, and a phone number.

"*Eema,*" one of them said as he pressed a note into my hand. I wrote out the word "Mom" in English.

Another: "Tell my wife I'm okay." He pushes a note toward me with a phone number on it.

Most of them just called out names and messages and phone numbers in a barrage of Hebrew I couldn't understand with everyone talking at once. Laura and Devorah were now next to me, reaching into their backpacks to pull out writing pads and pencils.

Long before backpacks were a fashion statement in the United States, Israeli schoolchildren, who didn't have their own lockers at school the way I had in Oak Park, carried their books and writing paper and all their other school supplies in canvas backpacks. I used to wince to see Becca trotting off to school at a forty-five-degree angle with her heavy books attached to her. It was as natural for a schoolgirl to toss on a backpack as put on her blouse.

Laura and Devorah were already talking to the soldiers in Hebrew, scratching notes on their writing pads, and taking down names and phone numbers as quickly as the soldiers called them out. I tore off a couple of sheets of paper and started writing, too. My notes were in English. Theirs were in Hebrew. The soldiers immediately spotted the difference and the English speakers pushed over toward me, many of them just to show off that they knew another language. The others crowded around the girls.

The messages were almost all the same. "My name is Avi. Please call my wife, we just got married last summer. The number is . . ."

"I'm from Tel Aviv. Write down this number. Tell my dad I'm okay. That I'm safe and they shouldn't worry." And always the reminder, "Don't tell them where you saw me." Even new recruits knew there are things you don't say.

Finally, the soldiers started to turn away from us. In twos and threes, they tossed a wave over their shoulders, some still calling out messages to us, and trotted back to their barracks. They had heard something we didn't hear and quickly disappeared. We were suddenly alone standing next to the sand-covered Volvo. We exchanged quick glances and busied ourselves trying to put the wrinkled notes and paper into some sort of neat pile. I looked at my watch. Although it seemed as if we had just arrived, we'd been there an hour already. And we were not alone, after all. My hitchhiker was still with us. As we crawled back into the car, he bent down toward me. "Thanks," he said in English, then turned his back on us and walked away. I watched him for a moment and hoped he would be okay, then started the ignition and headed back to Jerusalem. The girls and I didn't speak. We were still trying to sort out our emotions.

I pressed hard on the accelerator. It was already Friday afternoon, and it would take us at least an hour to get back home. And a couple of hours after that, *Shabbat* would begin. The war was still raging on two fronts. Hundreds of families had no idea where their sons were, whether they were in battle, whether they were still alive. And on *Shabbat*, Orthodox Jews won't violate the Sabbath by answering the phone. We had to get back fast.

Laura and Devorah were busy turning the fistfuls of notes right side up, pressing their wrinkled forms flat, and putting them together with my own hastily scribbled notes. They put the English names in one pile. That was for me. They divided the other names between themselves.

The traffic thinned out as I approached Jerusalem. As the hour grows late on Friday afternoon and families get ready for *Shabbat*, there are fewer cars on the streets. I was making good time and not driving as carefully as I should. As I got closer to home, I drove even faster, swung the car into Jabotinsky Street and up the hill to our *kikar*, bumping the curb as I braked the car to a stop in front of the Belgian Embassy across from our apartment.

None of us said a word. We threw the car doors open and started running up the stairs, each of us clutching a handful of notes. We tossed off a quick greeting to Rosalind who was in the kitchen and went up one more flight to the small room I used as an office. I grabbed the phone and set it on the floor, dropping down beside it. The girls sat down on either side of me. We stared at each other as if to decide who would go first. We only had one phone, this was not Winnetka. We would have to take turns. I nodded to Laura whose Hebrew was the best. Let her start, and we would work it out as we went along.

Laura dialed the number on the note on the top of her pile. I looked at my watch. Three-thirty. *Shabbat* would start in two hours. Laura held the receiver open toward us so we could listen. A woman answered.

"*Shabbat shalom*," Laura said in Hebrew. "I just saw Udi, and he sends his love." I heard screaming. Laura looked up quizzically and kept talking. "He's all right. He asked me to call you."

"Is he all right?" the woman shouted. "Is he all right?"

"He's all right," Laura said. "I just saw him. He's all right."

"Where did you see him? Where was he?"

"I can't tell you," Laura said. "But he's all right. He sends his love."

"You're sure he's all right?"

"I just saw him. Not to worry. He looks great!"

"*Toda l'El*," the Sephardic expression, "Thanks to God."

"*Shabbat shalom*," Laura said and eased down the phone. She looked up at me, and I saw her eyes holding back tears. "I didn't know what to say," she said.

"You did fine," I told her. "You were great." We looked at each other, half frozen in fear. How do you do this without making the family more scared? And what about all their unanswered questions after they hang up? And when we say we can't tell them where their son is, are they going to have worse fears? Or maybe their fears are already as bad as they can be. At least we got some word to them.

"My turn," Devorah says. She reaches for the phone and dials a number. Devorah speaks softly, and as she bends over the phone, we can hardly hear her words.

"*Shabbat shalom*. I saw your son this afternoon. He's okay. He's fine. He sends his love."

Devorah looks up at me. "She wants me to talk to the father."

We heard a man's voice yelling into the phone "*Shalom. Mee zeh?*" "Hello, who is this?"

"I saw your son a couple of hours ago. He's okay. He sends his love."

"Is this Varda?" the man asked.

"No," Devorah said. "I'm Devorah. I just happened to meet him. He asked me to call you."

And that's how it went. The same excitement, the same questions, the same frustration at not being able to answer the questions, not to be able to tell them more about boys who until a few hours ago we had never met.

Devorah put down the phone, and I grabbed it. My turn. The English speakers. I didn't even take time for *Shabbat shalom*. "I just saw your husband," I said. "He looks great. He sends his love."

And so it went as we raced the clock to finish before *Shabbat*. We heard every possible response.

"Here is his mother. Say it again to his mother."

"Where did you see him? How did he look?"

"Thank you, thank you. God bless you."

Sometimes hardly any words. Sometimes just quiet weeping. Not even questions. And then a soft "thank you."

At last, all the calls were finished. Quickly we showered, put on *Shabbat* clothes, and joined the rest of the family for *Shabbat* dinner. Rosalind lit the candles. We were one of the families with everyone together at the table that night.

I blessed the children. I filled the silver cup to chant in Hebrew the *Kiddush*, the blessing over the wine. I should have said the prayers with special feeling that night, but I didn't. I should have been thinking about God. But I was still thinking about the young soldiers crowding around us at the army base.

Chapter 19

Death in the Golan

There was a chill in the air that second week in October, a hint of November rains soon to come. At the outdoor market, I saw two Moroccan women, the collars of their light jackets turned up against the chill. Streaks of rust-colored henna in their shiny black hair sneak out from under brightly patterned kerchiefs. One of the women leaned across the large wooden bin of avocados to reach a mound of plump grapefruits. Between small fingers, she plucked one out and dropped it into the blue plastic basket on the mud floor next to her. She reached over for a second grapefruit, dropped that one in too, then picked up her basket and moved on, already evaluating the tomatoes ahead of her. A young Arab boy rushed past her wheeling crates of oranges stacked atop one another.

The air was crowded with voices. There was a bargain that day, someone called out, a special price for anyone buying two kilos of avocados. The *souk* was filled with shoppers, but not as many as usual. Everything seemed the same, but wasn't the same.

At the cheese stall, I didn't see the young man who was usually there chanting his litany of cheeses, the man with the dark curly hair and the red-checked shirt with a baker's apron over it. His mother was there alone, bent over a block of feta, cutting off a chunk for a customer and weighing it the old-fashioned way with the cheese on one scale and weights on the other.

I passed the stall where fresh fish flop around in a tub of water, oblivious to their pending fate. "*Dag chai!*" live fish, the fish man called out to anyone who would listen. The live fish—they were all carp—did short laps within their small space. There was hardly room for them all, and yet they smoothly swished past one another. "*Dag chai!*" he called out again. He was alone. I usually saw two sons working there with him.

At the far end of the *souk*, I came out on Jaffa Road. At the corner, two children leaned out from the curb to gauge the speed of approaching cars, then grabbed each other's hands and dashed across the street. There were a lot of cars on Jaffa Road. They honked their way down the street, weaving in and out of the black gases of old buses that plodded along. And yet with all the tumult, it was not as noisy as usual. And the faces, they were not the same. In Israel, people look directly at you when they walk down the street. Even if they don't speak, there is contact. It was different that day. People were caught up in thoughts they didn't want to think about.

Like the other men not at war, I went to work. I picked up my film crew and drove past the military cemetery and then down the winding hill to Hadassah Hospital. The dirt road is so narrow you feel you're going to tip over into the wild trees and bushes that grow down the hill into Ein Kerem, where John the Baptist was born. I drove a little further, and we were at the hospital, the one with the Marc Chagall stained-glass windows that all the tourists visit.

It's not the real Hadassah Hospital, not the original

one, but most visitors don't know that. The original one was on Mount Scopus in East Jerusalem. After the cease-fire that followed the 1948 War of Independence, Jordan took over the eastern part of Jerusalem and Jews weren't allowed to go there. Mount Scopus and the hospital lay abandoned in the dust of shattered walls and broken glass. So all those women of Hadassah who had raised money to build that hospital went out and raised money again and built another Hadassah hospital, where it was safe, in the Jewish part of Jerusalem. That's where we were that day to film more stories for ABC.

My cameraman strode in alongside me, the Arri 16mm camera perched on his shoulder, a quickly visible sign of power. It was a time when people were still awed by the sight of film crews. My soundman was a small Iraqi Jew whose short legs seemed to be pedaling to keep up with us and keep the heavy Nagra recorder from sliding off his shoulder. We were on our way to the third floor, surgery, to meet an American doctor who had agreed to let us follow him as he made rounds treating wounded soldiers that day.

I was just about to enter the elevator when from the corner of my eye I saw an attractive young woman leaning against the hospital's drab wall, her body shaking with sobs that couldn't come out. I recognized her immediately, a tall, dark-haired girl I had met six months earlier in Neuva, a small coastal town in the Sinai where the waters of the Red Sea swirl in over scattered stones in that same relaxed way the sea comes in on the Riviera. I was a friend of her brother, Yair, a handsome, solidly built young man of about thirty who had fought in Jerusalem in the Six Day War. Their father, Zvi, owned a couple of gasoline pumps that pretended to be a gas station in that sandy Sinai waste-land. Zvi pumped gas from a wheelchair, his powerful torso erect, the muscles of his sunburned arms rippling with every turn of the rubber wheels that moved it. His legs were gone, lost when fighting as an American in Italy during World War II. His wife helped him at the gas station. They had met during the war. She was his nurse. After the war, they moved to Israel.

Yair had invited me to bring the family to spend our first Passover in Israel with them in the desert, a setting not much different from where the first Passover began some 3,300 years earlier. We shared a few carefree days along nearby beaches still pristine, a seashore long protected by isolation. We were carefree in those days because like all the Israelis, we felt the security of the recent Six Day War victory. We felt carefree because of all the things we didn't know that April in 1973.

We didn't know that during that same month, the Egyptian president, Anwar Sadat, had committed to attacking Israel. We didn't know that a month later, Egyptians and Syrians would meet to plan their first air strikes against Israel. We didn't know that by June, the Soviet Union would ship hundreds of tanks and massive amounts of armaments to Egypt. We didn't know that in just six months, tank battles would rage across the Golan larger than those fought when the Germans invaded Russia in World War II. Nor did we know that Yair would be there.

All we knew as we bounced across the sand in his Jeep was that Neuva was incredibly beautiful, and it was good to be alive.

And then October came. Syria sent 700 tanks into the Golan. Between them and the towns of northern Israel were 176 Israeli tanks. The overwhelming barrage of shells and explosives sheared apart Israeli tanks and incinerated young soldiers. That's where Yair was sent during those terrible first days of the war. His tank was hit, he jumped from it, ran over to help another soldier, and was killed.

Those were the terrible words I heard from his sister as I held her close to me, feeling her body shaking against my chest. I tried to say words that would help, knowing that nothing would. I tried to make her feel not alone even as I knew I would soon leave her and she would be alone. I didn't know why she was in the hospital that day or how she got the news there, but that's where she was, and that's how I remember her, standing against the sand-colored plastered wall of the corridor, shaking as strangers hurried past. I have been haunted ever since by my memory of that moment, her grief and my helplessness, the thought that I should have done more even though I know that whatever I might have done or said wouldn't have mattered. There are times so terrible that nothing matters.

As soon as the war ended, I went up to the Golan to film where Yair had fought. I wanted people to feel the loss that is called victory, to sense the silence that hung like a shroud over the battlefield, to know the pain that I knew they could never know. It was something I had to do.

I called the documentary, *After the War*. I filmed the battlefields. I filmed the survivors. I filmed those who had been in battle and those who waited at home for soldiers who didn't come home.

On the Golan, I walked across the empty hills formed millions of years ago by a volcanic eruption that from deep within the earth tore out rocks and stone and ash. And now once again, the land was ripped open, this time by the clawing tracks of armored tanks. Rocks and stones spilled out in all directions.

There were goats there, too, trotting around ancient boulders and over the charred earth. Otherwise, all was emptiness except for the hulks of burned-out tanks that lay abandoned, like broken toys, along the rocky landscape.

The winds blew hard and cold. The brush trembled

backward before their force. From one tank, scraps of metal hung loose from the gun turret, scraps so thin that like paper they reeled back from the wind. Larger chunks of metal, torn and distorted, hung from other tanks. One was in the shape of an arm grotesquely bent backwards.

A few of the soldiers' belongings, so important to them so recently, were still there. Inside one of the tanks were a few playing cards, scattered across the metal floor. Inside another tank, a half-empty tube of toothpaste.

Everything lay askew, broken and twisted across that churned-up land. The only sign of life were the goats wending their way through the brown brush, trotting past the tanks with neither interest nor curiosity. They were looking for something to eat.

Except for the wind, it was quiet across those hills. As quiet as a cemetery.

The bodies of the soldiers, Yair and others, had been taken away, all the bodies, Israeli and Syrian. They were young men, all of them. They might have even liked one another if they had ever met. But the only time they saw one another was through the sights of machine guns and from the turrets of tanks. The only time they saw one another in life was as enemies, separate from one another, until it was all over and they were taken away together in death.

None of us spoke as we filmed. There was a holiness to the silence that should not be disturbed. Yair was dead and more than two thousand other Israelis, killed in just eight days of war. The number of Israeli soldiers killed in those eight days was comparable to twice the number of American soldiers lost in the entire eleven years of the Vietnam war.

But they were important, those first eight days. The war was different after that. The massive Syrian assault bogged down along those volcanic rocks of the Golan. In the south, the world witnessed one of the fiercest battles since World War II as more than a thousand Egyptian tanks clawed their way through the desert to attack 600 Israeli tanks in defensive positions. The Egyptian losses were devastating. For the Arabs, it was the beginning of the end. Yet the war dragged on, and the killing continued.

In contrast to the shrieks of men and machines on the battlefield, there was quiet in Jerusalem. People tried to live lives of normalcy at a time when nothing was normal. Sadness cloaked the days, silence the nights. The blackout continued. We lived our lives behind tightly closed shutters.

During those few weeks, it seemed as if the stars felt an obligation to compensate for the darkness. Their beauty seemed to mock the madness that raged across our little bit of land, and yet there was something nourishing about that beauty, a reflection of eternity that stirred hope.

But hope is fragile. It was hard to maintain hope as we followed doctors on their rounds and saw young boys in hospital beds and in wheelchairs. Some flashed a smile as they saw us. Some lay flat on their beds, staring toward the ceiling, lost in thought or trying to avoid thought. In the corridor, one hobbled along on his crutches, even managing to turn his head to follow the sight of the nurse who walked by. Another was being pushed in a wheelchair, his right leg sticking out straight from inside a cast. The light blanket that covered him hung limp where the other leg should have been.

We didn't enter the burn unit. Patients lying there with raw skin covered by ointments and thin protective strips that were made, ironically, from pigskin didn't need our germs. I was thankful we had an excuse not to go in. I had already seen burn victims.

Another day and once again we finished our work, left the hospital, and walked back to our car to mark the cans of film and get them ready for the late-night flight to the States. I was relieved to be out of there, away from the tension that filled the halls and the anxiety hidden behind plastic drapes pulled shut around patients' beds. I never liked hospitals. My discomfort must have been obvious early on because even my Jewish mother never suggested I become a doctor. It was worse during the war, of course. I filmed doctors saving lives, but what I saw was the pain.

The next day, I went to see Pinchas Peli, a renaissance rabbi with the improbable appearance of Santa Claus as a redhead. Pinchas was a seventh-generation native of Jerusalem. He was a descendent of Orthodox rabbis but his wide-ranging interests and unlimited energy drove him into myriad activities that made him suspect among his peers. He was true to the rabbinic world, yet for many of his peers he was too much of this world. Rabbis were just not all over the place the way Pinchas was.

He was forever writing. He wrote a book about his mentor, Abraham Joshua Heschel, and he wrote a book translating Rabbi Joseph Soloveitchik's classic, *The Lonely Man of Faith*. He wrote pamphlets, and he wrote a weekly newspaper column about the week's Torah reading. The only thing Pinchas relished as much as writing was talking. He ran seminars and he gave lectures. I liked him, liked the excitement his eyes projected, the warmth of his big round face, and the way he was always bursting with ideas.

The day I visited him during the war, even Pinchas was subdued. When I walked in, I didn't even greet him. I put my hand on his shoulder and walked past him. He nodded. I walked over to the window with no awareness of what I was seeing.

"Nothing ever changes," I finally said. "The world is always killing Jews." My words sped up as if rushing to be heard.

"Six million Jews killed in our own lifetime, And now we finally have our own country, and so what? They're still killing us!"

Pinchas didn't say anything. I was still facing the window. I wanted to look at him when I spoke, but I couldn't. My head was filled with the scenes at the hospital, with memories of Yair, the image of Ruth mourning for Jacob before she knew he was dead.

And I was angry at myself again, angry for bringing a family to Israel and ending up in the middle of a war. I wanted to be part of a dream. I was beginning to learn how dreams often end.

Pinchas reached over, gently put his large hand on my arm, and turned me around. We stood close, facing each other.

"It's different, Yale," he said. "It's different."

"It's not different," I said. I was almost shouting at him. "A Jew is always expendable."

I looked up and saw the hurt in his eyes. "It's different," he said.

"All through history," he said, "the slaughter in the Middle Ages, the pogroms in Russia, the Holocaust in Europe . . ." he paused for a moment, perhaps shocked at the inadvertent blasphemy of reducing such terrible events to a mere list, and then went on. "Through all those times," he said, "most of the Jews in a town or a country were killed, and only a few survived." He paused to make sure I was following him. "In Israel," he said, "in our own country, Jews are still killed. But there is a big difference. Today, in our own country, most survive."

He managed a slight smile even as he shook his head sadly. He put both his hands on my shoulders. "*Yeeheeyeh tov*," he said, the way every sad conversation in Israel ends. "It'll be okay."

I turned to walk away. I was glad I'd stopped by to see him.

The war continued into another week. The Syrian and Egyptian attacks had been blunted. But "blunted" was the kind of word newspapers use. The words of the people were hushed. There was not even a sense of relief. Fighting was still intense. Lurking within every person was the dread felt upon awakening, the dread that cast a shadow over you the entire day, that got in the way of trying to sleep at night and that wove its way through what restless sleep might come, the fear that a loved one—you mustn't let yourself think it.

On the battlefield, Israel slowly moved onto the offensive, but couldn't push forward without replacements for the thousands of lost tanks and airplanes. Military equipment was running low. Russia had sent weapons to Syria and Egypt. Initially, the United States delayed sending more arms to Israel. Both superpowers were using its surrogates to maintain their own influence in the Middle East while being careful to not be drawn into war with each other. The United Nations did what it always does, held meetings and passed resolutions. Meanwhile, Golda Meir pleaded with President Nixon to send Israel more arms.

And then at last, President Nixon broke the logjam. The United States began to airlift arms to Israel.

As Israel drove back the Egyptians and Syrians, there were occasional cease-fires. They were broken almost as quickly as they were agreed to as each side, like a tackled quarterback nudging the football an inch ahead, pushed for one last bit of territory.

At last, on October 24, there was a final cease-fire.

When the fighting ended, it didn't feel like an ending. There was no jubilation, no excitement. Nothing like the pandemonium I saw on State Street in Chicago at the end of World War II when soldiers and girls who had never seen one another kissed and hugged in the sheer abandon of being alive. There wasn't even the quiet relief that marked the end of the Korean War. In Israel, everyone was simply numb.

President Kennedy liked to quote the line that to be Irish is to know that the world will break your heart. The Jews know that, too.

There was not a family in that small country untouched by the war. Even we, in Israel only sixteen months, knew three young men who were killed. All of us struggled to retain the images of loved ones as they were in life and to forget the scenes at the cemetery that you can't forget.

I remember the military cemetery in Jerusalem, Mount Herzl, and walking along a narrow path there with friends, together and yet each with his own thoughts, walking so slowly and silently alongside grieving parents, walking behind six nineteen-year-old boys in army uniforms carrying a wooden box on their shoulders with a flag imprinted with the blue Star of David draped over the box and inside the box the remains of a boy who had already been buried once by sands that covered him amid tanks on fire and who was now being buried in a real grave that people could visit.

I remember the boy's company commander, a boy himself, standing at the foot of the grave and beginning to speak. A handsome boy, restlessly twisting his taut body as he spoke, as if to break out from some invisible constraints. He spoke directly to his fallen soldier as if the boy were still alive. He spoke to him quietly and with affection. And we who also grieved were at that moment intruders at a moment of intimacy between the boy and his commander.

For most of us, the war was over. The loss was terrible, more than 2,500 soldiers in eighteen days. But as Pinchas Peli said, it wasn't like the pogroms anymore or like the Holocaust. Most of us had survived, each returning to his routine, his work, or his make-work. Anything to stay occupied. No less so the mourners. There is only so long one can weep. With the ponderous passage of time, weeping subsides. The mourners return to the habits of their lives and to a rhythm of normalcy. The tears end while the pain hides deep inside.

A mother says to me, "Don't ask about the nights."

A father says to me, referring to the Jewish prayer for the dead recited once a year, "Every day is *yartzeit.*"

In Jerusalem the lights had flickered on again as if in compassion the gods had decided to share their starlight. You could feel the change in daytime a strange daytime that was without war and yet not as before.

I invent errands so I will have something to do, and I stroll into town to do them. It's easier to do than to think. Along King George Street the tourist shops are open, their windows filled with prayer shawls and silver candlesticks and camels of olive wood and Palphot postcards, but no one is there to buy them. Not even to look. The drugstore is open. There's always someone who needs something from a drugstore. Around the corner at Ben Yehuda Street, the small-boned Yemenite man with wrinkled skin and white shirt and black *kippah* is there at his juice stand pushing bright orange carrots into whirling blades while a soldier stands with his weight shifted to one foot watching the glass fill as if by magic with an orange-colored drink. Life hobbles on.

I keep walking but walking through Jerusalem isn't like walking anywhere else. As imperceptible as it may seem, there is always a latent sense that you are not alone, that you walk through the shadows of history. The artist Ivan Schwebel often paints a familiar Jerusalem street, Jaffa Road, or Ben Yehuda Street, or Zion Square at the end of Ben Yehuda. Time and again splashed against that scene is the figure of King David "dancing with all his might before the Lord." Wherever Schwebel looks there is King David.

In Jerusalem, prophets are never far away—Isaiah and Jeremiah, so many prophets. Simple people, too, and impoverished people, those who worshiped God and those who did not believe, all those long gone, and yet you feel their presence. No wonder psychiatrists and scholars have written serious tomes about the Jerusalem Syndrome, the whirlwind of spirituality that sweeps up so many pilgrims. One doesn't have to be a pilgrim or even religious to know that when you walk in Jerusalem, you do not walk alone.

As I moved on, the heaviness of eighteen days of tension slowly eased away. I began to walk more quickly, the way I usually walk. On the street named after the Talmudic scholar, Hillel, I passed the movie theater. A sensuous woman looked out at me from a poster of upcoming attractions, her eyelids lowered, her parted lips suggesting passion. I passed the toy store and stopped to look at the puppets and rubber balls and a red wagon in the window. People will be buying toys again. I was beginning to feel giddy with lightness, and I trotted across the middle of the street, not going anywhere, just moving because it felt good to move and to see people and shops even though there were not many people in the streets and even though not all the stores were open.

I walked on a few minutes more and suddenly realized I was passing the office of my lawyer, Johnny Heiman. I had seen him just before the war. As a matter of fact, we had made a date to meet again soon. Maybe he was there. I'd run in and say hello. Not to talk business. This was not a day for business. But at least to say hello.

I had known Johnny for just a year, and we had immediately liked each other. It was difficult for anyone not to like Johnny. He was the son of British immigrants. Even his Israeli childhood could not suppress the influence of their refined manners. Johnny was comfortably charming and debonair, the antithesis of the bluntly intense Israelis.

I met him because I needed a lawyer, but immediately felt a close connection to him that quickly grew into friendship. I could talk to him about the most personal feelings. I used to think that an intimate relationship could exist only with someone you've known forever. As I grew older, I realized that time was not the bond. Rather it was something that was beyond logic. As I grew older, I began to understand that truth dwells in the heart, not the mind.

He was about my age and like most Israelis had seen war. By the age of forty-one he had seen war twice. Like most Israelis, he rarely talked about those wars. Israelis don't do that. Over coffee a few weeks earlier, we talked about other things.

I ran up the stairs effortlessly. One flight, a second, and finally the third. Easier than waiting for the antiquated elevator to grind its way down and then up again. I was excited about seeing him and talking about all the things that had been happening. When I reached the third floor, a sense of foreboding came over me, but just as quickly faded away.

In Hebrew and in English, a shiny brass nameplate that was a little off-angle identified his small law office. Still caught up in the swift movements of racing up the stairs, I crossed the corridor with a couple of long strides and pushed the door open. The endorphins were pumping from running up three flights and I felt like I was flying.

The receptionist sat behind a dark wooden partition facing me, sipping tea. In Israel, secretaries are always sipping tea. The office was so small that with one step from the entrance, I stood immediately in front of her. I asked for Johnny. At the same time, from the corner of my eye, I saw it was dark at the end of the small corridor where his office was. He must have gone out.

I asked again, in Hebrew, nodding my head toward his office. "Is Johnny in?"

A shake of her head was her answer.

"When will he be back?" I asked, already sensing her mood, unwilling to acknowledge it.

The secretary still held her cup, balanced on a saucer. She answered me in English. "He's gone," she said.

"When will he be back?" I wanted to ask, but I didn't ask anything. My mind was racing. The war was over. The lights were on. And she answered me in English. Certainly she didn't understand the nuances of English. Of course, she simply meant that Johnny was not in the office. After all, I hadn't made an appointment. No one was expecting me. He didn't have to be there.

I had another idea. He must be in the army and hadn't come back yet. It hadn't even occurred to me that he was in the army. After all, how many wars can anyone be in? And he wasn't a kid. I knew, of course, that Israeli men can be called up until they are fifty, but for older men that was often for embarrassing jobs like checking women's purses somewhere. It can't be for war anymore.

I looked at her and was about to say something, but I didn't. Her eyes looked at me steadily. She said nothing. She just looked at me.

I had my answer.

I turned and closed the door behind me. Quietly. I turned toward the staircase and began to walk down. Slowly this time. Very slowly.

I don't know what I did after that. I don't remember anything about the day after that.

The war was over. My first. Johnny's last.

Chapter 20

After the War

The rains of autumn shrouded Jerusalem in gray. Streams of water splashed across the city's streets. The stone buildings soaked up the dampness. Sunlight broke through occasionally, but no one seemed to notice.

Spring was better. Elchanan, who lived downstairs, was home from the army. One night during the war, his parents joined us for dinner. His father sat there, his thoughts elsewhere, perhaps recalling his own years in the army. Or memories of the Germany he had fled. He didn't hear from Elchanan until the war was over. That was the first time he was able to call. Elchanan was safe. He had made it through another war.

Shula's son was back, too, the boy who shot down four Egyptian planes. So was Yitzhak Rogow, who the day before the war opened his own public relations firm by moving a desk, three chairs, and a filing cabinet into a small office and putting a sign out front. Now he was back. The sign was still up.

At our bank on Agron Street, one of the small cubicles

was empty. It had been empty since the war began. But now the war was over, and the cubicle remained empty.

I went to the bank again a week later. This time I saw someone sitting there, behind the small desk where Rony used to sit.

The streets still felt empty. I saw more men than before, but not a lot more. Families were going about errands as families do. But there were few tourists. I hadn't realized before how many tourists come to Israel, how they fill the streets. Without them, the streets were barren. It felt like the world had disappeared.

Some Christians had come in December. Most of them went to Bethlehem. More came for Easter, but not many. They went to the churches in Jerusalem.

Jews came who had relatives in Israel. Leaders of Jewish organizations also came, to show their support for Israel. They met with the prime minister and the foreign minister and other top officials. They had their pictures taken with them. Senators and congressmen came, met with the same important people, and had their pictures taken, too. Not many people came to just walk the city streets. You don't see many pictures of American Jewish leaders and congressmen shaking hands with ordinary people.

In May, it was Independence Day again, the twenty-sixth Independence Day. It seemed inconceivable that just a year earlier, like the rest of the Israelis, I had felt such a sense of euphoria. It seemed inconceivable that I was so naïve as to think that after centuries of persecution, Jews were at last secure somewhere. I believed what I wanted to believe. For at least a year.

The celebrations after the war were muted.

"For everything there is a season," Solomon wrote, if indeed it was he who wrote Ecclesiastes. Whoever wrote it was right, of course. Slowly we all resumed our routines, our small roles in life. Mercifully, mourning does not last forever.

The change of mood was almost imperceptible. I first sensed it early one morning when, lost in my own thoughts as I walked along near the President's House I realized that something had interrupted my concentration. Glancing up, I saw nothing unusual. There was no abrupt sound, nobody running past me, not even a car racing by. Still I knew that something had caught my attention. I looked around and found myself staring at two old men who had come upon one another about a half a block away. That's what I had seen. But why had they caught my eye?

I looked at them more closely. Their long coats were shabby. One wore a fedora and the other a beret, and they were talking with intensity, each leaning toward the other so that their two bodies seemed to form an arch. As I came closer, I saw one of the old men lightly throw his weight to one side and jab playfully at the arm of the other. The second man reached out like a big bear and patted the shoulder of his friend. They shuffled toward each other just a bit, their heads tilted to one side, and began chuckling together.

I walked on trying to figure out what it was about them that had interrupted my thoughts, and then I realized what it was. It was the first time since the war I had seen anyone smile.

Slowly, slowly, the burden of memory began to slip away. Yehoram and I went out filming again. One of the stories we covered was the arrival of three thousand American Jews, regular people who came to Jerusalem as part of a rally organized by the United Jewish Appeal. It was called "We Are One."

There was something electric about the sight of them. You could almost touch their optimism as they marched down Jaffa Road. They continued on to the Old City and then to the Western Wall where Teddy Kollek greeted them with his usual ebullience and assured them that Israel would carry on. Then a rabbi blew the shrill sounds of the shofar, the ram's horn that is sounded each year on Yom Kippur. Its powerful notes reverberated against the Wall's ancient stones that rose up fifty feet above the crowd. And then the men and women sang *Am Yisroel Chai,* the people of Israel live. Many sang with tears in their eyes. Even the Israelis, notoriously cynical, were stirred at the sight of those three thousand American Jews who had traveled seven thousand miles to be with them.

Yehoram, who himself had just returned from the war, filming with his right eye pressed against the camera lens and the other squeezed shut, opened his eye and glanced over at me with a big smile on his face. We were not alone after all.

Life reasserted itself in familiar patterns. Weddings that had been postponed by war were celebrated at last. At the ceremonies, the traditional dances of the men were charged with the intensity of pent-up energy, released now in a celebration that was a defiance of death. The men danced with their arms linked together, their bodies whirling in circles, their feet stomping against the floor to the beat of ancient rhythms. Every wedding became a reaffirmation of life.

Yehoram and I went down to the Negev to film a story about the Bedouins. Like their fellow Arabs, the Bedouins are nothing if not hospitable. You cannot approach a Bedouin without him offering you food, and you cannot possibly refuse to eat or drink with him because that would be a terrible offense.

Inside their tents of goatskins, the Bedouins sit on their haunches either brewing strong coffee or else boiling goat's milk over a fire and stirring in great doses of sugar.

Whenever I was among them they invariably offered me the boiling milk. As a child, I hated the taste of hot milk, especially when the cream coagulated into what to me was a sickening amalgam that would make me gag if I swallowed it. Fortunately, as a child I was taught that you must eat whatever is put in front of you whether you like it or not. By the time I met the Bedouins, I already knew the meaning of discipline and suffering. I would take the milk, look down so they wouldn't see me squeezing my eyes shut, and force myself to swallow that thick, sticky sweetness. But at least we got our story.

More and more, we were filming all over Israel. We filmed the Jewish National Fund dynamiting its way through rocky hills to build new roads. We filmed fish farming in northern Israel, skiing on Mount Hermon, and ski-surfing on the Kinneret. We filmed young violinists in a master class as Isaac Stern leaned forward into his own violin to illustrate his technique, and we filmed a new medical procedure that was viewed as a miracle back then, open-heart surgery. We filmed a story about the Christian kibbutz, Nes Amim. So much going on. It was as if Israel was a small country with a big country inside.

Kirk Douglas was in Israel filming a movie and told a friend at the Technion, the Israel Institute of Technology, that he'd be a spokesman in a documentary I was making for them. I was to meet Kirk at the movie set in Tel Aviv. I arrived early and finally spotted him at a small table in an outdoor café on the shore of the Mediterranean, sitting across from a stunning woman in a black cocktail dress. His eyes caressed her as he slowly raised his glass of wine. At just that moment, a small airplane swept in from over the water and someone called out, "Cut!" The 35mm camera stopped rolling.

Kirk put down his glass and waited. The woman

brushed back a strand of hair. Kirk smiled just slightly as the two of them gazed into each other's eyes, completely unperturbed as voices in the background called out "Quiet on the set. Stand by. Rolling. Take Four!" Obviously the airplane was not the first problem they had encountered that day.

Kirk looked into the woman's eyes with renewed intensity. Once again, he raised his glass. But the glass tipped slightly and a couple of drops of wine spilled out of it. He turned to the camera and waited for the word. There it was, "Cut!" After that, they did Take Five, then Six, then Seven. Take Eight and Kirk gazed once again and looked at the woman as if it was the first time. The actress spoke a few words. Kirk answered her briefly and then paused. "Cut! It's a take!" Kirk turned in his chair and got up. A makeup girl ran over to the woman. One more scene in the can. It takes a long time to shoot a movie.

An hour later, we were at the Technion, Kirk and I with my small camera crew and one 16mm documentary camera. Our set was a laboratory where the university had just completed another technological breakthrough. The idea was to explain the new phenomenon.

"Would you mind standing over there?" I said to Kirk, just as if I knew what I was doing.

"How about this?" he answered as he darted out of sight behind a big instrument case. I couldn't see him. "I'll step out from here and then start talking. That'll give you a chance to establish the place. That way it won't be the usual stand-up."

"Right on," I thought to myself. "Good idea," I said to Kirk, grateful to be working with a real professional, a guy much smarter than I was. But at least I was smart enough to take his advice.

"Ready?" he called to me from his hiding place.

"Stand by," I said, signaling to Yehoram. "Okay, Kirk," I said. "Rolling!"

Kirk stepped out from behind the instrument case, looked around in amazement at the lab's star-wars equipment, and began to extol the achievements of the Technion. It wasn't exactly what was in the script, but it didn't matter. It was better than the script. Blah, blah, blah, he went on. Then his voice edged down into a conclusion, and Kirk flashed a big smile right above the dimple.

"Cut," I said to Yehoram. "Great," I said to Kirk. This was a low-budget documentary, not a feature film. One take was about all I could afford. And with Kirk Douglas I didn't need more than that.

"Okay, Yale," he said, patting me on the back. With a graceful swing of his body, he was out the door and slid into a waiting car. The chauffeur stepped on the gas, and Kirk disappeared from view.

"What a guy," Yehoram said. We were happy campers.

In the United States in those days, the country was preoccupied with the threat to impeach President Nixon. For some bizarre reason, Nixon chose that time to visit Israel. I stood on the *kikar* one day and watched as his motorcade first appeared in the distance. It was so American, big, black, shiny cars charging up the hill and then swinging around the traffic circle and on to the President's House. As if in a reflex action, I thrust my arm forward and gave the president a big wave. I'm not the kind of guy who waves at presidents, especially if their last name is Nixon, but I was caught up in the emotion of the moment. I wasn't even sure if I was waving at the right car. Maybe it was a decoy car. It didn't matter. It felt great to be there. It felt even greater that Nixon was in Israel of all places.

The Israelis loved every minute of it. Nixon had sent Israel critically needed planes and armaments during the war. He may have been in trouble in Washington, but he could have been elected president of Israel in a minute.

The Israelis waved wildly as he went by. Nixon was probably happy to see them. We all want to be loved.

A couple of years later, another president was on his way to Israel. On November 19, 1977. That was really special. That president was Anwar Sadat of Egypt.

No one could believe it. Sadat, who just four years earlier on Yom Kippur had ordered the Egyptian attack on Israel, would arrive in Israel right after *Shabbat*. It was three minutes after eight, according to official reports, when Sadat became the first Arab leader to set foot in the Jewish state.

Technically, Egypt and Israel were still at war, a war in which Sadat lost his younger brother. There was only a tenuous cease-fire in place. And yet, there he was, the president of Egypt, walking down the red carpet to shake hands with Prime Minister Menachem Begin.

It takes a lot to impress Israelis, but this time they were more than impressed. They were amazed. On television, they saw Sadat's plane with the words "Arab Republic of Egypt" and the bold image of the red-and-black Egyptian flag. They saw the Israeli band standing smartly, or at least as smartly as Israelis can manage to stand, belting out the Egyptian national anthem followed by the somber notes of Israel's own anthem, with its one word title so appropriate for the occasion, *Hatikvah*, the hope.

Sadat shook hands with Golda Meir, who had been prime minister during the Yom Kippur War. He shook hands with Defense Minister Moshe Dayan, familiar to people all over the world for the black patch that covered the place where his eye was supposed to be. A bullet went through that eye in a battle before Israeli independence. It was an Egyptian bullet.

Sadat shook hands with Ariel Sharon, the general who led Israeli troops across the Suez Canal and surrounded Egypt's Third Army on Egyptian soil at Kilometer 101. The opposing forces were still in place there, just sixty-three miles east of Cairo, as Sadat and Sharon shook hands.

More than a thousand journalists were at the airport that night. Even in normal times, or as normal as Israel ever manages to get, the country is one of the most reported about nations in the world. It's the old bromide, Jews are news.

I would have loved to have been at the airport that night, but I didn't even try. I knew that security would be at an all-time high and that it would be impossible for reporters to get close enough to see anything let alone talk to anyone. So I found my own spot where I could see everything clearly. In front of my television set.

After the airport ceremonies, Sadat and his entourage drove to Jerusalem. Thousands of Israelis lined the highway cheering. A month earlier those same Israelis were cheering Sharon as he led Israeli soldiers across the Suez Canal and onto Egyptian soil.

Six weeks are a long time in the Middle East. That Saturday evening, Egyptian president Anwar al-Sadat went to bed in the King David Hotel in Jerusalem.

The next day, Sadat stood on the dais of the Israeli parliament and laid out his proposals for peace. Actual negotiations were scheduled to begin three weeks later in Cairo. History was being made, and I was determined to be there.

I was not the only one. Within a few days, several of us filmmakers, journalists, and assorted political junkies posing as newsmen decided to hire a private plane to make the one-hour flight to Cairo. We wanted to get there before the Israeli delegation arrived so we could see the whole story unfold.

Saturday, December 10, began like every other *Shabbat* in our home. I went to synagogue in the morning, and the children joined me soon after. Rosalind prepared Israeli salads and chicken for our usual *Shabbat* lunch. A few friends came over, we said the traditional prayers for the wine and bread, and passed the food around. The fiery conversations, usually political ones, that are typical of Israeli *Shabbat* gatherings had already begun. We had learned to be careful to not invite people with clashing political views to the same *Shabbat* meal. Feelings run strong in Israel, especially political beliefs that are so close to matters of life and death. *Shabbat* is supposed to be a time of peace, not arguments.

After lunch, we spent the afternoon resting, reading, and napping. The only difference that Saturday was that a few hours after *Shabbat* ended, I was in a taxi driving through the darkness to Atarot, a small airport north of Jerusalem. That's where our plane was waiting for a midnight departure.

I saw about twenty other men there when I arrived. I knew most of them, or at least recognized them from the endless array of news stories we had covered in Israel. Everyone spoke softly that night. No one knew what awaited us. This was not Ben-Gurion Airport from which we always left the country when going overseas and where Sadat had so recently landed. This was an airport that Israelis didn't use very much. There were no huge lights creating a sense of daytime. There was none of the reassurance of hundreds of other people getting ready to fly. There was only quiet. And a feeling of isolation.

We stood around for a while and waited to board. There was some small talk and a few weak jokes. Little more. And finally a voice from somewhere saying it was time to go.

One by one, we mounted the ramp, bending our heads beneath the metal of the top of the door as we entered the plane. I walked down the narrow aisle trying to figure out what kind of a plane we were in. I hadn't taken a close look when I was outside. It seemed to be a Russian plane, but I wasn't sure. I just kept inching along with everyone else. There were no assigned places. I spotted an empty aisle seat and wedged myself into it.

Out of habit, I reached for the seat belt and fastened it. I thought back to the time I was filming in Poland and flying in a small Russian plane owned by Lot Airlines. When I pulled up the left part of my seat belt, I found it dangling in my hand. It wasn't attached to anything. We took off anyway. I was wondering if this plane was any better.

There were no big announcements. All the seats quickly filled up, the metal door was pulled shut, the motors started, and the plane taxied down the runway. I looked out the window and saw my reflection staring back at me. I looked forward and saw the stewardess fastening herself into the small fold-down seat near the front facing us. The plane kept rolling down the runway, and then, at last, I could feel it rise slowly into the darkness.

After a few minutes, we began to relax. We introduced ourselves to men we hadn't met before and shared stories with those we knew. Reporters like to tell stories. A few of the men were standing in the aisle, and a couple of others sitting in front of them were beginning to laugh. Then we heard the voice of the stewardess. We had forgotten about her.

"We are now entering Egyptian air space," the voice said.

After that, all you heard was the steady hum of the airplane alone in the black sky. Each of us was alone with his thoughts. Never mind that Sadat had just come to Jerusalem. Egypt and Israel were still at war.

I started thinking about the controllers on the ground. I started thinking about the Egyptian air force. Some of them must be guarding Cairo, I thought. I hoped they got word that we were cleared for this flight. I've always believed in Murphy's law, that if something can possibly go wrong, it will. I tried to not think about Murphy.

Slowly the small talk resumed. Whatever would happen, would happen. The only thing we could do now was slide back into the comfort of denial. How else can a reporter go to so many dangerous places?

We did land safely, but it was nothing like Sadat coming to Jerusalem. Although we didn't expect klieg lights or a brass band, we felt there would be some aura of excitement. But Cairo airport is not Kennedy or O'Hare and arriving at one-thirty in the morning did nothing to make things better. As we walked toward passport control, I saw only a few cleaning women and uniformed police with big Kalashnikov rifles and big mustaches and empty eyes.

I looked at them closely as I walked by carrying my overnight bag. I wasn't sure whether they were looking back at me, just staring straight ahead, or had disappeared all together into some out-of-body experience, transporting themselves perhaps to a sandy beach in the company of voluptuous women. I quickly discarded that thought. No one could think about a voluptuous woman and look that bland.

When we got to passport control, I slid my Israeli passport under the glass partition, that opening where your hand barely fits. I had an American passport, of course, but I didn't want to make it too easy for the clerk. And I wanted to see his reaction. There was none. His job was to stamp. He grabbed a bulky metal holder, went bang against an ink pad, bang against the passport, and that was that. I recognized the gesture. I had seen it a hundred times in Israel. Stamps are power.

I joined the other Israelis who were standing together

with Egyptian minders whose job was to get us into a couple of vans and take us to our hotel. We were more than ready. Tired from both the hour and the tension, I followed the others and our security man into a van that would take us to the Mena House hotel just ten miles outside Cairo. That's where the official talks between Egypt and Israel were to begin on Friday.

Mena House was named after the first Egyptian pharaoh. The Jews know a lot about pharaohs. The sense of Jewish nationhood was first forged after centuries of slavery under the pharaohs when Moses led his people to freedom. The concluding sentence in the most important Jewish prayer, the Sh'ma, is a constant reminder. "I am the Lord your God who brought you out of the land of Egypt." To the Jewish people, God is not only the master of the universe, He is a God of history.

I was too tired to start thinking about Jewish history. But tired as I was, on some subliminal level, feelings about what it means to be a Jew were stirring within me. How could they not? I had just stepped onto the soil of the country where God was present when Jewish nationhood began.

As I walked into Mena House, the exotic scent of jasmine dispelled my weariness. I looked around and found myself transported into the Arabian nights. Forty acres of lush gardens guided me into a building of oriental mysticism where embroidered Persian carpets flowed beyond endless arches, past intricately carved paneling and inlaid mosaic and pearl tiles that merged into a visual rhythm that seemed to beckon me on forever. Nothing should surprise anyone who has lived in the Middle East, but Mena House, built by Indian hoteliers, was a surprise. Roosevelt, Churchill, and Chiang Kai-shek had met there during World War II. I liked their taste in hotels.

Security men were everywhere, not because of us, but

because this is where the Israeli delegation would stay when they arrived Tuesday. Policemen in black with Russian-made assault rifles stood guard. Khaki-clad regulars were stationed wherever I looked. Their presence made me feel safe, at the same time producing the reaction I always have at times like this. If there is so much security keeping me safe, there must be an enormous threat out there that they're protecting me from. That is one of the things I try to not think about.

I finally signed in and then followed the bellman—was he a security agent?—to my room where I collapsed into a world of oriental luxury or at least a roomful of it. Soft cotton sheets, subtle lighting as soothing as a lullaby, and the tranquilizing perfume of flowers that reclined nearby luxuriating in a vase of carved glass. It was the best that money could buy. Not my money, of course. It was more than I could handle. It was the Egyptian government's money. We were its guests.

I stepped out onto my balcony the next morning for my first sight of Egypt, the Pyramid of Cheops. Even the exciting news of peace talks vanished at the sight of the pyramids. The last time I had seen them was in a glossy photo in *National Geographic*, enormous, passive monuments. Suddenly they were real, close enough to walk to, which is exactly what I did. I even climbed its sloping side, step by step toward an entrance into one of its cavernous interiors.

Israeli Prime Minister Menachem Begin, during the period of negotiations with Sadat, often boasted that the Jews during their centuries of slavery built those pyramids. As everyone who has ever read a Passover haggadah knows, the Jews were indeed slaves placing brick upon brick, but I doubt whether anyone really knows exactly what they were building. Maybe it was a palace. Maybe a lot of palaces. No matter. Begin was a great orator with a performer's gift for theater. His was too dramatic a story to pass up.

Before I arrived, I made plans to film a few feature stories in advance of the Israeli delegation's arrival and arranged to work with an Egyptian cameraman the following day. My first day in Cairo was free. There was still time to visit the National Museum. At the hotel, I asked the doorman to tell the cabbie where I wanted to go, climbed into the small but shiny black car, sat back in my seat, and relaxed. For at least one minute.

We drove out of the hotel grounds and raced onto one of Cairo's wide boulevards, built about a century earlier in an attempt to emulate Paris. Paris is better. Cairo's boulevards were more like the Indianapolis 500 except that not everyone was traveling in the same direction. There were four lanes of traffic going our way and four lanes that I hoped were going the opposite way, plus all the variables such as my driver cutting left from the far right lane and crossing three other lanes of speeding cars. I found myself looking down at the floor instead of out the window, assuring myself that this, too, must end, though I wasn't sure just how.

God is kind to children and tourists in Egypt, and my driver finally slowed down as he turned into a narrow street of buildings whose facades had been corroded by unremitting pollution and left to their own fates by neglect. The people themselves—the men in their black suit jackets that Arabs wear against the heat, the women in their dark flowing dresses—seemed to be an extension of the black exhaust that permeates and darkens the air. My driver maneuvered past them, squeezed his taxi around other autos fighting for their bit of space, and past donkeys pulling wooden carts in the midst of chaotic crowds of Cairo's twelve million people, Egyptians, Arabs,

Africans—there are even more today—all of whom seemed to be deliberately crossing in front of us.

Above the crowds, banners stretched from one side of the street to the other bearing movie-star images of a smiling Sadat. He was an impressive-looking man and at least projected a more appealing image for Egypt than did earlier rulers such as King Farouk. My driver told me that the words that stretched out in the graceful Arabic script spoke of peace. I decided to take his word for it.

There were pictures of Sadat everywhere in all sizes, hanging from lampposts, nailed onto trees, and bandaged onto walls. In time, I learned that this was not just a matter of the peace process, but rather a common practice in Arab countries where the rulers, democratically elected by about 99 percent of the voters, like to show their appreciation by reminding the people wherever they go whom they voted for and, more importantly, who is in charge.

I felt my body hit the inside of the taxi as my driver made a sharp turn. There were people in front of us and on all sides of us as he maneuvered his car through the middle of the central bus station. People shoved one another into the buses, not with any hope of finding a seat or even standing inside, just for the privilege of placing one foot on the edge of the floor and finding something to hold on to as they hung out of the bus at a forty-five-degree angle. In Cairo, even a veteran of the New York subways could learn a thing or two.

The sound of a train caught my attention. I looked up just in time to see it chug by in the distance. Then I looked again, closely, to be sure I really saw what I saw. On the top of the train carriages were people, at least a hundred people, spread-eagled over the trains and grabbing tightly onto whatever they could reach. I was spellbound at the sight. I wondered what happens when someone falls off. On the law of averages, someone must fall off. I wondered if among those millions of impoverished people in Cairo, anyone would notice.

At last, I arrived at the city's world-famous Museum of Egyptian Antiquities, built more than a hundred years ago. I was grateful for having arrived at all. I stepped out of the taxi and paid the driver. He gave me a huge smile. That was the tip-off about the tip. I quickly reviewed in my mind the conversion rate of the dollar and realized I had tipped him well, about double the price on the meter. If you believe that there is a reason for everything, it might have been more than a mathematical lapse. It might have been a subconscious offering to the gods. And heaven knows, there are a lot of gods in Egypt.

Even in December, it was hot in Cairo. By then I was used to the weather in that part of the world. I started climbing up the stairs of the museum and kept on climbing and climbing. I thought about other museums I had been to and realized that at practically every one of them, I had to climb a lot of stairs. Perhaps like apartments in New York, the higher up you are, the more important the museum.

When I was about eight or nine, my mother would take me to the Field Museum in Chicago. It was an hour-and-a-half trip on two different elevated trains, but it was worth it so I could see the mummies, my mother's clever plan to introduce me to the magic of museums. I have been an authority on mummies ever since, a condition not particularly helpful at cocktail parties or anywhere else. At least, it had me primed for this visit. At last, I was where I belonged, in the company of mummies.

I entered and soon found the sarcophagus of the Pharaoh Tutankhamen. The path to where he lies and to his wooden throne took me past many glass enclosures within which were scores of more than a hundred thousand exhibits on display in the museum. I looked at those treasures in shock, saddened to see them abandoned to neglect. Dust and disinterest enfolded every casement. The explanations at each display were smudged typewritten sentences struggling to impart their fading words from small cards that, yellowed by the years, reeled back from the heat and retreated into tiny scrolls. Millions of Egyptians were living in poverty and yet no one seemed to care enough about the museum, or about the unemployed, to hire a thousand or more of those people to care for those treasures. I was learning more about Egypt than just its past.

The next day, it was time to begin filming. I went with my Egyptian minder to meet the cameraman who was assigned to me. He was a man of slight build with light wavy hair. He didn't look like other Egyptians, most of whom had darker skin. I had to remind myself to go beyond stereotypes, to remember how many civilizations over the centuries had traversed the trade routes and the paths of conquest, most recently the French and English.

The people at the Broadcasting Authority told me he was one of the very best cameramen in Egypt, that he would regularly film the public appearances of Sadat himself. That didn't reassure me. As a matter of fact, it worried me. He not only looked frail, unlike most cameramen who carry around heavy equipment from morning until night, but the fact that he filmed Sadat worried me. It doesn't take great skill to stand in one place with your camera on a tripod and record a speech. It does take skill to film while you are moving, to catch the magic of the moment when other people are in motion, to make the quick judgment about when to zoom in for that final bit of emotion as a speaker's story becomes poignant.

As it turned out, his frailty precluded my concern about

all that. Although I was told that we couldn't begin working with him before nine o'clock, a time in Israel when a
film crew would have usually been out working for three
hours, by one o'clock he told us his workday was over. I
didn't argue with him. It was obvious he couldn't go on.

It was annoying, but not critically important since I was
filming some soft-feature stories simply as an excuse to see
the country, and the presence of a camera usually gets you
in anywhere. What I hadn't thought about is that in a
police state, a camera can also get you in trouble. Driving
along the next day with a new cameraman, my old minder,
and all my appropriate credentials in place, I realized that a
black car had been behind me for some time. Just the traffic, I thought, as I kept on driving.

When I looked up again, I saw that the driver was signaling to me. First a "pull over to the side" gesture. I was
puzzled and slow to respond. When I looked again, I saw
he was waving his arm more aggressively. This time I got
the idea. I pulled over to the side of the road as he pulled
up alongside me. I don't know what he said, but he was
pointing to the 16mm motion picture camera that was on
the floor in the back. Even though I wasn't trying to hide
it, it was nonetheless out of sight, though somehow not out
of sight to him.

He pointed to the camera again and waved a finger at
me in a pronounced left-to-right-and-back-to-the-left
motion. Once again, I got the idea, sort of. I wasn't supposed to do whatever he thought I was going to do. The
minder, who doubled as a translator, agreed that I had read
him correctly. He said it would be a good idea to close up
for the day. A little shaken by my first introduction to a
police state, I told him I agreed.

I consoled myself that I did get one good feature that
day, a story about the city of the dead, the cemetery in

Cairo where hundreds of impoverished people live among the tombstones. But the story I really wanted would begin the next day when the Israeli delegation arrived. I told the cameraman to go home early and treated myself that night to an evening of Egyptian food with beer, kebab, kofta, which turned out to be meatballs, a green soup called mulukhia, a mix of rice and lentils called kusheri, as well as a lot of Mediterranean dishes I knew from Israel like eggplant, tahina salad, and grape leaves. I decided to skip the hamam mahshi. I never had a problem with squab, but the thought of a stuffed pigeon just didn't feel right. Maybe it reminded me of all the dirty pigeons that littered the platforms of the elevated trains in Chicago.

Tuesday at last. Not the official meetings yet, but at least the beginning of the beginning, the arrival of the first El Al flight from Israel. There was a lot of symbolism that day. The pilots selected to fly the plane had been prisoners of war in Egypt. One of the flight attendants had been born in Cairo.

The plane swooped into the airport, the word "peace" emblazoned on its fuselage in both Hebrew and Arabic. The Israeli delegation was headed by Eliahu Ben Elissar, director general of the prime minister's office. Major General Avraham Tamir, head of the strategic planning division of the Israeli general staff, came, too. My friend, Meir Rosenne, the legal advisor in the Foreign Ministry, was the third delegate. They arrived in Israel with two dozen other Israelis, assistants and technicians.

Some time after the plane was scheduled to arrive, I was standing on the outskirts of the city when suddenly I heard the sound of motors. I turned just in time to see the shiny black cars of the Israeli delegation racing down the wide boulevard. I caught a glimpse of Dan Patir, spokesman for the prime minister, and waved at him as his car swept by.

Dan waved back. It was too exciting a day for any of us to pretend to be dignified. We just wanted to jump up and down in excitement. Was it really possible there could be peace? After twenty-five years and four wars since Israeli independence? I even thought about it being thirty-five hundred years after the exodus from Egypt. You couldn't possibly be in Egypt and not think about that, especially at a time like that.

The entire group was quickly whisked off to Mena House to make final preparations with the Egyptians for the official opening of the peace talks on Friday. The meeting would take place in the hotel's posh Al-Rubayyat restaurant. The Israelis and Egyptians agreed on the removal of the tables and chairs from the long hall and the setting up of a conference table. It would be a round conference table. Nine microphones were made ready for the nine invited participants even though only four had accepted. Delegates from Egypt and Israel had agreed to be there, together with representatives from the United States and the United Nations. The PLO, Jordan, Syria, Lebanon, and the Soviet Union turned down the invitation. They kept the nine microphones ready anyway. This was the Middle East. You never know.

By Friday, you could almost touch the excitement. Outside Mena House, hundreds of journalists, photographers and cameramen pressed together toward the entrance to the meeting room where in a few minutes there would be a photo op of the participants, smiling together in their newfound camaraderie. There might even be a chance for a couple of sound bites.

As the time drew closer to that designated moment when the doors would finally open, everyone pushed even tighter together. That's part of the craziness of the news business, that events that are often little more than theater are portrayed as something serious. The dignitaries remember to sit up straight and smile for the cameras. If someone says something, it is usually polite and rehearsed. The photos show little more than a few men sitting together in a room, and the sound bites, if captured, are perfunctory parts of the performance. On the other hand, when those few men happen to be delegates of Israel and Egypt and they are talking about a real peace little more than two months after a vicious war, even theater becomes news.

The door was flung open, and in one reflex action everyone pushed forward. Above the crowd, I heard the voice of a red-headed Israeli I knew, Mickey, a cameraman who was the size of a football tackle. "Wait, everybody! Wait!" he called out. For just a second, the shoving stopped. Just a split second. That's all Mickey needed. I looked in the direction of his voice in time to see him lunge ahead, breaking through the line. I credited him with a gain of ten yards.

Inside, the meeting itself was brief, little more than ceremonial. Its purpose was simply to begin, to transform words into deeds, to show the world that both countries were serious about once and for all ending the bloodshed. Months of negotiations would follow with many setbacks along the way. Months became years and continued on into 1979 and the meetings at Camp David where United States President Jimmy Carter, alternating between charm, bluffs, and threats, finally succeeded in bringing Begin and Sadat together in a final agreement.

When the negotiations ended, Israel returned the entire Sinai Desert it had captured from Egypt in the 1967 Six Day War, including valuable airfields and oil fields. The agreement also meant giving up that beautiful Israeli-made oasis in the desert, the town of Yamit. More than anything, it meant that the right-wing Likud party, whose political religion was to expand Israeli settlements throughout all the land conquered in 1967, was violating its own dogma and surrendering that land and even a major settlement. The ramifications of that surrender reverberate to this very day.

And what did the Israelis get? Not one piece of land. Not one grain of sand. Just a piece of paper, a paper that promised one thing that every Israeli hungered for—peace.

When peace came, the Israelis were enthusiastic and almost stumbling over one another to create business projects with the Egyptians, tourism with the Egyptians, industrial and financial projects with the Egyptians. But that's not what happened. Hosni Mubarak, who has been the country's ruler for the quarter of a century since the assassination of Sadat, has discouraged relationships with the Israelis. Mubarak himself never set foot on Israeli soil until he was unable to avoid attending the funeral of Yitzhak Rabin. Nor has he come to Israel since then. It's been a cold peace, but any peace is better than war.

What the future holds, no one knows. But every Jew who knows his Bible knows about the time when Joseph was the trusted advisor of the pharaoh. And then the pharaoh died. And the Bible says, "There arose in Egypt a Pharaoh who knew not Joseph." No one knows what will happen when Mubarak is replaced by a new pharaoh in Egypt. The future is never certain. But at least for more than three decades there has been no war.

At that moment in Cairo, none of us knew how events would play out, but we were all filled with hope. The ceremonial meetings adjourned for a long weekend. It was Friday night, *Shabbat,* and we Israelis did what Israelis usually do on *Shabbat,* we gathered together with friends.

Long tables had been set with white tablecloths and beautiful dishes. It's hard to remember how many of us were there, maybe sixty, maybe more. Not everyone was religiously observant. It didn't matter. Just being together on *Shabbat* is what mattered.

For Israel's legal counsel Meir Rosenne, who was Orthodox, it was essential to observe the Sabbath. I sat next to Meir as someone lit the candles to signal the beginning of *Shabbat*. Someone else recited the *Kiddush*, the blessing over the wine. And the *motzei*, the blessing over the bread.

I'm sure that more than one of us also quietly recited the *Shecheyanu* that night, the prayer thanking God for preserving us in life and good health to witness that day. I'm sure that not one of us, even those who were not observant, was not moved at the thought of where we were, celebrating *Shabbat* in Egypt.

I looked over at Meir next to me. He knew all the songs, knew all the words, and was singing with gusto. Timorously, I joined in. Slowly, slowly, caught up in the emotion, I began to sing louder and louder as my voice blended in with the voices around me. We sang one song after another when I realized we had begun to sing *"Hinei ma tov umanaim, Shevet achim gam yachad."* "Behold, how good and how pleasant it is, for brothers to be dwelling together."

I loved it.

I couldn't believe it. The boy who grew up singing Christmas carols in Oak Park was singing once again, singing in Egypt where it all began. He was singing the psalms of his people. He was an irrevocable part of that people.

Sometimes journeys begin before we even know it. Sometimes they end further away than we ever imagined. Sometimes you have to travel far to come home.

Epilogue

*O*nce again, it is November. Twenty-eight years
have passed since that *Shabbat* in Cairo. And
now I am back in New York.

I walk along East End Avenue where once upon a time
Rosalind and I walked together pushing Laura and
Devorah ahead of us in the double stroller. We were filled
with energy and optimism. And ambition, too. Thirty-
three years old and already a network executive. What
more could I ask?

Israel? Never thought about it and certainly never
dreamed I would move there.

At that *Shabbat* dinner in Cairo, I never dreamed I
would ever leave Israel. But there's a Yiddish expression
that goes "Man plans, and God laughs."

I returned from Cairo a few days before Rosalind and I
celebrated our twenty-first wedding anniversary. After
seven years in Israel, we had many close friends and several of them came over that night to celebrate with us. I
enjoyed the moment. That much I had learned in Israel. I
had seen enough death and suffering to know that it was
important to enjoy the moment.

What I didn't know was the future. God spares us knowing the future.

I didn't know that three years later Rosalind would decide to end our marriage. Looking back, it's apparent she had been thinking about it for some time. I hadn't been thinking about it at all. Other people got divorced. We were a family. That's what I thought. I didn't know that within intimacy, people can be strangers.

As a woman said to me once, describing her former husband, "We traveled well together." Rosalind and I did everything well together, with decency and caring. We traveled well together, but by now I've learned that I never really understood the person I was traveling with. Rosalind apparently had that insight, realized that something was missing. I missed the whole thing.

I thought we had the perfect marriage. Our friends thought so, too.

We certainly had the perfect divorce. Heartbreak, yes, but no arguments over the children or over money. We were nothing if not rational. Still traveling well together, even while separating. In any case, Rosalind wanted out, wanted something different. She wasn't even sure what she wanted, but one thing was clear. Whatever it was it didn't include me.

Worse than the divorce—and that in itself must reveal something—was the breakup of the family. That was the most painful part of the whole experience. To me, the family was what it was all about. The kids were in their teens, and we had more than our share of teenage rebellion—who doesn't? I still believed we'd muddle through all that as most families do. I still believed in an old-fashioned way that we all belonged together.

A few years later, Rosalind married a man who made her happy. And then Rosalind who for years had never smoked, who exercised an hour a day, was a strict vegetarian and never complained about anything, began to complain. About pains in her stomach. By the time the doctors figured out it was ovarian cancer, it was too late. She was only fifty-five when she died. Just like Rita.

In the 1970s while Rosalind and I were still married, Becca, our youngest child, our promising writer and artist, began to suffer from manic depression. People didn't talk about depression in those days. Rosalind and I knew nothing about it, and it took us a long time to learn about lithium and the medications that were available. Meanwhile, I could see Becca's torment as she mysteriously changed from the excitement of embracing life to the despair of being overwhelmed by it. Rosalind and her new husband were living in Boston when we tried to get help for Becca at nearby McLean Hospital. It was a famous psychiatric hospital that had treated such famous writers as Sylvia Plath. McLean treated her but didn't save her. They didn't save Becca, either. One night, the struggle to live was too great for her. She was in her room in a halfway house. It was Friday night, *Shabbat*. That's when she swallowed all her pills. She died the next day.

Laura had already moved back to the United States. She returned to her native California and studied at Berkeley. Years later, she married and had two sons. Need I say they are handsome and smart?

Devorah, our family *rebbetzin*, married an Israeli, remained a devout, Orthodox Jew, and today lives with her husband and seven children on a hilltop near three Arab villages. She calls the area by its biblical name, Judea. The newspapers call it the West Bank.

David, after acting out his rebellion by briefly dropping out of high school—assuring me that he could live happily ever after playing piano in a piano bar—did his compulso-

ry military service, which he hated, and subsequently studied at Brown University, ending up with a Ph.D. in psy-
chology from Columbia. He is not religious and lives with
his wife, a native of Jerusalem, and their three children in
Ramat HaSharon in Israel.

I remarried a year before Rosalind did. I didn't think I
would marry again. I didn't think that would happen.
Unlike a lot of men, I can spend time alone. And I still had
children and grandchildren nearby in Israel. But it did happen and once again in a strange way.

It began with Rita who with Mike had visited us in
Winnetka and first talked about our moving to Israel. And
it was Rita, ten years after that, who told a woman she
worked with in New York that if she needed a film made in
Israel about her mental-health organization, she should call
me. She did, and that's how I met Anita. I liked her immediately, right from that first phone call. Nothing strange
about that. I liked many of my clients. Anita was married,
lived in New York, and for years she was just a client.

But in time I fell in love with her. I hadn't expected
something like that to happen. When it did happen, she
stirred within me feelings I had never felt before. And
Anita's own marriage was falling apart.

Becca was only sixteen, a teenager who needed her
father around. David was eighteen and going into the army,
a young man who needed his father around. And regardless
of the children, I would never leave Israel.

But I did. When you're in love, you do a lot of things
you never thought you would do. My love affair with Israel
brought me to Israel in the first place. My love affair with
Anita took me away from Israel, though not completely.
The trade-off was that I would live with Anita in New
York, but that we would keep a home in Jerusalem and go
to Israel several times a year. Which is what we did. Older

now, I travel there less. Still there is not a day I am not passionately involved with that land.

The memories of Israel are always in my mind and in my heart. I walk down a hospital corridor and suddenly remember another time and another doctor wearily telling me about his wartime hours in an operating room. I walk down the street and see the handle of a tennis racket sticking up from a young man's backpack, and in my mind's eye it's a rifle on the back of an Israeli soldier. The memories will own me forever.

More than three decades have passed since my adventure began. The Oak Park *goy*, as my mother used to call me, the very proper Republican who ran for Congress from the very proper North Shore of Chicago, now has ten grandchildren in Israel.

Rosalind lies buried in Jerusalem. Becca lies buried in Jerusalem. I will be buried there, too.

The years with Anita have been more blessed than anything I could have ever imagined. After almost twenty years of marriage, we are still in love.

Anita has my heart.

My soul is in Jerusalem.